THE
GAZA
MARINE
STORY

THE GAZA MARINE STORY

THE POLITICS AND INTRIGUE BEHIND PALESTINE'S UNTAPPED GAS WEALTH

MICHAEL BARRON

NOMAD
PUBLISHING

The Gaza Marine Story
The Politics and Intrigue behind Palestine's Untapped Gas Wealth
Michael Barron

Published by Nomad Publishing in 2025
Email: info@nomad-publishing.com
www.nomad-publishing.com

ISBN 978-1-917045-02-5

CIP Data: A catalogue for this book is
available from the British Library.

"All peoples have the right of self-determination and control over their natural wealth and resources and, accordingly, have the right to freely determine the form of their political structure and to freely pursue their economic, social and cultural development."

Article 2, The Arab Charter on Human Rights

CONTENTS

AUTHOR'S NOTE

Most of this book was researched and written prior to the events of 7 October 2023 and the subsequent conflict in Gaza. I have ended the story of the Gaza Marine gas field for now at that point but in the conclusion examine the role that Gaza Marine could play in the rebuilding of Gaza by Palestinians. As the book goes to print, the conflict in Gaza seems set to escalate again after hopes of a ceasefire. Also, US President Donald Trump has made his suggestion that the US takes over control of Gaza but does not appear to have taken any action to make this happen. As this book makes clear, Gaza Marine gas belongs to the Palestinians and it should be a future Palestinian government's decision on how to exploit, if at all, this valuable resource for the benefit of the Palestinian people and their economy.

Finally, a note on terminology as the natural gas industry is full of jargon. I have tried where possible to avoid jargon. Units of measurement for natural gas are usually expressed in terms of volume or in terms of its energy value. Volume e.g. millions of standard cubic feet or metres are typically used when talking about the amount of gas reserves or level of production e.g. so many million standard cubic feet per day. Natural gas is usually priced in terms of its energy value e.g. so many million British thermal units (the standard unit) per US dollar. One million British thermal units is approximately 252 million calories. Prices and financial values are given in US dollars, in most cases, as this is the currency normally used in the natural gas business. A few values are given in pounds sterling as that is the relevant currency for the specific agreement being discussed.

MB
June 2025

INTRODUCTION

Around the table in the hotel conference room sat the special advisor to the Israeli prime minister, two senior Israeli civil servants, the deputy prime minister of the Palestinian National Authority (PNA), head of the Palestinian Energy Agency (PEA), an executive of the Palestinian Investment Fund (PIF), a former British cabinet minister, a commercial manager from a private Palestinian-owned oil and gas firm, a senior vice president from a large British publicly listed gas company, one of his commercial managers and one of the company's government relations managers. They are meeting in a Tel Aviv hotel in 2013 to discuss the Gaza Marine natural gas project. It was one of a handful of times that representatives of all the main players in the project had met in the same room in the fourteen or so years since the project's start. All the participants were polite, very polite, to one another. The two main protagonists, the Israeli and Palestinian officials referred to each other as "*my colleague*" or "*our friend*" or "*our partner*". There was no raising of voices or thumping of tables but there was tension. Both the Israeli and Palestinian representatives seemed reluctant, even unable, to utter the name of the other side. For the first half of the one hour meeting, the Israelis avoided using the word "*Palestinian*". The Palestinians avoided using the terms "*Israel*" or "*Israeli*". The government relations manager noted this circumlocution. At about the halfway point of the meeting, the Israeli prime minister's advisor hesitated as he searched for another form of

11

address. He could not find one and uttered the word *"Palestinian"*. The taught band stretched between the two sides slackened, a little. Both sides referred to each other by name repeatedly for the rest of the meeting. That slight easing of tension did not lead to any breakthrough at the meeting. Positions were stated and repeated. There was no agreement on any solution to the obstacles facing one of the largest potential economic prizes for the Palestinians, which could alter the direction of the Palestinian/Israeli conflict.

The advisor to the Israeli prime minister was Yitzhak Molcho, a lawyer who acted as the prime minister's trouble shooter with the Palestinians. The Israeli civil servants were from the staff of the National Security Council and the Ministry of Finance. The Palestinian Deputy Prime Minister was Mohammad Mustafa, who also held the title of Economic Advisor to the Palestinian president Mahmoud Abbas. The head of the PEA was Omar Kitaneh and the PIF representative was Durgham Maraee. The PIF is the Palestinian's sovereign wealth fund. The former British cabinet minister was Stephen Byers who was advising the Palestinian-owned Consolidated Contractors Company (CCC) and with him was his colleague Yasser Burgan. The British company at the meeting was BG Group plc (BG) and its representatives were Mark Rollins, Victoria Farrelly and the author. BG had once been part of British Gas, privatised under Margaret Thatcher.

BG and CCC were partners in the Gaza Marine natural gas project. The project represents the Palestinians' largest mineral resource with the potential to provide a vital source of revenue and energy and alter the dynamic of the relationship with Israel. The project involved the exploration and discovery of natural gas beneath the sea off the Gaza Strip and the future development of that gas for supply to power stations or for export. BG and CCC acquired the licence to explore for gas from the PNA in 1999 and discovered gas in 2000. BG spent $25 million exploring and drilling for gas and another $75 million trying to find a market for the gas. The company estimated that it would cost $700 million to install the equipment, pipelines and processing facilities to get the gas to a market. That market could be the Palestinian's only power station, which is located in the Gaza Strip or Israeli power stations or Jordanian power stations or export to Egypt, where again it could be used to generate power or continue onto world markets via Egypt's gas export facilities. The market could be more than one of these options but not all of them. There is not enough gas for that. Getting the gas to market could earn total revenues of $4 billion to be divided (not equally) between BG, CCC and the PNA. The PNA's share could be around $100 million per year for 15 years, the expected productive lifetime for the gas field. This sum would not turn the Palestinians into the next Qataris or Singaporeans, but it would be their own revenue and not aid, on which the Palestinian economy remains dependent. The revenue could contribute to rebuilding houses, offices, hospitals, roads and other essential infrastructure destroyed since October 2023 in the Gaza Strip.

The supply of gas to the Gaza power station combined with sensible investment of the revenue from gas exports could have a revitalising impact on the Palestinian economy and particularly the Gazan economy. The volume of gas discovered makes the Gaza field commercially viable, but it is not a large discovery by regional or international standards. BG's experts calculated that the volume of gas in the Gaza Marine field is 1 trillion cubic feet (tcf). This is equivalent to approximately 170 million barrels of oil. In 2007, BG calculated that Gazan gas could generate enough electricity to supply Tel Aviv for 50 years. The Gaza Marine gas could meet Gaza's current electricity demand for many times more years than that. This is not a fair comparison as supplying the Gaza power station with gas would create a reliable electricity source for the territory and would spark an increase in energy use. Rather than relying on intermittent supplies of diesel subject to Israeli restrictions, Gaza would have 24 hour electricity supply. Factories, workshops and businesses would increase production. Gaza's residents could rely on the electricity supply for cooking, washing, lighting, heating and cooling, watching television, charging devices and powering appliances. Hospitals and schools would be able to function efficiently.

Even before the conflict that started on 7 October 2023, Gaza suffered from an energy shortage. Electricity was only available for a few hours every day. Essential services like hospitals relied on diesel-fuelled generators. The availability of diesel for both generators and the Gaza power station was uncertain and at the discretion of the Israeli authorities. Diesel for the power station is imported by truck. Since 2006, the Israeli government has imposed a blockade on the Gaza Strip and controls all but one of the border crossings into the territory. It has used this control to apply pressure on the Hamas-led government that seized power in that year. The other border crossing, at Rafah in southern Gaza, is controlled by Egypt. The Egyptian government has also restricted the access of goods (and people) at Rafah. The Egyptian government is also no friend of Hamas and values security co-operation with Israel. Diesel was also smuggled in from Egypt through tunnels under the border. This is a precarious trade route with persistent Israeli and Egyptian efforts to destroy the tunnels.

The Israeli blockade of Gaza reinforced a process of separating the territory from Israel. This separation included progressively tighter restrictions on the ability of Palestinians to enter Israel from Gaza (and for Gazan residents outside to return) so that very few Palestinians were able to leave the Gaza Strip. This separation also included the construction of a fence along the whole border with watchtowers, barbed wire and no access to a wide strip of land on the Gazan side (enforced by shooting anyone who dares to enter). This separation also included the removal of all Israeli settlers in Gaza in 2005 and the demolition of all the settlers' buildings including those such as greenhouses and factories that the Palestinians could have put to good economic use.

This separation was not complete and irreversible. At the same time, the Israeli government exerted total control over the Gaza Strip. It controlled who went in and out, including foreigners and members of the PNA travelling to Gaza. It controlled what goods went in and out of Gaza including essential food and medical supplies. It controlled the air above Gaza and it controlled the sea off the Gaza. Israel imposed tight limits on the waters where Gaza fisherman can operate and it prevented boats arriving from overseas to bring humanitarian aid. This control also extended to the gas resources under the seabed. The Israeli government has prevented the development of the gas field and imposed conditions on any future development. Israeli officials, including Yitzhak Molcho, have stated that the pipeline delivering the gas to shore must land on Israeli territory first (not in the Gaza Strip or in Egypt) and the gas must first enter the Israeli gas market. This arrangement would give the Israeli government complete control over the flow of gas and the resulting revenue. Israel has not yet gained access to any of Gaza's gas resources.

The Gaza Marine project highlights this contradiction in Israeli policy towards the Occupied Palestinian territories (OPT). Israel wants to control the OPT and at the same time to separate itself from the OPT. Israel's arc lamps of control and separation have cast shadows over Gaza Marine, throwing some features into relief and casting others into darkness. The control/separation paradox has picked out Israel's control over the Palestinian economy and the Palestinian's reliance on Israel for economic development. Some of the measures it uses to exert that control remain cloaked in darkness. Also, in the darkness lies an appreciation of the mutual benefit that could be gained from Israeli and Palestinian collaboration on the development of natural resource and economic co-operation. This contradiction has thwarted this collaboration to the detriment of both Israelis and Palestinians. The impact of this contradiction is felt not just in the economy but also on the politics and the security of both populations.

Penetrating the shadows cast around the Gaza Marine project

reveals a great deal about how Israel exerted close control over the Palestinians while also attempting to separate itself from the Palestinians. The project provides a case study on the political, economic, diplomatic, military and security measures that Israel used towards the Palestinians. The project shows how Israel worked to increase Palestinian dependence on Israel while at the same time trying to push Palestinians away and separate them from Israelis. Gaza Marine provides a microcosm of interactions between Israelis and Palestinians on many levels from the highest peaks of government through the bureaucracy and military through to ordinary people on the ground both in Israel and in the OPT.

Looking at Gaza Marine through night vision goggles also reveals a multitude of other aspects about the Israeli-Palestinian conflict. Looming out of the blackness is the reluctance (or is it inability) of the PNA to commit 100% to pushing for its national interests. This reluctance may stem in part from the asymmetry in the Israeli/Palestinian power balance. There are, though, other aspects of this asymmetry beyond the PNA pulling its punches. Pushing back the shadows from Gaza Marine also shows the role that business, both Palestinian and international, plays in the Israel/Palestinian conflict. International companies are just one category of many external actors in the conflict and should have some impact especially when large sums of money are at stake. In the case of Gaza Marine, very large sums of money are at stake, but the prospect of these sums has not bought success. The project has instead displayed the limits of these external players. It is not all negative. The Gaza Marine project also provided a glimpse of a path towards a different future. It has shown the potential for energy to bring Palestinians and Israelis together for their mutual benefit. That future of mutual benefits remains a distant hope for now.

Like the smoke from chimneys that combined with fog to create London's pea-souper fogs in the 1950s, there is a dense cloud blocking a clear view of Gaza Marine. The cloud of corruption hangs low over the project. From its earliest days, the Gaza Marine project has been subject to allegations of bribe paying, conflicts of interest, favours sought (and given) and influence peddled. Even before Yasser Arafat established the PNA, he had a reputation for corruption. His relocation from exile in Tunis to Ramallah on the West Bank along with his cronies also brought the relocation of his corrupt practices. The new regime in parts of the West Bank and the Gaza Strip also created new opportunities for making money. A swarm of middlemen buzzed round these opportunities. Some were Israelis who traded on their past covert relationships with the Palestinians, some were Palestinians and others were foreigners. While Arafat and his representatives may or may not have corruptly acquired Israeli acquiescence to award the Gaza Marine licence, representatives of the Israeli government may also have tried to influence the project in unethical ways. The companies involved, both BG and CCC also have questions to answer about some of the methods that they used in attempts to advance the project.

The Gaza Marine project provides a case study on how corruption allegations become attached to a large natural gas project. The industry globally has a poor reputation for corruption and many of the underlying reasons for that are present in the Gaza Marine project. It was negotiated in an opaque manner with an unequal balance of power and knowledge between the two sides, the inexperienced PNA on one side of the table and a major international gas company on the other. At the same time, there was the unequal power balance between the PNA and Israel. There were also large sums of money at stake. BG would have to spend hundreds of millions of dollars to develop the field with thousands of suppliers and contractors, including companies in Israel, the Palestinian territories, Egypt, Europe, North America and Asia. The Gaza Marine field, once the gas was flowing, would generate even larger sums in revenue for the PNA, BG and its partner CCC. Given these fertile conditions for corruption, it is not surprising that allegations of bribe-paying, soliciting bribes and bribe offering have dogged the project. There are allegations that $40 million was paid as a bribe to acquire the licence and that Israeli representatives demanded exorbitant payments from BG as the price for allowing the project to go ahead.

Whatever the truth regarding corruption, the Gaza Marine project offered the prospect of substantial legitimate investment in the Palestinian territories. It would represent one of the largest single foreign investments in the Palestinian economy. Such opportunities are rare due to the uncertainty that surrounds the Palestinian territories while Israel's occupation persists, the violence continues and the long-term future of the PNA is unclear. When the PNA was established under the Oslo Accords in the mid 1990s, it was intended to be a five-year temporary arrangement while a permanent peace agreement was negotiated. The Gaza Marine project shows that there are business opportunities that can play a role in building confidence between the two sides in the conflict. Gaza Marine sheds a light on these business opportunities and the role of the private sector in the conflict. Private sector companies such as BG Group and CCC bring more than money, technical expertise and commercial acumen, they also bring political influence and lobbying power. BG could round up a posse of international players in support of the project, including the British government, the EU, the US and the Egyptian government. BG was one of the ten largest companies listed on the London Stock Exchange and one of the largest corporate taxpayers in the UK. It was also a significant participant in the European gas market, had major business interests in the US and was one of the largest foreign investors in Egypt. CCC also brought important political connections to the project. It has close connections with the PNA and has a strong Palestinian identity. The company also had links with other governments in the Arab world, where most of its business was conducted. The willingness of each company to use their lobbying power, the manner in which they used it and the effectiveness of any deployment of this power would also play a role in steering the project's direction.

Some commentators and experts have blamed the discovery of natural gas off the Gaza Strip coast in 2000 for adding to the tensions between Palestinians and Israelis and feeding a cycle of violence that erupted with the second Intifada on the day after the discovery was announced (see Chapter 8). The same experts have accused Israel of trying to gain control of the Palestinians' gas reserves for their own benefit. Rather than trying to gain control of Gaza gas for its own economic benefit, Israel has blocked the Palestinians ability to derive economic benefit for political reasons. Both the Palestinian and Israeli economies would benefit from the development of the gas reserves. Palestinian gas production, especially if it had happened in the early years of this century, would have altered the nature of the Palestinian-Israeli relationship. It would have given the Palestinians some economic independence and would have made Israel partly dependent on the Palestinians for an important energy source. Such a change in the relationship could have reduced the risk of violence and possibly even built enough confidence and trust to allow a breakthrough in the peace process. Instead the story of Gaza Marine gas sheds light on Israel's policy of exerting total control over the Palestinian territories including through methods that involve alleged corruption, highlights aspects of the relationship that are little discussed or studied such as economic issues, shows the limitations on the role of external parties even when large sums of money are at stake and may have played a role in the cycle of violence that erupted in late 2000 and continues to this day.

Gaza was not alone in the region in having substantial gas reserves located off its coast. The region was already known to have gas-prone geology. Neighbouring Egypt was already producing gas from its Mediterranean waters and discoveries had also been made offshore Israel. Exploration for oil in Israeli waters dates back to the early 1960s when primitive methods using dynamite were used, leading to Palestinian residents of Jaffa claiming that those involved had "*burnt the sea*.[1] In later years, Cyprus would also discover gas and Lebanon would start the process of exploration as well. The presence of this gas in the rocks beneath the seabed is a recent phenomenon in terms of geological time. It is the result of rivers laying down silt rich in organic matter during the Pliocene epoch which started around 5.3 million years ago. At that time the climate was warmer and wetter. Large river systems flowed to the sea. Over the millennia new rock layers were deposited. Under the resulting heat and pressure, the organic material was turned into methane (chemical symbol, CH_4), otherwise known as natural gas. The natural gas is trapped in layers of sand and prevented from escaping by overlying rocks. Barring major seismic shifts, the gas will stay there until the political and economic conditions above ground are right for its exploitation. In the mid 1990s, a seismic political shift appeared to signal the start of a new era that would allow the Palestinians to take advantage of their potential mineral wealth.

---

1 LeBor (2007), p207

CHAPTER 1

OSLO ACCORDS (1993-1999)

The modern story of the Gaza Marine natural gas project starts with the Oslo Accords. The agreements and the process behind them created the political and legal framework that allowed the exploration for natural gas to take place in the sea off the Gaza Strip. The Oslo Accords are a series of agreements negotiated between the Palestinian Liberation Organisation (PLO) and Israel in the mid 1990s. The breakthrough resulted from a series of secret contacts between Israeli and Palestinian academics, brokered by the Norwegian government in the first eight months of 1993. Ironically, in light of the fact that Gaza Marine was the largest economic project to emerge from the Oslo process, the first contacts involved economists. Later, official representatives from both sides were brought into the process. These talks were occurring at a time when it was illegal in Israel to have contact with the PLO. The Oslo back channel emerged due to frustration with the US-led peace process that had followed the end of the Gulf War in 1991, precipitated by Iraqi President Saddam Hussein's invasion of Kuwait in August 1990. Saddam had linked his actions to the Israeli/Palestinian conflict and had fired Scud missiles at Israel. Peace between Israel and the PLO became a priority. US Secretary of State James Baker established a multi-lateral peace process that became known as the Madrid Process after the first venue for the talks. The PLO was specifically excluded from Madrid as Israel would not agree to their presence. Instead the Palestinians were represented in a joint Jordanian-Palestinian delegation by prominent, nominally independent, figures such as the writer Hanan Ashrawi and the doctor and activist Dr Haydar Abdel-Shafi.

The first Oslo agreement was signed in Washington DC on 13 September 1993 in a landmark ceremony on the White House lawn. The iconic image from this ceremony shows President Bill Clinton, his arms outstretched, overseeing then Israeli Prime Minister Yitzhak Rabin and PLO President Yasser Arafat meeting and shaking hands for the first time in public. Looking on are other key figures in achieving the agreement, then Israeli foreign minister Shimon Peres, Arafat's deputy Mahmoud Abbas as well as then US Secretary of State Warren Christopher and Russian foreign minister Andrei Kozyrev. These four also signed the agreement. Also, in the audience were many Arab leaders, notably from the Gulf States, who did not recognise Israel. After that initial handshake, Rabin and Arafat made speeches and then shook hands with all the other signatories and VIP guests.

At the time, I was working in the newsroom of the Saudi-owned television station Middle East Broadcasting Centre (then based in London). My colleagues and I were gathered around a screen watching these events unfold as colleagues in Washington reported on them. The question hanging in the newsroom air was this: would the Saudi foreign minister shake hands with Rabin? If he did, this would be the first public contact between the Saudi and Israeli governments and would mark a major break with Saudi policy. The anticipation (in the newsroom) built as Rabin and Arafat made their way along the receiving line. There appeared to be no hesitation on either side, the Saudi minister offered his hand, Rabin shook it. A cheer went up in the newsroom.

That euphoria in the newsroom was echoed around the world. An end to one of the most intractable international conflicts seemed to be within reach. A new era of peace was just around the corner. Peres and other leaders put forward grand plans to give tangible form to this new era such as a canal linking the Red and Dead Seas. As we now know, a new era of conflict and violence appeared from around the corner. That was to come. Before that, officials on both sides, helped by the US and others focussed on putting into effect the agreement signed in Washington.

The agreement signed on that sunny September morning in Washington is officially titled, *"Declaration of Principles on Interim Self-Government Arrangements"*. Unofficially, it is referred to as Oslo 1. As its full name suggests, the agreement was intended to put in place temporary self-government arrangements as a step to full statehood for the Palestinian entity that it created. The Accord set a five year period for negotiation of a final status agreement. More than 30 years later, the *"interim self-government arrangements"* remain in place and the prospect of a final status agreement is as distant as ever.

Oslo 1 set the framework for self-government. It called for elections (which duly happened), establishment of self-rule, first in Gaza and the West Bank city of Jericho, and the creation of a Palestinian police force. The Palestinians in Gaza and Jericho were granted self-government over a limited number of areas including health and education. Also, Oslo 1 laid the basis for Palestinian control over the economy, including energy. At first this would be limited to issues such as direct taxation and tourism. The agreement does though make reference to oil and gas.[2] It calls for the creation of a joint Israeli-Palestinian committee to co-operate over the development of energy resources. Annex 3 *'Protocol on Israeli-Palestinian Cooperation in economic and development programs'* states, *"The two sides agree to establish an Israeli-Palestinian Continuing Committee for Economic Cooperation, focusing, among other things, on the following:"*. The third

---

2 Text of Oslo Accords downloaded from: https://www.jewishvirtuallibrary.org/israel-negotiations-with-the-palestinians

item on the list that follows is, "*Cooperation in the field of energy, including an Energy Development Program, which will provide for the exploitation of oil and gas for industrial purposes, particularly in the Gaza Strip and in the Negev*". This co-operation never happened.

During the year or so that followed the signing of Oslo 1, Israel and the PLO negotiated a series of agreements to implement the Accord. Two of these agreements have direct relevance for the Gaza Marine story and set the framework that allowed for the exploration and discovery of natural gas offshore the Gaza Strip. The first of these agreements was the Paris Protocol, signed on 29 April 1994 in the French capital. This Protocol was incorporated as Annex 4 of the other key agreement in 1994, the "*Agreement on the Gaza Strip and the Jericho Area*". Israel and the PLO signed this agreement on 4 May 1994 in Cairo, Egypt. The Cairo Agreement sets out the detailed arrangements for the establishment of the Palestinian self-rule entity, the Palestinian National Authority (PNA). The agreement specifically states that the PNA's rights extend to the territorial waters and the subsoil. Article 5, clause 1.a states, "*Territorial jurisdiction shall include land, subsoil and territorial waters, in accordance with the provisions of this Agreement.*" Such rights are a vital pre-requisite for the licensing of mineral exploration and exploitation rights. Further, the Cairo Agreement gives the PNA the right to conclude economic agreements with international organisations (Article 6, clause 2.b). Of direct relevance to oil and gas exploration, the agreement also gives the PNA control over surveying activities (in Annex 2, Article 2.B.3).

The significance of the Cairo Agreement also lies in the security arrangements it established for Gaza's maritime area. These are set out in Annex 1, Article 11 along with an accompanying map, labelled Map 6. The agreement's text describes three security zones, known as K, L and M. Zone K extends along what could otherwise be the maritime border (that term is not used) between the Gaza Strip and Israel. It extends 20 nautical miles from the northern Gazan coast and is 1.5 nautical miles wide. Zone M extends along what could be the maritime border with Egypt and has the same dimensions, i.e. 20 nautical miles in length and 1.5 nautical miles wide. Both these zones are deemed *"closed areas"* and only the Israeli navy may sail in these areas. Zone L occupies the area between Zones K and M and also is 20 nautical miles in length from the Gazan coast. The same article also explicitly states that economic activity is permitted in Zone L (clause 2.b).

The creation of these zones in Gaza's maritime area was for the purpose of security control only. They did not indicate that Israel claimed any sovereignty over the maritime area. The question of sovereignty and who (if anyone) had the right to award exploration licences for the area would come to be contested in the Israeli courts. When the time came to undertake exploration activity, the companies conducting seismic surveys and drilling wells had to co-ordinate their activities with the Israeli navy. This involved providing details of the vessels and crew, the type of activity and regular communication. These activities were allowed in Zone L. Vessels were barred from sailing in Zones K and M but at this early stage, entry to those areas was not required. However, development of the Gaza Marine field would require access to at least one of these 'no-sail zones'.

While the Cairo Agreement is clear about the legal and security framework that would be relevant for any economic activity in the waters off the Gaza Strip, Annexe 4, the Paris Protocol, is less clear. The Protocol gives the PNA a general right to economic decision making for its own development and economic priorities. It also contains detailed mechanisms for areas specifically under PNA jurisdiction such as import and export of goods, taxation, agriculture and tourism. It also gives the PNA control over industrial policy. However, the Protocol is silent on exploitation of oil and gas or any other natural resource. Indeed, the protocol contains very few references to energy.

A more detailed protocol, which specifically mentioned energy issues, was to follow. Again in Cairo, on 27 August 1995, Israel and the PLO signed the *"Protocol on Further Transfer of Powers and Responsibilities"*. This covered eight economic areas, referred to in the text as the *"eight spheres"* and each has an annexe providing the detailed provisions. The Protocol gives the PNA authority, power and responsibility over these eight spheres and the right to legislate. Gas, energy and petroleum is one of the spheres and is the subject of Annexe 3. The Annexe specifically mentions oil and gas exploration and states that the PNA has the power and responsibility over oil and gas exploration. For exploration activities, the most significant provision in the Annexe is that the PNA is required only to *"notify"* Israel of any exploration conducted rather than requiring any approval or permission.

This series of declarations, agreements and protocols, the Declaration of Principles, Oslo 1, the Cairo Agreement (including the Paris Protocol) and the August 1995 Protocol set in motion the establishment of the Palestinian self-rule area, first in the Gaza Strip and Jericho and later extended to a large part of the West Bank. They set out the areas over which the PNA had power and responsibility and granted the PNA legislative power over those areas. Of direct relevance to the future exploration for natural gas, the agreements granted the PNA jurisdiction over territorial waters and the subsoil, albeit with an Israeli security overlay. The agreements and protocols also granted the PNA power to legislate on oil and gas matters, including exploration without the need to gain prior approval from Israel. They also gave the PNA the right to reach agreements on economic matters with international partners.

These agreements were having an impact on the ground in both the West Bank and the Gaza Strip. In July 1994, Arafat made a triumphal return to his homeland, arriving in Gaza City by helicopter. It was his first known visit to the land of his birth since he had led guerrilla raids across the River Jordan in the late 1960s and early 1970s. The Palestinian flag, whose public display was banned under the Israeli occupation, was now flying from almost every building in every town in the Gaza Strip and the West Bank, including East Jerusalem. Arafat's image was also everywhere. Shortly after Arafat's return, I made my only visit to date to the Gaza Strip. By this stage, I had left MBC and joined the political risk consultancy Control Risks Group (CRG). For my first research trip for the company, I visited Beirut, Jerusalem and Gaza City. In the summer of 1994, it was possible to take a shared taxi from East Jerusalem to Gaza City. So that is what I did. This involved driving across Israel and passing through a checkpoint at Erez on the Israel-Gaza border. There was only a cursory inspection of my passport. I spent the day in Gaza City and then caught a shared taxi back to East Jerusalem. I was able to wander around the city centre and the waterfront to soak up the atmosphere.

The Oslo Accords are a complex set of documents and implementation was beset by problems almost from the start. Agreeing the details and mechanics of implementation, such as which Israeli forces would withdraw from where, when and how far, took far longer than anticipated. The eight month gap between signature of the Declaration of Principles and the Cairo Agreement setting out the withdrawal from Gaza and Jericho was caused by just such delays. In the intervening period, the violent backlash against the peace process started. On 25 February 1994, an Israeli far-right extremist Baruch Goldstein opened fire on Palestinian worshippers at the Cave of the Patriarchs in Hebron in the West Bank, killing 29 people and injuring many more. Goldstein was a supporter of the far-right Kach group which advocated the expulsion of all Arabs from Israel. The Israeli government banned the group which is also proscribed as a terrorist organisation in the EU, the US and Canada. The Cave of the Patriarchs is sacred to all three monotheistic religions as the site of the tomb of the Old Testament prophet Abraham. A mosque, known as the Ibrahimi Mosque (Ibrahim being the Arabic for Abraham), stands on the site. The Palestinian militant group, Hamas, used the attack as a pretext to launch its own violent campaign. Forty days later (the traditional Islamic mourning period), a Hamas suicide bomber attacked a bus near the town of Afula. He killed eight people and injured many more. This was the first suicide bomb in Israel itself and the first of many in a Hamas terror campaign.

More violence was to follow. On the evening of 4 November 1995, while addressing a peace rally in Tel Aviv, Israeli Prime Minister Yitzhak Rabin was assassinated by another Israeli far right extremist, Yigal Amir, who was opposed to the Oslo Accords. Rabin's death deprived the peace process of one of its most credible advocates. As a former Chief of Staff who had overseen Israel's victory in the June 1967 Six Days War, he could not be accused of being soft on security. He was a highly trusted politician and his death was a severe blow to both Israeli politics and the peace process. The peace process never really recovered. While most of the key agreements had already been signed, implementation proved long and difficult. In the September before his death, Rabin had signed an agreement that became known as Oslo 2. The agreement was officially titled the "*Interim Agreement on the West Bank and the Gaza Strip*" and was signed on 28 September 1995 in Washington DC. The agreement extended the interim self-rule arrangements set up under Oslo 1 to the rest of the West Bank beyond Jericho. There were no significant amendments as far as economic matters were concerned. The agreement also re-affirmed control over territorial waters and subsoil (Article 17, clause 2.1).

Israeli far-right extremists were not the only opponents of Oslo to use violence. The Palestinian extremist group Hamas opposed the Oslo peace process. In the spring of 1996, it also resorted to violence as part of its campaign to derail the Accords. Hamas staged a series of suicide bomb attacks in Israel, mainly targeting buses and public spaces. These attacks marked a change in tactics by Hamas and an escalation in its campaign against Israel. Hamas had assumed the mantle of leader of the resistance to Israeli occupation that the PLO had vacated by entering into the peace process. Hamas would come to replace the PLO as the enemy in the eyes of many Israelis. The group would now be a key player in the Israeli/Palestinian conflict. Its main support base was in Gaza and would eventually become a factor in the attempts to develop the Gaza Marine field.

The initial euphoria created by the 1993 Declaration of Principles was now giving way to suspicion, mistrust and cynicism as delays in implementation mounted and violence returned. On top of these challenges, it was also becoming clear to both Palestinians and Israelis that there would be little real change to their lives. For Palestinians, much of the harshness of the occupation would stay in place and there was little prospect of an improvement in their standard of living. Checkpoints and restrictions on movement would remain and indeed intensify in some cases e.g. more restrictions on Palestinian workers gaining access to jobs in Israel and therefore having a negative impact on their livelihoods. Even for those Palestinians living in areas now under the administration of the PNA, they had exchanged the brutality and indignity of Israeli occupation for a corrupt and brutal police state. For Israelis, peaceful co-existence with their Palestinian neighbours and an end to security threats seemed as elusive as ever.

Although the Oslo Accords were intended to be *"interim"* and lead to a permanent settlement, that has not happened. Instead, the institutions set up under the Accords and the arrangements put in place have acquired a semi-permanent character. They have sustained for more than 30 years despite the collapse of final status talks in 2000, the deaths of leading protagonists in the peace process (Rabin, Arafat and Peres), the end of office of others, doubts over the legitimacy and binding nature of the Accords, periodic escalations of violence and the establishment of an alternative Palestinian regime in the Gaza Strip under Hamas. One effect is that "Oslo" is now almost four-letter swear word in both Israeli and Palestinian political discourse and the reputation of the process and its outcomes is the subject of ridicule, denigration and outright hostility. The high hopes and euphoria of that sunny September 1993 morning in Washington have certainly not been met and indeed dashed.

Despite all the brickbats thrown at the Oslo Accords, they continue to provide the framework in which Israel and the PNA conduct affairs. While it is customary now to focus on the failures of the Oslo process, there have been some achievements. The exploration for and discovery of a substantial natural gas field offshore the Gaza Strip is one of the outcomes of the Oslo process. Without the arrangements put in place under Oslo, this exploration is unlikely to have taken place and the field would have remained undiscovered. The lack of progress from discovery through development to production of the Gaza Marine field symbolises the lack of progress in the peace process since Oslo and is due in part to the tension between Israel and the PNA that has grown since the late 1990s.

The Oslo Accords clearly give the PNA jurisdiction over territorial waters, the subsoil, power to legislate over oil and gas exploration and to award licences to do so. Control over natural resources was an important element of Arafat's state-building agenda. Israeli exploitation of Palestinian resources was (and remains) a central part of the conflict. Arafat established the General Administration for Natural Resources. This department was headed by Ismail Al-Misshal, a Palestinian geologist who had worked in the oil and gas industry in Iraq and Libya before returning to the West Bank following the Oslo Accords. He wrote to Arafat in December 1995 to inform him of the possibility that there were hydrocarbon resources beneath the seabed off Gaza. He recommended that aerial and seaborne surveys be conducted in order to assess the extent of any resources. On 5 May 1996, Arafat replied to Al-Misshal and gave him the authority over this issue. However, it was not until 1999 that the PNA legislated on natural resources. In 1999, it enacted the Natural Resources Law which included provisions that all natural resources are publicly owned.[3] The 1999 law also put on a legal basis the General Administration for Natural Resources. Under the Oslo Accords, the PNA also had responsibility for energy matters. One of the earliest agencies that the new-born PNA established was the Palestinian Energy Agency (PEA) to oversee all aspects of the energy sector in the territories under its control. The PEA would come to play a major role in the Gaza Marine project.

These powers and the resulting legislation could still be invalid if the Oslo Accords are not legally binding documents. Critics on both sides have argued that the Oslo Accords are not binding.[4] However, it has been convincingly argued that the Accords are binding. Not least, both sides have always acted as though they are binding. Despite the clarity in the Oslo Accords and their binding nature, who owned the mineral resources lying beneath Palestinian administered territory became a central question which dogged the efforts to develop Gaza Marine's resources. Some in Israel claimed that it retained ownership and that Israel had gifted the right to exploit them to the PNA, but this was a gift that could be taken back. In 2000, a group of US and Israeli companies that held exploration licences offshore Israel took legal action to prevent BG drilling offshore Gaza. The court did not, in the end, reach a definitive conclusion on who owned the resources. The court accepted the Israeli government's case that the waters offshore Gaza were 'no man's water' and that Israel did not own the resources but could not say for certain who did. The issue of ownership would become more vexed after 2006 when Hamas took control of the Gaza Strip.

Ambiguity over the rights of the PNA to award exploration licences for the Gaza maritime area stems from two questions: did the PNA, as a non-sovereign entity, have the right to award exploration licences?

---

3   Palestinian Legislative Council (PLC) Law No. (1) of 1999 for Natural Resources, article 6.

4   Watson (2000)

Did the PNA have rights over the maritime area beyond its territorial waters? The Oslo Accords had granted Palestinians self-rule over parts of the West Bank and Gaza Strip. They had not established these areas as an independent and sovereign state. It is a well-established principle that sovereign states can grant mineral exploration rights rather than any sub-national or non-sovereign entities. For example, following devolution in the UK, it is the national government in London that grants oil and gas exploration licences in the North Sea, not the Scottish government. On this basis, the PNA did not have the right to award an exploration licence as it was not a sovereign entity. There is, though, a complicating factor. The PLO signed the Oslo Accords on behalf of the Palestinians. Many countries around the world recognise Palestine as a state and the PLO as its representative. Moreover, the PLO enjoys permanent observer status at the UN as a non-member state, a status shared by the Vatican State.

On the second question regarding whether the PNA had any rights over the whole maritime area offshore the Gaza Strip, there is no clear answer here either. The Oslo Accords categorically give the PNA rights over "*territorial waters*". This term is used in the documents. Territorial waters are usually defined as the waters up to 12 nautical miles from the coast. By this definition, the PNA did not have the right to award licences beyond this limit. The licence area extends in a wedge-shaped area more than three times this distance. Sovereign states also enjoy rights to an exclusive economic zone (EEZ) up to 200 miles from the coast. The Oslo Accords are silent on the PNA enjoying an EEZ and as non-sovereign entity, it would not normally possess an EEZ. The Accords do, though, set up security zones that go beyond the territorial waters and encompass part of the waters under which the Gaza Marine field lies (although this was not known at the time the Accords were agreed). The PNA though would award a licence for an area that extended beyond this security zone.

So, what was the entity that the Oslo Accords established? In many respects, it resembled a sovereign government and this was deliberate on the part of the PLO. The organisation viewed self-rule as a steppingstone to full, independent and sovereign statehood. The PLO negotiators insisted on the word "*national*" in the name to suggest a nation. Israeli and many Western commentators routinely drop the "*national*" and refer to the entity as the Palestinian Authority (PA). The head of the PNA was Yasser Arafat, who had become the iconic leader of the Palestinian struggle for statehood. His title was "*rais*". This is the term used in the English language version of the Accords, which is the reference text. Again, this was deliberate ambiguity that could be used by the Palestinians. In Arabic, the word can mean either president (the Palestinians' preferred translation) or chairman (preferred by Israelis and many others). Arafat was confirmed as PNA president in the first presidential election held on 20 January 1996, when he won more than 88% of the vote against Samiha Khalil a prominent charity worker who gained 11.5% of the vote. Arafat appointed a cabinet of ministers to oversee the portfolios for which the PNA had responsibility such as interior affairs, security and tourism. This cabinet included a minister for energy. The PNA also established an extensive bureaucracy, security apparatus and judicial system to administer the areas under its control. As well as executive and judicial branches, the Oslo Accords allowed for the establishment of a legislative function. The first elections for an 88-member legislative council also took place on 20 January 1996. Arafat's Fatah party, which dominated the PLO, won an overwhelming majority, gaining 55 seats. Less than two and half years after the signing of the first Oslo Accord in Washington, the Palestinians had gained a measure of self-rule and the trappings of government.

One of my BG colleagues used this ambiguity about the PNA to avoid intrusive questions from Israeli immigration officials when passing through Israel's Ben Gurion airport on the way to meet PNA officials. Knowing that if he admitted that he was on his way to meet the PNA, he would face extensive questions and long delays. So, when the immigration official asked who was going to meet, he would answer with the concise, "*the government*". He may not have been telling the whole truth, but he was also not telling a blatant lie.

The January 1996 presidential and parliamentary elections held out the hope that a democratic and pluralistic entity would emerge under the PNA's leadership. The elections were heralded at the time as a rare example of democracy in the Arab world. This was despite Hamas and other militant groups boycotting the elections. These hopes proved to be over optimistic. The regime that emerged under Arafat turned out to be in the same model as many other regimes in the Arab world at that time: a despotic police state with high levels of corruption and a circle of crony capitalists around the leader. Power and decision-making were concentrated in Arafat's hands. Despite the institutions set up under the Oslo Accords, he would take decisions without consultation and would rely on a small circle of advisors. This should not have come as a surprise. Prior to Oslo, Arafat had ruled over the PLO in the same style. The PLO had become notorious for corruption and the self-enrichment of its officials. Arafat was reputed to be worth several hundred million dollars at the time of the signing of Oslo 1.

The implementation of the Oslo Accords allowed Arafat and his cronies to transplant the same system to the West Bank and the Gaza Strip and to develop new sources of personal enrichment. The Oslo Accords gave Arafat territory to administer, a well-armed security force and bureaucracy to enforce that administration and access to funds. These funds came from donor governments and international institution aid budgets, repatriation of diaspora Palestinian wealth and business opportunities. The hopes of peace and reconciliation persuaded many around the world to support the emerging Palestinian entity. There was much talk of confidence building measures and projects to take advantage of the new and more peaceful situation such as the idea of a canal linking the Dead Sea to the Red Sea that could generate hydroelectricity and desalinate water. That particular project remains on the drawing board more than 30 years later.

Palestinian and Israeli entrepreneurs saw the opportunities in the establishment of a separate jurisdiction in the West Bank and the Gaza Strip. One of the more incongruous opportunities that came to fruition was the construction and operation of a casino on the outskirts of Jericho. Gambling is illegal in Israel but is popular. Until the mid-1990s, Israelis had to travel to Turkey or further afield to satisfy their urge to gamble on the roll of dice, the fall of the roulette wheel or the turn of the cards. In the mid-1990s, Turkey banned casinos and so that avenue was closed. The new administration in the West Bank presented an opportunity to open a casino close to Israeli cities. In 1999, a group of foreign investors opened the Oasis Casino near Jericho. Among the group of investors was an Austrian businessman Martin Schlaff, who would become associated with the Gaza Marine project but in what capacity is a long running mystery.

Conducting business between the PNA and Israel was not straightforward. Tight controls remained in place for people and goods to cross between the West Bank or Gaza Strip and Israel. Permits and approvals were needed from both the PNA and Israel. Despite the goodwill created by the signing of the Oslo Accords, suspicion and mistrust persisted on both sides. The resumption of violence created tensions. In a sign of hardening attitudes on the Israeli side and a more sceptical view amongst Israelis of the peace process, the right-wing politician Benjamin Netanyahu was elected prime minister in June 1996. While professing support for the Oslo Accords, he took a harder line against the PNA and Arafat.

When it came to business and making money, Arafat entrusted matters to Mohammad Rashid (also known as Khaled Salam), an Iraqi Kurd. Rashid played a number of business related roles for Arafat. He sought new business opportunities, he negotiated deals, he managed Arafat's investment portfolio, he acted as a channel to Arafat for approval for new business projects in the West Bank and Gaza Strip and in doing so, ensured that Arafat received a slice of the profits. Nominally, Rashid acted for the PLO and the Palestinian people but the division between his public role and representing Arafat's private interests was blurred. Rashid headed the Palestinian Commercial Services Corporation (PCSC), which was in effect the PNA's sovereign wealth fund. It held the PNA's stake in commercial enterprises.

Rashid started his political career in the Iraqi Communist Party but was forced to flee to Beirut in the late 1970s after a crackdown on its opponents by Iraq's ruling Baath Party under Saddam Hussein. In Beirut, he made common cause with Palestinian refugees and eventually joined the left-wing Democratic Front for the Liberation of Palestine (DFLP), one of the constituent parties in the PLO. Through this he came into contact with Arafat and despite his communist background proved adept at capitalism. Arafat tasked him with undertaking a small investment in Spain from which Rashid earned a significant profit. This cemented his relationship with Arafat and when the PLO was forced into exile in Tunis in 1982 after the Israeli invasion of Lebanon, Rashid accompanied Arafat as his economic advisor. With the establishment of the PNA in Ramallah following the implementation of the Oslo Accords, Arafat tasked Rashid with building up an investment portfolio in the newly acquired territories. Rashid made investments in local telecommunications, hotels, the local Coca Cola bottling plant and a diverse range of other businesses. In 2012 Rashid was sentenced in absentia by a Palestinian court to 15 years in prison for embezzlement. He currently resides in Cairo and Dubai.

The Oslo Accords had created new facts on the ground in the West Bank and the Gaza Strip. Business opportunities in this new situation, whether building a casino or exploring for natural gas, required engagement with both the Israeli government and with the PNA. Despite all the goodwill created by the Accords, there was still a great deal of mistrust between the two sides and many officials from both sides had never dealt directly with their opposite numbers. Individuals who did have good relations with the other side became sought after as intermediaries, especially for those seeking lucrative business opportunities in the brave new world of peace. Some of those individuals were from overseas, such as Schlaff, who leveraged his existing relations with Israel and gained the trust of some in the PNA, including Rashid. Others came from one side or the other.

One such figure was Yossi Genossar, a former Israeli military intelligence officer who had established strong links with Arafat and Rashid. Lithuanian by birth, Genossar emigrated to Israel in 1946 as a child. After his military service, he joined military intelligence and worked his way through the ranks, including serving as an undercover agent in Gaza, before eventually being appointed head of the northern district in Israel. In 1986, Genossar was forced to resign for his role in the Bus 300 affair in 1984. In April 1984, four Palestinian militants from the Gaza Strip hi-jacked a bus travelling from Tel Aviv to Ashkelon (route 300) and held most of the passengers hostage. When negotiations broke down, Israeli special forces stormed the bus killing two of the hi-jackers but capturing alive the other two. The two surviving hi-jackers were then taken by intelligence officers to a field and summarily executed. Israel's security service Shin Bet, whose officers, including Genossar, had killed the two surviving hi-jackers then embarked on an elaborate plot to cover up the incident. The plot was led by the head of Shin Bet, Avraham Shalom, and included Genossar. The plot involved lying to the investigating authorities and a deliberate campaign to blame the then Israeli Chief of Staff Mordachai, who was tried for the killings but acquitted. The cover up plot started to unravel when press photos came to light showing the two surviving hi-jackers being led from the bus by Shin Bet agents. This was reported first in the international press and then the Israeli media. The result was an outcry both in Israel and overseas. The government held an enquiry and in 1986 several officials were forced to resign, including Genossar.[5]

Genossar also played an instrumental role in another cover up whilst serving in the northern district including southern Lebanon, which Israel had occupied following its 1982 invasion of the country. The 1980s saw the establishment and growth of Hezbollah, a militant Shia organisation founded by Iran to project power in the region, including confrontation with Israel. Hezbollah, under Iranian guidance and using the theological justification put forward by Ayatollah Khomeini, developed suicide bombing as a terror weapon. In November 1982, a Hezbollah suicide bomber drove a truck loaded with explosives at a building in south Lebanon used by Israeli forces. The resulting explosion killed more than 70 Israelis. It was the first suicide bomb to target Israel and remains the deadliest suicide bomb targeting Israel. Realising the devastating impact that the attack would have on morale in Israel, Genossar covered up the real cause of the explosion. His official report blamed an accident involving bottled gas in the building's kitchen.[6]

Following Genossar's resignation from the intelligence services over the Bus 300 affair, Ariel Sharon, then Minister of Trade, appointed him to head the country's export institute. Genossar also seems to have maintained the trust of the country's leaders. Successive Prime Ministers including Yitzhak Rabin, Shimon Peres and Ehud Barak used him to conduct clandestine contacts with Arafat and the PLO.[7] With the implementation of the Oslo Accords, Genossar realised the potential value of the access he had to Arafat and his close circle. He appears to have come to an agreement with Rashid to co-operate on exploiting business opportunities created by the establishment of the PNA. Shortly after the formation of the PNA, the Israeli companies

---

5 For a detailed account of the Bus 300 affair and the ensuing cover up including Genossar's role, see Bergman (2018), Chapter 17.

6 See Bergman (2018).

7 Barak (2018), p350

Dor Energy and Nesher Cement hired Genossar to obtain exclusive rights to supply electricity and cement respectively to the PNA.[8] The two appear to have had an agreement to share any commissions earned. In a sign of Genossar's continuing importance to relations between Israel and the PNA, he was a member of the Israeli delegation to the Camp David talks in 2000.[9] By that time, he was already involved in one of the most significant business opportunities to arise from the Oslo process: the exploration for natural gas offshore the Gaza Strip.

At some point in late 1998 or early 1999, a consortium consisting of the US oil and gas exploration company Samedan and the Israeli company Delek approached Genossar for help in mediating with the PNA. The consortium was known as Yam Tethys. The waters offshore Gaza were already known to be prospective for natural gas. Samedan, later to be renamed Noble Energy, and Delek already held licences offshore Israel where they had discovered natural gas. The US-Israeli consortium wanted to persuade Arafat to award them the licence for exploration offshore Gaza. However, they lacked access to Arafat and so turned to Genossar for help. This was exactly the kind of business opportunity that Genossar was looking to exploit and earn commission from. This was, though, an opportunity that was a magnitude greater than any previous project. The natural gas exploration business requires large sums of money, specialist technical know-how and carries a high degree of risk. Genossar may have felt out of his depth or he may have felt under some obligation to other acquaintances. In any case, it is not clear why he brought other intermediaries into this opportunity. He teamed up with Schlaff and a Swiss entrepreneur Richard Samocha. The three of them expected to earn significant commissions from any deal the Yam Tethys consortium signed with the PNA. Genossar, Schlaff and Samocha took the opportunity to Rashid and Genossar arranged for Samedan

---

8 Roy (2016), p372.

9 Barak (2018), p361.

executives to meet with Rashid and Arafat in early 1999.

Samedan and Delek were not, though, the first oil and gas companies to come knocking at the PNA's door asking for a licence. In late 1997 or early 1998, BG Group made contact with the PNA through CCC. Wael Khoury of CCC introduced Hugh Miller of BG to Walid Najjab, a consultant who worked with Rashid at the PCSC. Miller was then BG's country manager in Egypt and had travelled to Israel to seek new business opportunities. Miller was originally from the US state of Alabama and like many US oilmen preferred informality. So, he rarely wore a suit and tie. He met Najjab at the Dan Hotel in Herzliya, just to the north of Tel Aviv. Najjab then took Miller to meet Rashid in the Israeli town of Rishon Hetzion. Rashid asked Miller if he wanted to meet Arafat. Miller was keen but did not think he was suitably dressed and then worried that he did not have a camera to record the occasion. Rashid assured him on both counts and took him the next day to meet Arafat in Ramallah. The PNA ensured there was a photographer on hand to record the meeting.

When the idea of exploring for natural gas offshore Gaza was first put to Arafat, he was sceptical and was not convinced that there was a real opportunity here. He wanted advice from those who knew the natural gas sector, had contacts with international oil and gas companies and who could be trusted to look after the Palestinian's national interest. Among those he sought advice from was the then Egyptian petroleum minister Hamdi El-Banbi and Wael Khoury of CCC. El-Banbi recommended that Arafat contact BG Group who were emerging as one of the most successful gas explorers in Egyptian waters. Khoury also pointed Arafat towards BG. Khoury convinced Arafat that there really was the prospect of significant natural gas in Gazan waters but made clear that it would need international expertise to make the project happen. If there were significant natural resources to be found off the Gaza coast, Arafat was clear that he did not want an Israeli company involved in their exploitation. This would not be popular with ordinary Palestinians. This would have to be a Palestinian affair with the support of neutral parties. Khoury advised Arafat that he could find a suitable international partner and form a consortium to undertake the exploration of natural gas offshore Gaza. Khoury had turned to BG, with which CCC already had a relationship as it was a contractor on a major BG project in Kazakhstan, the Karachaganak gas and condensate project. As far as CCC was concerned, BG was the ideal partner. It was a blue chip gas exploration company, listed on the London Stock Exchange, had enjoyed considerable success exploring for gas offshore Egypt and CCC had an existing relationship with it. BG was also convinced there were further gas discoveries to be made in the area, given the knowledge they were acquiring through exploration and development activities offshore Egypt's Mediterranean coast. After those initial meetings with Hugh Miller, further meetings followed. At a meeting on 8 February 1999 in London, Khoury and BG Group's Tim Forbes appear to have formally agreed to bid for the Gaza Marine licence. Forbes was the BG vice president with responsibility for new business in the Middle East.

Arafat tasked Rashid with leading the negotiations for the Gaza Marine exploration licence. Arafat did not dismiss the proposal from Yam Tethys. While he did not want Israeli participation in the exploitation of Palestinian natural resources, he saw the benefit of maintaining competitive tension between two rival bidders: the Yam Tethys consortium and the CCC-BG partnership. Other companies had also expressed an interest in acquiring the licence, amongst them the Eilat-Ashkelon Pipeline Company (EAPC). This was a joint venture formed in the 1970s between Israel and Iran, then under the rule of the Shah who had established good relations with Israel. EAPC, as its name suggests, had been created to build an oil pipeline across Israel linking the Red Sea with the Mediterranean to by-pass the Suez Canal and facilitate the export of Iranian crude to Europe and North America. The pipeline was never built (in 1979, the Iranian revolution and Israel's peace treaty with Egypt changed the geopolitical dynamic). EAPC did though still own land in an industrial park outside of Ashkelon and was looking for sources of revenue. In the late 1990s, the Iranian government still held its stake in the company but with the hostility between the two countries was not able to play any role. Any EAPC revenue was directed into an escrow account and did not flow to Tehran.

Whichever company eventually won the Gaza Marine licence, Rashid realised that Israeli acquiescence to granting the licence would be needed in addition to future co-operation in allowing exploration activities to go ahead. Rashid needed a green light from the Israeli government for the PNA to award the licence. Under the terms of the Oslo Accord, approval for granting a licence was not strictly required but realpolitik dictated that it would be needed. Rashid understood that without Israeli approval, the licence would be worthless. If he did not consult Israel on the licence, then the risk that they would block exploration activity in future increased markedly. Israeli security control over the Gaza maritime area established under the Oslo Accords (zones K, L and M) gave Israel an effective veto over any offshore activity. Rashid almost certainly used Genossar as his emissary to the Israeli government, then led by Benjamin Netanyahu. However, Netanyahu was forced to call an early general election in May 1999 having lost a vote of confidence in the Israeli parliament, the Knesset. He lost the resulting election to Ehud Barak, who after the horse trading that follows Israeli elections formed a government in July 1999. Rashid gained the green light that he needed. In later years, Israeli critics of the Gaza Marine project would describe the licence and the right to explore offshore Gaza as a "*gift*" from Barak that could be taken back.

The right to award the Gaza Marine licence may have been less of a "*gift*" and more in the way of a purchase by the PNA or by BG. Did the PNA pay a bribe to the Government of Israel to secure the right to award the Gaza Marine licence? Or did the PNA bribe someone (perhaps Genossar) to persuade the Israeli government to allow the PNA to proceed with the Gaza Marine licence? What is certain is that allegations that a bribe was paid surfaced some years after the event. The Israeli journalist Ben Caspit and others have alleged that a bribe of $40 million was paid to secure the Gaza Marine licence. Caspit accuses BG of paying the $40 million bribe. The allegation takes various forms. Some have the PNA paying the bribe, others allege that BG Group paid the bribe to secure the licence. It is not certain that any bribe was paid. Indeed, the evidence that any bribe was paid to secure Israeli acquiescence to the Gaza Marine licence is weak. As noted above, there are differing versions of who is alleged to have paid any bribe and who is alleged to have received any bribe. Also, the motivation for any bribe is not clear. Was it to secure Israeli approval or to obtain the licence itself? The $40 million sum itself is exactly the same amount that BG was prepared to state in public as the amount it would spend to explore for gas in Gaza's waters. The Israeli press would erroneously report this sum as the actual amount BG paid to acquire the licence. In reality, it represented the cost of hiring a drilling rig and associated services to undertake exploration in Gaza's waters.

While standards of corporate governance were less strict in 1999 than they are today, even then, paying a bribe of $40 million for a company like BG would have been extremely difficult. That would have been a large sum for BG to pay for a licence in 1999 and would have required the co-operation, conspiracy and cover up of a large number of people, probably including its auditors, to go undetected. Also, BG did not have motive. The company was not so enthusiastic about the prospect of exploring offshore Gaza that it would have been prepared to pay a bribe of that magnitude to secure the acreage. This was not highly sought after acreage and BG was not facing fierce competition to gain access.

In 2007-8, BG commissioned a law firm to conduct an investigation into the manner in which the company had gained the licence. The conclusion of this investigation was that if any bribe had been paid, BG had not paid it or allowed it to be paid on its behalf. The investigators delivered their report in 2008. By that time, the allegations of corruption and unethical conduct in the Gaza Marine project had already been circulating for some time and the damage had been done. BG had been involved in the project for nearly a decade at that point with very little to show for it. The company was having regrets about becoming entangled in the project.

CHAPTER 2

A CLOUD OF SECRECY
(1996-1999)

How did BG Group plc, a blue chip, FTSE 100 listed gas company become entangled in the politically treacherous and commercially risky arena of the Israeli/Palestinian conflict? BG Group plc was the UK's third largest oil and gas company and listed on the London Stock Exchange where it was one of the 10 largest companies and at times one of the largest corporate taxpayers to the British treasury. It was one of the successor companies to the state-owned British Gas, privatised under Prime Minister Margaret Thatcher in 1986. The publicity campaign to sell the shares to the public used, as its strap line, "*Tell Sid*" and became one of the iconic privatisation campaigns of the Thatcher government. When it was a state-owned entity, British Gas held monopoly control over the whole of the gas value chain in the UK from exploration and production in the North Sea, gas storage, transmission of gas around the UK, distribution to individual businesses and homes and even the retail of gas appliances such as heaters and cookers. After privatisation, it gained the freedom to expand overseas and faced competition from new entrants in the UK as the gas market underwent liberalisation. In the late 1980s, British Gas took advantage of this new freedom to invest in new markets including Egypt through the acquisition of independent exploration and production company Tenneco in 1988. Through the 1990s, as it acquired new gas-prone acreage offshore Egypt in the Mediterranean Sea, British Gas established a strong position in Egypt. Back in the UK, as a response to reform of gas market regulation, British Gas made the decision to de-merge parts of its operations. First in 1999, the high-pressure gas transmission system was spun off into a separate company, Lattice (later to merge with the electricity transmission operator National Grid). In 2001, the second de-merger saw the UK gas storage, distribution and retail business separated as Centrica. At this point BG Group plc was created which contained all the international businesses and the North Sea oil and gas fields. To signal its new identity, BG Group stopped using the name 'British Gas'. Also, it had licensed the name to Centrica to use for its retail business in the UK. So, Centrica's customers in the UK would still receive a gas bill headed 'British Gas'. BG Group held its international businesses in various subsidiaries. The Gaza Marine licence was held by BG Great Britain Ltd, which was a wholly owned subsidiary of BG International, in turn 100% owned by BG Group plc. In February 2016, BG Group plc was acquired by the oil and gas super major Royal Dutch Shell (Shell). So, Shell became the owner of the 90% share in the Gaza Marine licence along with CCC holding the remaining 10%.

BG's journey to Gaza Marine started in 1996 but like many visitors to the Occupied Palestinian territories, it travelled via Israel. The Gaza Strip was not the original destination. The skills and the experience the company had gained from operating across the gas chain in the UK was one of its strengths. Its strategy as it embarked on international expansion in the late 1980s and early 1990s, was to promote that gas chain expertise as its unique selling point to governments looking to develop their gas sectors and to City investors as setting the company apart and making it an attractive share to buy and hold. However, by the mid 1990s, BG's ability to point at successful examples where it had deployed this expertise were scarce. The then Chairman of BG's Board of Directors Richard Giordano set out to change that and saw an opportunity to do so in Israel.

In 1996, he visited Israel as part of a delegation of British business looking for new opportunities and keen to take advantage of the peace dividend that was then being much touted in the aftermath of the Oslo Accords. Also, on the delegation was Lord Young (David Young), a former trade minister in Thatcher's government who had close ties to Israel. Lord Young appears to have played a key role in persuading Giordano of the merits of Israel and would later sign a contract to act as a consultant on the Gaza Marine project with a hefty success fee.

Israel seemed to offer BG the chance to display its gas chain skills. The Israeli government was offering licences to explore for gas offshore and was seeking to gasify its economy through construction of a gas transmission network and conversion of its power stations to gas from coal and oil. This was exactly the type of gas chain that BG wanted: exploration and production of gas through to transmission of that gas for use in power generation. However, Giordano, who was a larger than life American and not known for his diplomatic skills nearly ended BG's ambitions before they had started. As part of the trade delegation, Giordano was asked to address an audience of senior Israeli government officials and business leaders. This was an opportunity to promote BG's gas chain skills and explain the benefits of BG investing in the country. He summarised them in a way that could have caused huge offence, "*we are going to gas Israel*".

Despite this gaffe, BG was able to establish a presence in Israel. Building a gas chain in Israel did make strategic sense for BG at the time. It was the type of integrated business it wanted to invest in, and it was already building a substantial business next door in Egypt. BG was looking for further growth areas in the region and so embarked on an Eastern Mediterranean strategy, hence Miller's visit to Israel. BG did succeed in finding new opportunities in Israel but did not achieve the original aim of developing a gas chain. In 1997, the Israeli government engaged BG as a consultant to give advice on designing and building a natural gas transmission network in the country. This placed BG in a strong position to lead the work on constructing and operating the network. After a protracted and politically controversial tender process, BG declined to bid for this project as it did not make economic sense to the company. Meanwhile, at the other end of the chain, BG also acquired exploration licences in Israeli waters. The acquisition of a substantial business in Israel posed risks to its business in Egypt and aspirations in the wider region. Despite the peace agreement between Egypt and Israel, relations (particularly commercial relations) with Israel remained controversial in Egypt. To balance, its position in Israel, BG took the opportunity to acquire the Gaza Marine licence offered by the PNA.

Secret Shareholders

At various times in the Gaza Marine saga, journalists and BG's competitors have asked questions about the true owners of BG and made accusations of secret shareholders on the BG side. These accusations persisted despite BG's listing on the London Stock Exchange. As a result of the public sale of shares in 1986, BG Group plc had thousands of individual shareholders as well as pension funds and other institutional investors. At any given time, there were tens of thousands of shareholders and no one shareholder had more than a 3% stake in the company.[10] While there were no secret shareholders, there were some stakeholders who kept to the shadows. Various well-connected politicians and consultants were used in the early days of the project. Some of these consultants were well known figures such as the former British trade minister Lord Young, noted above. Others were more obscure including former Israeli intelligence officers. The obscurity of such consultants concerned their precise role on the project and what they stood to gain financially.

By the late 1990s, Egypt was becoming increasingly important to BG. BG had acquired a number of gas prone licences in Egyptian

---

10 Under LSE listing regulations, 3% is the threshold for identifying a shareholder

waters and it was clear that there were significant gas resources there. At the same time, BG's acquisition of licences in Israeli waters risked undermining its reputation in Egypt and prevent it for building relations of trust, which would be needed for success. Although Egypt and Israel had signed a peace treaty in 1979, relations remained cool. BG did not want to place the Egyptian government in an awkward position and likewise Cairo would be reluctant to use valuable political capital with its own public opinion in defending a company with ties to Israel that was taking an increasingly prominent role in an important economic sector in Egypt.

The prospect of acquiring the Gaza Marine licence would allow BG to counteract opposition to its Israeli interests and show that it was also investing in the Palestinian economy. This did not, though, make Gaza Marine a vital part of the BG portfolio. It was a *"nice to have"*. While there was an expectation that the company would discover gas, there was no anticipation of a gigantic discovery that would be transformative for the company or for the Palestinians. Gaza Marine and Israel were seen very much as annexes to the Egypt business. It was the prospects for natural gas discoveries in the Egyptian sector of the Mediterranean that were of most interest to BG at this time. In 1999, it was at the start of its exploration campaign. The success of this campaign would eventually make BG one of the most important foreign investors in the Egyptian economy. It would also create an opportunity for the development of the Gaza Marine field that did not involve Israel. All that was in the future, for the moment, it was interested in securing the Gaza Marine licence.

The informal agreement between BG's Tim Forbes and CCC's Wael Khoury on 8 February 1999 to form a partnership to bid for the licence had to be turned into a formal contract. Each would have to obtain approval from their respective Boards for this partnership and for the terms under which they would submit a binding bid to the PNA. Forbes immediately wrote a memo to the BG Chief Executive Frank Chapman, reporting on his meeting with Khoury and setting out the case for teaming up with CCC to explore offshore the Gaza Strip. The partnership with CCC would take the form of an unincorporated joint venture, a common arrangement in the oil and gas sector. The two partners would not form a separate company but, would each hold their share of the licence in a subsidiary.

CCC, the Palestinian Partner

Who was this company that BG were teaming up with to explore offshore the Gaza Strip? Said Khoury (father of Wael Khoury) and his cousin Hassib Sabbagh along with a third Palestinian Kamel Abdul-Rahman founded The Consolidated Contractors Company (CCC) in 1952 in Lebanon. Abdul-Rahman left the company in 1980. Sabbagh and Khoury were from the town of Safad, now in northern Israel and until 1948 part of the British Mandate of Palestine. Safad is also the hometown of Mahmoud Abbas, the PNA president. Sabbagh and Khoury were forced to flee Safad during the 1948 war that followed the declaration of the State of Israel when Arab armies invaded the territory and the Israelis forced thousands of Palestinians to flee as refugees. Both men played prominent roles in the PLO and became close to Arafat as advisors. The sons of both men now control the company. Khoury's sons Tawfik, Samer and Wael all play leading roles as do Sabbagh's sons Suhail and Samir. The company started as a sub-contractor on construction projects in the Middle East. It has since grown to become one of the most successful Arab-owned companies in the world undertaking projects across the globe and remains family owned. It has undertaken a string of large construction projects in the Middle East including airports, roads, hotels and embassies as well as oil and gas facilities. It was originally based in Beirut but as a result of the civil war there in the 1970s relocated to Athens, which remains its headquarters. The company has maintained close links with its Palestinian roots and has significant business interests in the Palestinian territories including construction and energy. CCC owns the majority of the power station in Gaza City, the only electricity generating plant in the Palestinian territories. Although construction is its prime interest, CCC has an oil and gas exploration arm. This subsidiary is registered in Beirut and is the entity that holds CCC's share in the Gaza Marine licence. The BG-CCC relationship had some unusual features that caused concern for some BG staff who encountered it.

Licence Acquisition
On 13 May 1999, Forbes received the first of the approvals he needed to proceed when BG International's new ventures committee gave the green light to seek the acquisition of exploration acreage offshore Gaza. While Forbes or one of his team may have verbally informed CCC of the decision, BG did not confirm the decision in writing to CCC until the end of the month when Hugh Miller wrote to CCC's legal department to confirm that BG were going ahead. Detailed discussion must already have been underway, as a month later on 29 June 1999, BG and CCC initialled the agreement that would govern the relationship between the two companies on Gaza Marine. This agreement was called the Area of Mutual Interest (AMI) agreement. At this point, though, some of the key terms were not agreed, as negotiations with the PNA on the licence terms had yet to get underway. However, the outline agreement with CCC allowed Forbes to get the next approval he needed. On 1 July 1999, BG's investment committee gave the go ahead. The next day Wael Khoury (note not Tim Forbes) wrote to Walid Najjab of the PCSC requesting the formal start of negotiations for the Gaza Marine licence. It seemed that CCC, rather than BG, were in the driving seat. This is despite BG bringing the bulk of the finance and the technical know-how to the joint venture. BG would be appointed as "*operator*" of the Gaza Marine field.

The pace of events then picked up. On 6 July, discussion of the Gaza Marine opportunity was on the agenda of BG's executive committee. This was the same day that Ehud Barak won the Israeli election. On 21 July, BG's executive gave firm project approval and on 30 July, the project got its own budget in BG. On 2 August, Arafat gave his blessing to the project in a meeting with Miller and Rashid. BG and CCC signed the final version of the AMI agreement on 23 August. Among the key terms of this agreement was the equity split in the licence. This would initially be 90% to BG and 10% to CCC but when the project received its final investment decision, which would happen after exploration and signal the start of the field's development, this split would change to BG 70%, CCC 30%. The agreement also contained provisions to allow for the PNA to acquire a direct equity stake in the project. CCC could allocate up to 50% of the additional 20% it acquired on project sanction to the PNA at cost i.e. CCC could not sell the equity to the PNA at a profit. However, CCC was under no obligation to do this, so there was a risk that the PNA would end up with no direct stake in the project if CCC was not minded to take advantage of this provision. Other key clauses including an agreement that BG would meet 100% of the exploration costs, known in the oil and gas business as a "*carry*". CCC would repay its share of those costs and its share of the development and operating costs once production started i.e. when it started receiving revenues from the field. The PNA would also be responsible for its share of the costs if it did indeed acquire any equity stake. If the PNA did acquire a stake, under the agreement terms, the final shareholding in the project once development work on the field started could be BG 70%, CCC 20%, PNA 10%. An intense period of negotiation followed between BG and CCC on one side and the PNA on the other to agree the terms of the licence. These negotiations took place in several different locations: London, Athens, Ramallah and ultimately Vienna.

Licence Signature
Rashid, Najjab and others were in Vienna in mid-October 1999 for an event to mark one year since the opening of the Jericho Casino.

BG and CCC used the occasion to finalise the negotiations and reach a deal. Arafat was due to visit London in mid-November and the PNA wanted a landmark deal for him to sign. At this eleventh hour, the PNA made a demand, they wanted a guaranteed equity stake in the project. They wanted to be sure that they would receive at least 10%. It is not unusual for a host government to demand some equity share for their state oil company. In the case of the PNA, they did not have a state oil company and this last-minute demand threatened to delay any agreement. Any share would be held by the PCSC. The demand for a guaranteed share would mean CCC being obliged to give up some of its share and thereby dilute the value they would obtain from the project. Despite some frantic last-minute negotiations immediately before the agreements with the PNA were to be signed, this issue remained unresolved until July 2000.

Despite the lack of agreement on the extent of the PNA's direct participation, on 19 October 1999 in Vienna, the Gaza Marine project agreements were signed by Tim Forbes on behalf of BG, Samer Khoury for CCC, Maher Masri, the Palestinian economy minister at the time on behalf of the PNA and Harbi Sarsour for the Palestinian Petroleum Authority. There were two principal agreements signed in Vienna. The first known as the Upstream Agreement set out the terms and conditions for BG and CCC to undertake exploration activities offshore the Gaza Strip and the procedure to follow in the event of a discovery. The second agreement was the Downstream Agreement. This committed BG and CCC to invest in gas infrastructure in the Gaza Strip to allow gas to reach the Gaza power station and for the construction of a gas distribution network in the territory. The second agreement would become a source of tension with the PNA. Signature of the agreements was celebrated in conjunction with the anniversary of the Jericho Casino. So, the event was also attended by Martin Schlaff who had played a role in getting that project off the ground. In his remarks at the event, Schlaff got the name of the company confused and referred to "*BP*" rather than "*BG*".

The agreements were now ready to receive Arafat's blessing during his visit to London. A signing ceremony was held on 10 November 1999, overseen by then British Prime Minister Tony Blair. Arafat signed the Upstream and Downstream Agreements for the PNA, BG CEO Frank Chapman signed for BG and Wael Khoury for CCC. The Upstream Agreement granted BG and CCC a licence to explore for oil and gas in the area offshore Gaza. This is a wedged shaped area of approximately 1300 square kilometres that stretched beyond Gaza's territorial waters and beyond the security zones set up under the Oslo Accords. BG and CCC had committed to acquiring seismic data over a large part of the area and drilling four exploration wells. The agreement set out three exploration phases: an initial phase of one year, a second phase of 18 months during which at least two wells must be drilled and a third phase of 18 months during which two further wells must be drilled. Once this exploration was complete, the agreement obliged BG and CCC to relinquish at least 50% of the acreage in 25% tranches. The first tranche would be released 18 months after 19 October 1999 and the second tranche a further 18 months after that. BG and CCC would retain rights over any acreage needed for the development of the field in the event of a commercial discovery. Such arrangements are typical in the oil and gas sector. They allow governments to recycle acreage and encourage further exploration activity.

There was also an immediate, but modest, financial windfall for the PNA. Under the terms of the agreement, BG and CCC agreed to pay a signature bonus of $250,000 to the PNA. Again, such bonuses are a typical feature of oil and gas upstream licence agreements. This was a modest sum for a signature bonus, which can run into many millions of dollars (even at this time in the late 1990s) for highly sought after acreage. The modest sum reflects the high risk nature of the Gaza Marine acreage. This was unexplored territory in a politically complex environment and there was not a great deal of competition for it. This appears to be the only sum that BG paid to the PNA for the licence. As BG was paying all the costs at this point under the carry arrangement with CCC, BG paid the signature bonus in full. BG also went to considerable lengths to ensure that the signature was paid into a bona fide PNA account and not into the personal account of Arafat, Rashid or any other PNA official. As a result, it was 13 June 2000 before the signature bonus was paid to the PNA. A BG in-house lawyer who was working on the project at the time, verified that the account belonged to the PNA's petroleum authority and that this was the authorised bank account to receive the payments. The lawyer also created an audit trail within BG and ensured all the requisite internal approvals were obtained for making the payment. Furthermore, the lawyer ensured that payment of the signature bonus did not break any British laws relating to financing terrorism or money laundering. The extent of work required to make this modest payment highlights the difficulties anyone working for BG would have encountered in trying to make a $40 million payment as a bribe.

Signature of the Upstream and Downstream Agreements marked a significant moment for the PNA. The agreements secured investment from a blue chip oil and gas company, was a step forward on the road to recognition of Palestine as a state and signalled a way forward for the PNA to secure its own revenue stream in due course. It was also a rare tangible success stemming from the Oslo process. If the project progressed through to development and production, it would undoubtedly be one of the largest investments in the Palestinian economy. It would though take several years before the licence holders would be ready to undertake any sizeable investment. In the meantime, BG established a presence in the Palestinian territories. BG opened offices in both Ramallah and Gaza City. Since the PNA was based in Ramallah, an office there made sense to represent BG and liaise with the administration. The office in Gaza City was essentially to demonstrate commitment to Gaza and show intent on transferring knowledge to the Palestinian economy. The intention was to have some of the engineering work undertaken by Palestinian staff based in Gaza. In Ramallah, BG rented office space in a building owned by CCC. As country manager, they took on a CCC employee Wael Abulaila. He was a Jordanian citizen of Palestinian origin and so as a non-resident was entitled to a generous expatriate package. BG did not employee him on a staff contract but rather as a consultant. Also, in the office were a finance manager, a PA/receptionist and an office assistant. The Gaza City office had two employees. As well as these two offices, BG already had an office in Tel Aviv, where some of the exploration and drilling team would be based. Hugh Miller was now BG's country manager in Israel and would lead the effort to persuade both the Israeli government and the PNA to co-operate and allow the project to go ahead. Forbes and the rest of the Gaza Marine management team were based at BG's head office on the outskirts of Reading, west of London.

BG and CCC gained the Gaza Marine licence as a result of direct negotiations with the PNA rather than as the result of a bid process. While direct negotiation is not unknown in the industry, it has disadvantages for both the licensing authority, in this case the PNA and the companies involved. An open bid process allows the licence authority to gauge the level of interest in the licence on offer and to create competition between bidders. The result should be the best deal for the economy. An open bid process can also give confidence to citizens and other stakeholders that the licence has been won fairly and that the government has gained the optimum deal. Such an open process therefore reduces the risk to companies of later accusations of unethical conduct in obtaining the licence or that the licence terms are inequitable. By contrast, direct negotiations do not always allow for competitive tension and therefore the licensing authority cannot be sure that they have obtained the best deal. This is a particular risk for entities such as the PNA that are not accustomed to negotiating such deals. The lack of transparency around the Gaza Marine licence award was one factor that allowed accusations of corruption to dog the project. At the same time the corporate governance around such new ventures was not as vigorous as it would become. There was not a comprehensive assurance process to examine the terms of the agreement, any existing data on the geology or the political, economic and social context into which BG was entering. The company had undertaken almost no due diligence on CCC as its new partner nor on the PCSC. The agreements and particularly the Upstream Agreement contained some terms that would cause difficulty for BG in the future. A considered review of the agreement at the time may have led BG to demand changes during drafting which would have led to a more balanced agreement in some areas. When BG many years later tried to sell its stake in Gaza Marine, some of these terms, the lack of governance and due diligence would cause significant issues for the company.

At BG in 1999, Gaza Marine came under the responsibility of the Middle East group headed by Tim Forbes. He was a flamboyant figure who looked like he should have been working in advertising rather than the oil and gas sector. He had the reputation of being a maverick and for liking the finer things in life. He drove a Bentley to the office. He had also secured a prime corner office for himself. He had reportedly turned his nose up at the standard office furniture and brought his own. He had spent his career in the oil and gas sector. Before joining BG, he had worked as a senior vice president at the French major oil company Total. His strength was finding the opportunities and landing them. He relished being the hunter and the challenge of the chase. Forbes was given a long rein by the BG Chief Executive Frank Chapman to pursue deals. He seemed particularly attracted to politically difficult parts of the world where others feared to tread. As well as Gaza, he had got BG into Iran, an easier task then than today but still a risky venture. There was also a rumour that he had attempted to get BG into Syria, but this was vetoed by Chapman who had first-hand experience from his time in Shell. Outside of the Middle East, Forbes had also courted the military junta in Myanmar.

Pride of place on his office wall was a framed photo of him meeting the generals. This was another opportunity deemed too hot to handle by Chapman. Next to the photo of Forbes with the Burmese generals was a photo of him shaking hands with Yasser Arafat.

Forbes would meet with Arafat several times as part of his efforts to ensure that the Gaza Marine project went ahead. After the signing of the Gaza Marine agreements in London in November 1999, the next occasion would be a visit to Israel and the West Bank by Frank Chapman in March 2000. The visit's objective was to demonstrate BG's level of commitment to Gaza Marine and reinforce political support for the project. Chapman spent around 24 hours in Israel and the West Bank. He arrived on 6 March and left the next day. Accompanying him on the visit was Forbes and BG's then head press officer Peter Crumpler as well as Hugh Miller. The delegation flew into Tel Aviv's Ben Gurion airport. The first meeting was with the British Ambassador to Israel, Francis Cornish, who served them tea in the grounds of his residence. Rather, his staff served the food and drinks but showed their lack of familiarity with traditional British afternoon tea by serving the cakes before the sandwiches, irritating the ambassador.

The next meeting on Chapman's schedule was with the Israeli Minister of Infrastructure, Eliyahu Suissa, whose portfolio included energy. The meeting had been arranged by Yossi Langotsky, a consultant hired by BG to act as their government relations advisor in Israel. His tasks included getting permits for drilling activities offshore Israel. Suissa reiterated Prime Minister Ehud Barak's support for the project. The BG delegation then travelled up to Jerusalem where they checked into the American Colony Hotel in East Jerusalem. This is one of the top hotels in the city and especially in the predominantly Arab east of the city. Its central courtyard shaded by lemon trees with a fountain gurgling in the centre is a favoured meeting place for international visitors and Palestinians. Here, Crumpler had arranged for Chapman to meet Israeli journalists to get some press coverage of the visit and PR for the project. One question took Chapman and Crumpler by surprise, why was the BG delegation staying in this hotel and not in Israeli West Jerusalem? Choosing to stay at the American Colony was taken as showing bias towards the Palestinians.

The next day, Chapman and the rest of the BG delegation were waiting for the phone call to confirm the meeting with Arafat before they set off for his headquarters in Ramallah in the West Bank. To pass the time, while they were waiting, Miller suggested a tour of Jerusalem's Old City which is just a short distance from the American Colony. However, just as they were about to set off, the call came through that Arafat would meet them. Like all visitors to the West Bank, Chapman and the BG delegation had to make sure they travelled in a car with the correct registration and permissions into cross into PNA-administered territory. Cars with Israeli registration plates are not permitted to do so. The delegation changed cars mid-way through the journey so that they arrived at the Israeli checkpoint in the correct vehicle. They were then driven to Arafat's heavily guarded headquarters in Ramallah, known as the Muqataa.

The meeting, intended to build goodwill with Arafat and the PNA, came close to an embarrassing fiasco. Arafat was using the new millennium to promote the Palestinian territories and particularly Bethlehem as the birthplace of Jesus. The Bethlehem mayor accompanied him to the meeting. Arafat presented the BG delegation with Bethlehem 2000 medals. Chapman and the BG delegation had nothing to present to Arafat in return. This was a major diplomatic gaffe, would embarrass BG and potentially undermine any attempt to build goodwill. Chapman was wearing a BG lapel badge. He unpinned the badge and presented it to Arafat. The Palestinian President was happy. So happy, he immediately pinned it to his lapel. A diplomatic gaffe had been averted and turned into a PR coup for BG.

Arafat was still wearing the BG lapel badge the next day when he held talks with the Israelis as part of efforts to salvage the Oslo process. The talks made headline news and the following day, 9 March, Arafat was pictured on the front page of the Financial Times clearly wearing the BG pin badge. The BG team were ecstatic. This was the kind of publicity that money could not buy and potential embarrassment had been averted. However, the incident over the gifts revealed BG's naivety and lack of understanding of the business culture in which they were operating in the Middle East. Forbes and his team had not done their homework. Staying at the American Colony Hotel could have compromised them in Israeli eyes and they nearly embarrassed themselves in front of the Palestinian leader. This lack of homework and preparation had more serious implications than getting the diplomatic niceties wrong. The BG team also lacked a deep understanding of the political situation they were entering and the risks this posed to the project. While they seemed to have the right instinct in balancing their interests in Israel with those in Palestine and trying not to show any bias, BG had not undertaken deeper analysis. This would prove a costly oversight.

The 10% Share for the PNA

The exploration of minerals such as natural gas held the prospect of the PNA developing a measure of financial independence. Its main sources of funds were contributions from international donors and customs dues collected on its behalf by Israel. Under the agreement signed with BG and CCC, the PNA would earn revenue through tax and royalties on gas production. The royalty rate was 12.5% and the corporate income tax rate was 25%. This represented marginally more generous terms for the PNA than offered under the equivalent Israeli regime in place at that time. Nevertheless, as noted above, the PNA demanded a guaranteed direct equity stake in the project. This would mean a larger slice of the revenue from the project through its share of profits and dividends. Underlying the PNA demand was its concern that it would suffer political backlash from civil society and opposition groups for selling access to a prime Palestinian asset too cheaply to foreign interests. The PNA's demand was a classic example of resource nationalism. The PNA was demanding a greater share of resources for the national interest. BG and CCC were both reluctant to accede to the PNA's demand, primarily because it would reduce their returns from the project.

This issue became known as the "*surplus interest*" issue as that was the term used in the agreement that finally settled the matter. Agreement came in the form of Schedule 3 to the AMI between BG and CCC. Both companies signed the agreement on 11 July 2000, marking completion of the agreement between BG and CCC on their participation in the Gaza Marine project. In Schedule 3, BG would assign a further 10% share, the "*surplus interest*" to CCC on the condition that it assigned a 10% share to the PCSC at cost. Also, in the agreement was a profit sharing arrangement should the PCSC ever sell its stake at a profit. In that case, BG and CCC would split the profits 50/50. BG had no separate agreement with the PNA or PCSC on the surplus interest. This was not part of the agreements signed with the PNA on 19 October 1999 or in London on 10 November. CCC's agreement to assign 10% to the PCSC was contained in a separate letter signed only by CCC and the PCSC. These changes in the equity share of the Gaza Marine project would only take effect once the project was sanctioned and work on developing the field started. At that point the shareholdings in the licence would change to BG Group 60%, CCC 30% and the PNA 10%. The PNA would hold this 10% share through its investment arm the PCSC. In the meantime, through the exploration phase, the shareholdings would remain at BG Group 90%, CCC 10%.

CHAPTER 3

"A GIFT FROM OUR GOD"
(1999-2003)

Under the terms of the Upstream Agreement, BG and CCC held a four-year licence to explore for gas offshore Gaza. The agreement was due to expire on 19 October 2003. During that four-year period, BG and CCC were obliged to drill four wells. This four-year exploration period was divided into three phases. Phase one was one year and during that time BG and CCC were required to undertake initial exploration activities including the acquisition of data. Phase two was 18 months and during that time, BG and CCC were obliged to drill at least two wells. Phase three was the final 18 months and there was an obligation to drill another two wells in that period. The validity of the Upstream Agreement could only be extended beyond these four years if BG and CCC made a discovery that was economic to develop and the PNA had approved a field development plan.

Four years was not a long period for an exploration programme and so BG immediately got to work having established a presence in the Palestinian territories with the offices in Ramallah and Gaza City. In all cases where there is more than one company involved in an exploration programme, one of the companies is appointed "*operator*". It is the operator who is responsible for ensuring that the exploration work happens and happens to the appropriate standard. The operator organises tenders for the various contractors that are required such as supplying a rig and all the specialists that are needed to drill wells. In the case of Gaza Marine, BG was the operator so would undertake the work on the concession. The costs of this work would be met by both partners, BG and CCC in proportion to their shareholding, so 90:10. However, as BG had agreed to carry CCC's and the PNA's costs until development of the field was sanctioned and the shareholding changed to 60:30:10, BG paid 100% of the exploration costs of Gaza Marine and costs associated with finding a market for the gas. At the point the shareholding changed, CCC would pay 30% of costs occurred to that point and of the costs after that point. At the same time, the PNA would become liable for 10% of past and future costs.

Between 1999 and 2014, those costs amounted to around $100 million. As the project has not reached the point of final investment decision and the shareholding has not changed from 90:10, BG has paid all these costs. CCC and the PNA have not made any financial contribution to the Gaza Marine project. Although it was operator, BG was not completely free to make decisions on Gaza Marine. Major decisions, including annual budgets required approval by CCC as a partner with a financial interest. In keeping with standard industry practice, a series of committees were set up to act as decision-making bodies. These were an operations committee (opcom) that would oversee all activity on the concession and two sub committees, a technical committee (techcom) to consider aspects such as drilling and engineering and a finance committee (fincom) to consider budgets and other financial issues. From the start, discussions in these committees, especially opcom and fincom proved contentious. One significant area of disagreement was costs. Each year, BG diligently produced a budget and largely kept within it. However, CCC avoided approving any budget or costs. Since a majority was required for decisions and spending to go ahead, CCC with a 10% stake could not block decisions. CCC avoided approving budgets so as to give themselves maximum room for negotiation when the time came to agree past costs at project sanction. As long as it had not approved budgets and costs, it was not committed to meeting its share. This would be a weeping sore throughout the project's existence. Relations between BG and CCC would at best be civil and at times were extremely tense. They were rarely if ever warm.

One other peculiarity of Gaza Marine partner meetings was the presence of PNA representatives. It is highly unusual for representatives of the licence granting authority to be present at such meetings unless it has a direct stake. In this case, the PNA did not yet have a direct financial stake. The intention for them to back into the licence at project sanction provided justification for their attendance. Partner meetings would frequently involve discussion of issues that would require eventual PNA approval such as requests for permits. The partners needed to discuss these first and agree a common position before making a case to the PNA and be able to present a united front.

The first task was to assess the potential of the concession area and to acquire data on what lay beneath the seabed. To achieve this, BG undertook a seismic survey over 1000 square kilometres of the concession area. Shooting seismic is a typical early stage in understanding the potential of a concession area. In maritime areas, it involves a ship bouncing sound waves through the rocks below the seabed and then picking up the echo through a series of microphones trailing behind the vessel. As sound travels through rock at different rates depending on the density of the rock, a picture of the rock structure below the surface is obtained from analysing the data. Interpretation of the data suggested that there was a substantial gas bearing structure around 36 kilometres from the Gaza shoreline. There were also smaller structures to the west, closer to what could be the maritime border with Israel. Based on this analysis, BG proposed to the PNA and CCC that it drill the first exploratory well in the large structure. In the event of success, a further well would be drilled to appraise any discovery.

Legal Challenge

Before drilling could start, BG faced another challenge. On 21 August 2000, the Yam Tethys partners launched a legal case in the Israeli High Court claiming that the Israeli government rather than the PNA possessed the right to licence the Gaza Marine area. Yam Tethys sought an injunction against BG to prevent it drilling in the Gaza Marine licence area. Yam Tethys argued that as the PNA was not a sovereign state, it could not grant licences and that the Israeli government had not consented to the licence award. The consortium also argued that in any case, the PNA had no jurisdiction over natural resources. In effect, BG and CCC's rights to the licence were invalid and therefore they could not undertake any exploration activity. BG was not an original party to the lawsuit as Yam Tethys were suing the Israeli government but petitioned successfully to join the legal case as an interested party. BG threw considerable resources at the case. It hired a Paris-based lawyer who was one of the leading experts in this field. It also brought in prominent academic experts, including Vaughan Lowe QC, Professor of Public International Law at Oxford University. BG's counter arguments drew on precedents of other non-sovereign or quasi-sovereign entities awarding exploration licences and the law of capture. The law of capture applies to areas of land or water that are not claimed by any state and so the first state to assert possession gains rights under this accepted principle of international law. The Israeli government also invoked international law in stating its position. The government's position was that it did not have any sovereignty claim over the Gaza offshore area and this was in effect 'no man's water'. Based on this position, the law of capture may well apply. In the end, the court dismissed the Yam Tethys petition on 23 November 2000, but it did not give a definitive ruling on the question of who had the right to award any exploration licence in the waters offshore Gaza. Instead, the court accepted the Israeli government's position, but it did not rule on who did have any rights. The various Israeli administrations since 2000 have not changed this position. This appears to be a tacit acceptance that the rights granted under the Oslo Accords for control over the subsoil and right to explore for hydrocarbons are valid. However, the lack of definitive legal ruling has created an element of uncertainty around the status of the Gaza Marine licence.

Drilling for Gas

BG did not wait for the outcome of the court case, it carried on with its plans to drill the first Gaza Marine well. It was a success. On 27 September 2000, BG Group announced the discovery of gas around 36 kilometres offshore the Gaza Strip. BG Group made a big show of the announcement. Arafat travelled on a fishing vessel, named the *Jandaley*, to within sight of the rig and gave the signal for the lighting of the flare on the rig to celebrate the discovery. He described the gas discovery as "*a gift from our God to our people, to our children, to our women, to our people inside and outside, to our refugees and those who are living here on our land*".[11] It was a much welcome and needed piece of good news at a time when the peace process was in trouble and Arafat's dream of a Palestinian state was slipping away. BG Group had just discovered the future state's largest natural resource. Arafat declared that the discovery was, "*a strong foundation for a Palestinian state*".[12]

The spectacle of the celebration continued. Both flares on the rig were lit, sending flames shooting out over the Mediterranean Sea. This became an iconic photograph of the project: the almost perfect symmetry of the rig with flares lit. It provided visible evidence of the resources beneath the seabed. Ironically, many years letter, the brand police at BG Group outlawed use of the photo in BG promotional material. Attitudes to flaring had moved on as the damaging

---

11 Orme, William, "Arafat Hails Big Gas Find Off the Coast Of Gaza Strip", The New York Times, 28 September 2000

12 Ibid.

environmental consequences of the practice became better known. As a result, any images depicting flaring were banned from use in BG publicity.

The rig in the photograph was the Atwood Southern Cross. It was standing in 603 metres of water and had drilled several thousand metres below the seabed to make the discovery. Drilling on the well had started (known as spudding in industry jargon) on 29 August and had taken four weeks to drill. The results of the well proved the analysis conducted after the seismic programme. A significant gas-bearing structure existed. Tests conducted on the well showed gas flowing at around 37 million cubic feet per day. BG's initially estimated that the gas reservoir contained around 60 billion cubic metres of gas. At least one further well would be required to gather more information and obtain a clearer idea of how much gas was down there.

Trouble Flares

Before that second well could be drilled, political events deflated the high hopes and expectations that had ballooned following the gas discovery. The day after the blazing announcement of the gas discovery, the right wing and controversial Israeli opposition leader Ariel Sharon made a visit to the Temple Mount in Jerusalem. Sharon made his 28 September visit to underline Jewish claims to the site where Judaism's first and second temples are thought to have stood. The site is now occupied by Islam's third holiest site, the Temple of the Rock and the Al-Aqsa mosque. The visit was a provocative political statement designed to boost Sharon's standing in his own Likud party and embarrass then Prime Minister Ehud Barak. Sharon was far advanced in his rehabilitation from disgrace following his role in the 1982 massacre of Palestinian refugees in the Sabra and Shatila camps in Beirut during Israel's invasion of Lebanon. Sharon was now poised to become leader of his party and prime minister.

The reaction to Sharon's visit was immediate and violent. Clashes flared during his visit in the immediate vicinity of the Temple Mount as Palestinians protested his presence. Those clashes set off a firestorm throughout the West Bank and Gaza Strip. Sharon had ignited the second Intifada. This uprising would last until February 2005 and result in around 3000 Palestinian deaths, 1000 Israeli deaths and 64 foreigners losing their lives. The uprising also saw the effective end of the peace process started by the Oslo Accords. The uprising and the accompanying tensions and hostility between Palestinians and Israelis would hamper efforts to make progress on the Gaza Marine project but would not put a total stop to activity, at least not immediately.

Was it a coincidence that Sharon timed his visit to the Temple Mount for the day after the announcement of the Gaza gas discovery? The answer is almost certainly yes. While Sharon was not a supporter of the Oslo peace process, his motivation behind the 28 September visit lay in Israeli domestic politics rather than an overt attempt to frustrate the peace process. This outcome of his visit was secondary but one he could support. Any direct linkage between the visit and the gas discovery announcement the previous day was unfortunate timing. Although Sharon would certainly have known that BG was exploring off the Gaza coast, he is unlikely to have known the results of the drilling or the exact date of the announcement in advance. He would though not have been disappointed to wipe news of the gas discovery off the front pages and focus attention elsewhere.

A Second Well

Despite the outbreak of the second Intifada, BG Group went ahead with drilling the second well in the Gaza Marine licence area. Indeed, the violence had very little practical impact on BG's ability to operate in Gaza's waters. There was no need for vessels, their crews or materials to pass through any areas affected by violence. Vessels entered the licence area from international waters and used Israeli ports when necessary. Relief crews and contractors could fly into Israel's main international airport, Ben Gurion, and be ferried to the rig and vessels from Israeli ports.

BG once again contracted the Atwood Southern Cross to drill the Gaza Marine 2 (GM-2) well. Drilling started on 16 November 2000 and took about four weeks to drill. This well was located around 35 kilometres from the Gaza coast. This time the rig was standing in around 535 metres of water. The GM-2 well was an appraisal well. The objective for this well was to confirm the presence of natural gas and to obtain more data on the structure to get a more accurate picture of the size of the resources. Based on the data obtained during the drilling of both wells, the experts at BG now estimated that the resources amounted to approximately 1 trillion cubic feet (tcf) or around 40 billion cubic metres of gas in place. This estimate of the volume of gas would later be confirmed by independent experts. The cost of drilling the two wells was approximately $40 million.

In order to conduct the activities so far - the seismic survey and drilling two wells - BG and the contractors undertaking the work co-ordinated with the Israeli navy. All this work took place in Zone L, set up under the Oslo Accords. Co-ordination included informing the navy in advance of the planned activities, the names of vessels and their intended routes, allowing navy personnel on board for inspection and daily contact with the navy during operations. At no time during these operations did the navy deny permission to BG or its contractors. Also, this co-ordination did not cause any significant delays to the work.

Building on Success

Having discovered a significant volume of gas, the Gaza Marine project team embarked on three parallel work streams. The first was to understand if there were any other resources to discover in the concession area. The second was to plan and undertake the design and engineering work necessary to develop the field, including designing the facilities to extract the gas, bring it to shore and process it to allow it to be used. The third work stream was to secure a market for the gas.

The BG team spent most of the following year, 2001, evaluating the results from the two wells and deciding on a preferred development concept for the field. In this work they were helped by engineering consultants who presented a range of options for developing the field. The technical aspects of developing the Gaza Marine field were relatively straight forward. The development did not seem to present any particular engineering challenges. It was not in particularly deep water nor was it an extreme distance from shore. The development was well within the parameters of technology current at the time. It would be a similar development to that BG was undertaking next door in Egypt with great success. The option that was chosen in 2001 was that all the facilities required for extracting the gas would be situated on the sea floor and would be operated remotely from a processing plant on the shore via cables. A pipeline would connect the gas gathering facilities to the processing plant. There would be no platform on the sea surface to indicate the location of the field. Any maintenance or repairs required once sea floor facilities were operational would be conducted by a remote-controlled robotic submarine launched from a surface vessel. This sub-sea development concept remained the preferred option for the rest of the time that BG held the licence.

While BG was working on the design of the facilities that would extract and process the gas, the political, legal and commercial environment for the project was becoming more difficult. Throughout 2001, the second Intifada raged on and made the political situation increasingly uncertain. On the commercial front, BG was struggling to secure a market for the gas, one of the three work streams required to allow field development to go ahead.

Running Out of Time

BG was also running out of time to undertake one of the other priorities, which was to assess whether there were any further resources to be discovered in the concession area. Under the terms of the Upstream Agreement, BG and CCC were obliged to relinquish 25% of the concession area 18 months after signature. That deadline was 19 April 2001. There was now insufficient time to undertake further exploration activities in the area due to be relinquished. On 18 April 2001, BG's Tim Forbes wrote to Mohammed Rashid requesting a one year delay on relinquishment. In view of the challenges that BG and CCC were facing and probably because he did not want to antagonise major investors, Rashid agreed to the one year delay.

BG was becoming concerned that it would not be able to fulfil its obligations before the Upstream Agreement expired on 19 October 2003. Faced with this increasing political, legal and commercial uncertainty, BG now had to consider its options. It could walk away from the project and return the licence to the PNA. This would mean writing off the expenditure incurred to date against its profits. This would not look good to its shareholders. BG was carefully crafting a reputation in the City as a reliable and prudent company. Another option would be to declare *force majeure* i.e. circumstances beyond the company's control prevented it from going ahead. This would place the project in a state of suspended animation. BG would retain the licence but all work on the project would stop. Both these options were not only unpalatable to BG, but were also opposed by the PNA and CCC. The PNA did not want to lose a blue chip investor and the project's abandonment would be a blow to its ambitions for Palestinian statehood. CCC did not want to let the project go as it was an important part of their portfolio, would damage their reputation in their home territory and would undermine efforts to gain more business from BG projects elsewhere in the world. Furthermore, BG's interpretation of the Upstream Agreement was that it could only claim *force majeure* if it had entered the third and final exploration phase and was then unable to meet its commitments, which were the drilling of two wells.

An Outline Development Plan

The solution agreed between BG, CCC and the PNA was contained in an exchange of letters in early 2002 that circumvented the licence terms and allowed BG to hold the licence, engage in minimal activity but without declaring *force majeure*. In the normal course of events, once BG and CCC had met their exploration commitments, were able to demonstrate to the PNA that the gas discovered was commercially viable for development and had submitted a field development plan that met with the PNA's approval, the Upstream Agreement would then be extended for 25 years. This time period was to allow sufficient time for the field's development, production for around 15 years and then abandonment of the field. This time period is typical for development and production licences in the industry. However, without a clear route to market and the prospect of not being able to meet the exploration commitments, producing a field development plan was impossible. The plan would need to include parameters such as the volume of gas production, the capacity of the pipelines and receiving terminal, the final specification of the gas and the daily flow rate.

The solution that BG proposed to the PNA was for the PNA to allow BG to submit an outline field development plan that only covered the parameters in general terms. BG and CCC would enter Phase Three of the exploration programme, meeting its commitments but BG would not declare a commercially viable discovery. In return the PNA would grant a 25-year extension to the Upstream Agreement. In April 2002, BG and CCC wrote to Mohammed Rashid to confirm they were entering Phase Three. They now had a year in which to drill two more wells. On 25 May 2002, Rashid wrote to BG and CCC to confirm approval of the outline field development plan and granting the 25-year extension. As BG had not made a declaration of commercial viability, no change in the shareholding was triggered. The shareholding structure remained at BG 90% and CCC 10%.

While BG had agreed to enter the third exploration phase, it did not want to drill two more wells in the concession. BG had agreed to enter Phase Three under pressure from CCC which was anxious to fulfil the commitments of the Upstream Agreement. Based on its analysis of the seismic acquired over most of the concession, the geologists at BG did not believe that there were any further significant resources to discover in the area. On top of that, the growing political, legal and commercial challenges would make it more difficult to justify further exploration activity and gain the approval of BG management to spend more money on exploration. Having entered the third phase, BG now came under pressure from CCC and the PNA to drill two more wells. Forbes negotiated with the PNA to find alternatives to drilling the two wells and to obtain an extension to the deadline for Phase Three. The result was that in place of drilling the third well, BG would acquire more seismic data over the remaining concession area near to the Gazan coast. BG undertook this seismic programme in early 2003. The exchange of a well for more seismic appears to have been reached in a verbal agreement between Forbes and Rashid. Later in 2003, a BG lawyer noted that there was no formal agreement to this change in the exploration commitment. Forbes also obtained a six-month extension to the third phase.

The deadline for the second relinquishment of 25% of the concession area was approaching. The Upstream Agreement set a deadline of 36 months after signature, so 19 October 2002. On 14 October 2002, Forbes wrote to Rashid proposing the area to be relinquished. However, the PNA were concerned at the perception that would be created if the relinquishment went ahead. The PNA believed that this would send a message that the acreage was not prospective and therefore undesirable for other investors. Rashid replied on 20 November 2002 and informed BG and CCC that he was unconditionally deferring all relinquishments "*until a future date to be determined solely by the PNA*". While BG and CCC could not hold on to all the concession area, the PNA could now demand relinquishment at any time.

CCC and the PNA still wanted another well drilled so that the exploration commitment was met. Their pressure on BG to drill what would now be the third Gaza Marine well increased following a discovery in Israeli waters. In early 2003, the Noa gas field was discovered close to the putative maritime border with Israel. This field appeared to lie partly in Palestinian waters. BG and CCC dubbed this the Border field. CCC and the PNA now demanded that BG drill the third well to confirm the Border field's existence. In addition, CCC and the PNA wanted any gas discovered to be developed for supply by pipeline direct to the power station outside Gaza City. This was the only potential large-scale consumer of gas in the Palestinian territories and was majority owned by CCC. BG still did not want to drill another well. However, BG's analysis showed that development of the Border field for supply to the Gaza power station was potentially an economic prospect. Also, it did not want the reputation damage that would ensue from failing to meet its exploration commitments. BG opened negotiations with the PNA on a memorandum of understanding (MoU) to cover this new aspect of the Gaza Marine project. These negotiations led to a suspension of the Phase Three deadline. As well as an MoU covering the Border field development, the two sides also had to negotiate a gas sales agreement for sale of gas to the power station.

By this time, BG was negotiating with a new entity in the PNA, and Mohammed Rashid was no longer in his post. In 2003, international donors demanded reforms to stem corruption in the PNA and introduce greater transparency. Arafat appointed former IMF official Salam Fayyad as finance minister. Fayyad was respected and trusted by donor institutions and governments, including the Israelis. At the same time, a system known as the single treasury account was set up to bring a greater degree of transparency to the PNA's accounts and the flow of revenues, including those remitted by Israel. The reforms also included the dismantling of the PCSC and the establishment of the Palestinian Investment Fund (PIF) that unlike its predecessor is subject to external audit. This was the organisation that BG now negotiated with. Its first chief executive was Walid Najjab who had served as a consultant to Rashid and the PCSC and had made the first introduction of BG to the PNA back in the late 1990s. The PIF acts as a sovereign wealth fund for the PNA. It holds assets on behalf of the PNA in the local telecoms network and in real estate development companies. The PIF succeeded the PCSC as the PNA entity that would hold the PNA's 10% share following project sanction. CCC had brought Najjab and BG together and now played a role in the PIF as well. Samer Khoury, one of three brothers at the helm of CCC sat on the PIF Board.

Israeli Co-operation and Competition

The exploration activities conducted offshore Gaza in 2000-2003, the two seismic campaigns and drilling two wells also highlighted the need for co-operation with the Israeli government. To carry out those activities, BG and its contractors needed to co-ordinate with the Israeli authorities and particularly the Israeli navy. All these activities took place in Zone L, one of the security zones set up in the Gaza maritime area by the Oslo Accords. Co-ordination with the Israeli navy is required to sail any vessel or rig into Zone L. The navy co-operated during the exploration phase, but that co-operation is not guaranteed in the future. Since the seismic survey and drilling activities that BG undertook in 2000-03, the circumstances offshore have changed considerably. Israel perceives an increased risk in this area. Israel has prevented vessels from overseas that are protesting at the situation in Gaza from entering the waters. It has also imposed constraints on the ability of Palestinian fisherman to operate, even in water close to the shore. During peak construction of the field, there could be a fleet of approximately 20 vessels working in the area. Specific permission is required to enter the no-sail zone along the putative Israeli- Palestinian maritime border (Zone K). Ships will need to enter this zone to carry out seabed surveys along the pipeline route and other vessels will need to sail through this zone to lay the pipeline and cables.

While the Israeli government has no direct commercial stake in the Gaza Marine field, it has a loud, even controlling voice in the project. The development of the Gaza Marine field cannot go ahead without the Israeli government's approval and continued co-operation. Israeli government officials have repeatedly made it clear that they will only allow Gaza Marine development to go ahead under circumstances where Israel retains control over the gas and the flow of funds. Following the discovery of the field, Israeli government officials stated in meetings with BG that the receiving terminal must be located on Israeli territory and all the gas must land in Israel. At times, it has blocked progress on the project, citing fears that the revenues would end up in the hands of terrorists.

Until considerable gas resources were discovered in its waters in 2009-10, some in the Israeli government also saw gas from Gaza Marine as making an important contribution to meeting its own energy needs. There was however little apparent co-ordination between the various entities with a stake in meeting the country's energy requirements. These entities included the state-owned power generator IEC (which until recently enjoyed a monopoly), the Ministries of National Infrastructure, Finance and the Prime Minister's Office. Some, especially in IEC, were keen to secure Gaza Marine gas but there was a lack of political will at the very senior level to make the compromises necessary to secure an agreement. Such compromises risked undermining the wider attempt to maintain control over the PNA and to reinforce the country's security. Supply of Palestinian gas to Israel would have given the PNA a degree of leverage over Israel and altered the nature of the relationship between the two.

Gaza Marine was not the only gas field that BG had discovered in the waters of the eastern Mediterranean. In 1999, BG had acquired a 50% share in five licences offshore Israel, known collectively as the

Med licences. These were in the waters immediately adjacent to the
Gaza Marine licence. Its partners in these blocks were a collection of
Israeli companies including Delek. The other partners were Isramco
and a consortium of industrial companies who were potential
customers for the gas known as Middle East Energy. BG drilled
two wells in one of the blocks, Med Yavne in 1999 and made two
discoveries, named Or and Or South. In the summer of 2000, while
it was preparing to drill the first Gaza Marine well, BG drilled a well
in the Med Ashdod block and made the Nir discovery. Meanwhile,
in June 2000, it had allowed the other three Med licences to expire
without undertaking any exploration activity. All three discoveries
were very small accumulations of gas and BG eventually relinquished
all the acreage and handed the licences back to the Israeli authorities.
In December 2000, BG acquired six further licences in Israeli waters,
collectively known as the Gal licences. Four blocks were located in
deeper water adjacent to the northern end of the Gaza Marine licence.
The other two blocks were further north off the coast of Haifa. BG
acquired 3D seismic over most of these blocks but did not conduct
any further exploration activity despite identifying a potential large
field in one of the northern blocks named Michal. However, BG was
reluctant to drill a well. BG's experts assessed that the well would be
technically challenging as it was likely to encounter high temperatures
and pressures in the gas reservoir. This would make it a very expensive
well. BG was struggling to find a market for its gas in Israel and
could not make an economic case for further exploration activity in
Israeli waters. BG eventually relinquished all the Gal licences. Some
of these, including Michal were eventually acquired by Noble and
Delek. They would go on to drill a well on Michal in 2009, which
did indeed prove to be one of the most expensive offshore wells
drilled anywhere in the world up to that time. However, the well
also marked the discovery of one of the largest gas fields found up to
that point in Israeli waters as well. It would have an impact on Gaza
Marine but more on that later.

CHAPTER 4

"THE RACE IS FIXED"
(2000-2002)

B G was not the only company that had discovered gas in the area in 1999-2000. The Yam Tethys consortium of the US-based Noble Energy and the Israeli company Delek discovered the Mari B field in March 2000. The field was, at that time, the largest discovered in Israeli waters with reserves of around 1tcf of gas - a similar size to the Gaza Marine discovery. The field was located just north of Zone K, the security zone dividing Palestinian and Israeli waters under the Oslo Accords and was closer to the shore. As noted above, in August 2000 BG discovered the Nir field, around 12 miles offshore. This was a much smaller discovery at around 274 billion cubic feet of gas.

The Israeli Gas Market: A Pipe Dream
In the late 1990s, the Israeli government encouraged gas exploration as part of its strategy to switch power generation in the country from coal-fired to gas-fired. Recognising that it would take many years from the first exploration activity for gas to the first molecules flowing to Israeli power stations, the government also sought other sources of gas and made plans for the pipeline infrastructure to transport the gas to Israeli power stations and industry. Since 1994 in the afterglow of the Oslo Accords, Israel and Egypt had been in intermittent discussions on an agreement to supply Egyptian gas to Israel. Such a supply would require building a pipeline from Egypt,

dubbed the *"peace pipeline"* and a pipeline network within Israel. The Israeli government also investigated the feasibility of importing gas from further afield, including Russia and Nigeria, in the form of liquefied natural gas (LNG). The plans to import LNG plans did not make any immediate progress. The proposals to import Egyptian gas also made little progress as Egypt focussed on developing gas for its own use and prioritised LNG export schemes as economic relations with Israel remained controversial amongst the Egyptian population. At the same time, the Israeli government did not always take a strategic approach to important national projects such as energy supply and the necessary infrastructure. At one point in the mid 1990s, two government-owned companies were proposing rival gas infrastructure projects and came close to launching competing tenders for the same project. After becoming Prime Minister in June 1996, Netanyahu created the Ministry of National Infrastructure and appointed Ariel Sharon as the first minister of this new department.

Led by Netanyahu and Sharon, the Israeli government pushed on with plans to construct a national gas pipeline network. One question that the government wanted to answer was how to prevent one company or consortium gaining monopoly control through owning the physical infrastructure and supplying the gas. As a small country with a limited number of large companies, successive Israeli governments have taken care to prevent monopolies and Israel has stringent anti-trust laws. The issue of monopoly supply of gas would re-emerge in the future with potential benefits to the Gaza Marine project. In the meantime, the government placed conditions on the pipeline project, including a limit of 26% ownership of the pipelines by any company that supplied gas. The government also demanded that local companies team up with an international partner. In March 1997, the government launched an international tender process for the project. Initial interest was strong with 22 companies expressing an early interest. Among the companies expressing interest was BG Group, then still known as British Gas. It teamed up with two local companies, Mashav and the Dankner Group. When the deadline for submission of bids arrived in March 1998, five consortia entered bids. The Ministry of Infrastructure was reported to be disappointed with only five bids after the initial interest. These consortia consisted of 11 companies in total. The Ministry undertook to make a decision by the end of May 1998 to keep to the project schedule which called for much of the project to be in place by 2000 to allow gas to flow. The Ministry did not keep to the schedule. The pipeline project was beset with delays. As the months passed, the bidding companies became frustrated at the process and one by one dropped out. Attempts by some companies to have the restrictions on ownership eased to make the project more economically attractive failed. The delays were caused in the main by political indecision over Israel's preferred source of energy for the 21st century. Sharon had set the end of December 1998 as a decision point but in November put off the decision for another year. At this stage the only options for a gas supply were from overseas, either from Egypt next door or sources further afield such as Russia. In all cases, this posed considerable risks to Israel's energy security as the country could find itself in the situation of relying on one source of gas and a potentially unreliable source. Coal and oil, on which it relied, could be imported from a variety of sources and there was a well-developed global market in both.

At the time of Gaza Marine's discovery in 2000, perceptions inside the Israeli government and the business community on energy security had shifted. Discoveries of gas in Israeli waters in 1999 and 2000 and then the Gaza Marine discovery demonstrated that Israel had access to gas resources close to hand. It did not need to import Egyptian gas (not just yet anyway). Switching to gas would also mean cheaper and less polluting energy sources to meet growing energy demand. The potential demand for gas would mean that by the middle of the decade, Israel would consume more gas than its own Mari B field would be able to provide. Israel was becoming an attractive market for natural gas and would need other sources of supply. For BG and its partner CCC, Israel provided the only viable market in the region for the bulk of Gaza Marine gas. A small amount of the gas could also be used in the Gaza Strip. However, all potential suppliers of gas to Israel faced a major hurdle. In 2000, very little of the gas transmission system had yet been constructed. So, there was no pipelines to transport natural gas from southern Israel (or the Gaza Strip) where most of its gas fields had been discovered to power stations and industry in the north. The backbone of this gas transmission system would be an offshore pipeline parallel to the Israeli coast. At this stage there were still four consortia, including BG and its partners, in the race but the government had not yet come to a decision. The government was now grappling with the challenge of choosing a long term gas supplier. This would now take priority over the pipeline project but the two would have to come together at some point in the future if Israel was going to be able to take advantage of its own gas resources. The pipeline project would also provide a possible route to securing Israeli government approval for the development of Gaza Marine. That was for the future.

In the meantime, local companies such as Isramco, that had been successful in finding gas in Israeli waters were pressing for the government to prefer Israeli suppliers first. It received a sympathetic hearing in some parts of government, which was now led by Prime Minister Ehud Barak with Eliyahu Suissa as infrastructure minister. In June 2000, Suissa stated his preference to use Israeli gas first. His definition of Israeli gas extended to any Palestinian gas. At this point, the Gaza Marine field had yet to be discovered but the potential for gas resources to exist was suspected. BG had started exploration activities. When the extent of the Gaza Marine field was known in late 2000, Suissa and others in the Israeli government appreciated that it was a potentially valuable source of energy for Israel. The Gaza Marine discovery was larger than any discovery to date in Israel. Next door, Egypt was also enjoying even greater exploration success.

Egypt was becoming self-sufficient in gas and was looking for export options. Importing gas from Egypt was back in the frame as a realistic possibility.

Choosing Gas Suppliers

Israel would need to source gas from beyond its own borders and faced the enviable position of having multiple, low cost, choices to meet its gas demands: its own gas, Palestinian gas or Egyptian gas. The Egypt option was taking more definite shape. A specific proposal had replaced the government level discussions of the mid-1990s. A partnership of Egyptian and Israeli entrepreneurs, known as Eastern Mediterranean Gas (EMG), was putting together a proposal to construct a pipeline across the Sinai Peninsula to supply Egyptian gas to Israel. The Israeli partner was Yossi Maiman, who allegedly had close links to the Israeli intelligence agency Mossad. The Egyptian partner was Hussein Salem who had close links to then Egyptian President Hosni Mubarak. The EMG project would later become embroiled in allegations of corruption, particularly on the Egyptian side.

Faced with at least three potential gas suppliers, the government charged the Israeli Electric Corporation (IEC, the state owned power generator) with selecting a long term gas supplier. IEC was looking for 15 years of supply with an annual supply of around 3 billion cubic metres of gas. There was a great deal at stake in this tender for both Israel and for potential gas suppliers. Israel was securing an important component of its future energy supply. For the suppliers, this was a lucrative and long term business opportunity. IEC would be spending hundreds of millions of dollars per year to buy gas. This process provided a potential route for Gaza Marine gas to be sold into the Israeli market. However, Gaza Marine would face strong competition from the other two potential suppliers: the Yam Tethys consortium and EMG. In the spring of 2000, IEC asked all three potential suppliers to set out their offer. Yam Tethys confirmed that they could supply the country's gas needs for 15 years from its gas resources discovered in Israeli waters. EMG not only confirmed that it was also capable of exporting sufficient volumes of Egyptian gas to meet Israel's requirements for 15 years but had secured an Egyptian government guarantee for that supply. On 6 June, BG was the third and last supplier to make an offer to supply Israel's gas needs for 15 years. In July 2000, the IEC negotiators embarked on discussions with the three potential suppliers, visiting first Cairo and then London to hold talks. Ostensibly, the tender process would use the clear and well-tested government procurement procedures. In reality, it would be a murky and bruising experience, especially for BG. IEC's strategy was not clear. Would it favour Israeli domestic gas over imports? Was it looking for one supplier for all the volumes for 15 years or would it seek more than one supplier to avoid a monopoly situation? Gaza Marine's discovery in late September 2000 (and the size of the discovery) appeared to influence government thinking on its supply options. Government officials indicated that they would prefer Palestinian gas over other import options (i.e. Egypt). Within a month, with the second Intifada raging, Israel's finance minister Avraham Shochat denied press reports that the government would block Palestinian gas imports. On 6 November, Shochat intervened again in the gas supply bid process in a much more dramatic way. He announced that there would be no preferment of Israeli domestic gas for supply. IEC should make its decision on purely commercial terms. Politics should play no part. Two days later, IEC asked all three bidders to submit detailed price proposals for their supply options.

From the start, the odds were stacked against BG Group. The structure of BG's bid was more complex than the other two and in Gaza Marine, it had a partner with a strong Palestinian connection and that was based in Lebanon, a country with which Israel was still at war. Under trading with the enemy laws in place since the British Mandate period, Israeli companies are barred from doing business with Lebanon-based companies. BG focussed on promoting its own bid and its credentials. There was an extensive campaign of meetings with relevant stakeholders in Israel, including government officials and key IEC representatives. BG also ran a public relations campaign including arranging for key journalists to visit its head office in the UK. BG's bid was more complex as it was proposing to supply the required volume of gas but was not identifying a specific source for the gas. In the event that it was one of the selected suppliers, it would supply the gas from a combination of Gaza Marine, its Israeli fields and from Egypt. This was in contrast to the Yam Tethys bid which would supply from a designated field, Mari-B and the EMG bid which would supply gas from Egypt, where there was already known to be plentiful supply (and a government guarantee). The structure of BG's bid also meant that it would face competing pressures from its partners. Its Israeli partners, Isramco and Middle East Energy, would demand that it favour Israeli gas in meeting its supply commitments whereas CCC and the PNA would demand that it favour Gaza Marine gas. On the same day that the High Court ruled on the Yam Tethys petition, BG signed an agreement with its Israeli partners to submit a joint bid for gas supply including provisions that gave Israeli gas preference over Palestinian gas to meet contractual supply obligations. BG further reinforced its commitment to Israeli gas in December 2000 when the government awarded it the Gal exploration licences offshore Israel.

BG needed to reinforce its commitment to Israel to counteract the negative impact of having a Palestinian element to its bid as well as being the most complex supply option. BG also seemed to face another source of opposition in the form of external political pressures. BG managers involved in the project at the time detected the influence of the US government on the bid process. One of the partners in the Yam Tethys consortium was the US company Noble. While it was natural for the US government, through its embassy in Tel Aviv to support Noble's bid as an American company, the US government appears to have gone further. The US government also appears to have advocated in favour of the bid from EMG. It saw geopolitical advantage in ensuring a direct commercial link between Israel and Egypt in order to support the peace treaty between the two countries.

IEC's Decision

IEC did not take long to reach its decision. On 25 January 2001, the company announced the results of the bid process to supply Israel with gas for 15 years. The result was a shock. IEC announced that it would buy 53% of its gas needs (1.7 billion cubic feet per year) from Egypt. It would buy the remaining 47% from Yam Tethys. IEC did not reveal the details of the winning two bids such as price. However, press reports indicated that the EMG price was 20-30% lower than the Yam Tethys price. BG also knew the price of gas in Egypt and suspected that EMG had offered an unrealistically low price. The low price that Egypt sold gas to Israel would become politically controversial in later years as well as cause BG's business in Egypt severe problems. In the end, it was not surprising that BG was not successful in the bid for gas supply to IEC. Faced with strong competition from consortia with strong Israeli connections and outside political pressure from Egypt and the US, BG was always going to be at a disadvantage. However, BG also did not help its own cause. It appears to have put in the most expensive bid, with a headline gas price some fifty US cents per million thermal units more than the competing bids. This may not sound much but when multiplied by the volume of gas required, made a considerable difference. Also, BG does not appear to have used the British government effectively to support its bid although it would ask for British intervention at the highest level in the years to come. BG would now need to find another way to access the Israeli market which was still the only viable market for Gaza Marine gas.

The IEC decision was not the end of the story and provoked controversy. Leader of the opposition, Ariel Sharon voiced opposition to importing Egyptian gas (or Palestinian gas) and called for the country to use its own gas first. Speaking to a business audience the day after the IEC announcement, he said, "*Israel must gain independence in the supply of natural gas*".[13] Prime Minister Barak addressing the same audience supported the IEC decision, saying it was economically rational. The reaction from some of those involved in the process, especially in the Yam Tethys consortium was stronger. David Cohen, CEO of Avner Gas and Oil Exploration, a partner in Yam Tethys claimed, "*The race was fixed*". He went on, "*The Egyptians put intense pressure on the IEC.*" He also claimed that the low prices offered by EMG were, "*price dumping, below US and European costs*". Gideon Tadmor, CEO of Delek, another Yam Tethys partner, said that "*Israel missed an historic chance to use local natural gas.*"[14] Many commentators in Israel questioned the wisdom of relying on Egypt for its gas supply. This reflected suspicion of Arab motives as the Intifada continued to rage. There were also appeals to patriotism and to support development of Israel's gas resources.

IEC now had to negotiate final supply agreements with both EMG and Yam Tethys. IEC's 25 January decision had fired the starting gun on another race, one whose finish was also uncertain. As well as the pressure in Israel building against Egyptian gas imports, IEC was also under scrutiny on how it had reached its decision. In February 2001, the State Comptroller announced an investigation into IEC's conduct of the bidding process. IEC added to the uncertainty two months later in March 2001 by changing its mind. On 12 March, IEC announced that it would now buy 50% of its gas supply from Yam Tethys and 50% from Egypt. The volume of gas sourced from Egypt would remain at 1.7 billion cubic metres per year. IEC would now buy the same volume from Yam Tethys. In announcing its policy change, IEC acknowledged the strategic

---

13 The Jerusalem Post, "IEC chooses Egyptian natural gas" 26 January 2001
14 Ibid.

value in sourcing gas from Israel's own gas resources. The company also stated that it was in detailed discussions with both Yam Tethys and EMG to reach agreement on a full gas supply agreement. Also adding to the uncertainty over gas supply was the lack of pipeline network to transport natural gas from the gas fields (once developed) to the power stations and industrial users. The negotiations with the two selected gas suppliers continued throughout the rest of 2001. At the very end of the year, there was a breakthrough, both on the tender to build the pipeline and on the gas supply agreement. On 30 December, the Ministry of Finance announced that one consortium had submitted a bid to build the pipeline. On the same day, IEC announced that it had reached an agreement with Yam Tethys to supply gas from January 2004. Yam Tethys had won the race to be Israel's first long term gas supplier.

The Pipeline Opportunity

A consortium consisting of the Belgian engineering company Tractebel, Israeli conglomerate Africa-Israel and Paz Oil which distributed and sold oil products in Israel was the only bidder and had won the tender for the pipeline. The other consortia, including the group headed by BG, were either disqualified during the process or withdrew from the process. Interest from international companies in investing in Israel was waning as the second Intifada continued and seemed to be getting worse. In the early months, Israel suffered a series of suicide bomb attacks. The most serious came in March 2002 on Passover eve when a suicide bomber killed 30 people, mainly elderly, at a hotel in the northern coastal town of Netanya. This attack shocked not only Israel but also people around the world and highlighted that the violence of the Intifada was not confined to the Occupied Palestinian territories but was being felt in Israel itself. In late April, Tractebel announced that it was withdrawing from the pipeline consortium. The two remaining Israeli partners now needed to find a new international partner. Under the terms of the project, the consortium had to include at least one international company. A month later, the Israeli partners announced that they were in negotiations with BG to bring it into the consortium. BG saw an opportunity here, beyond construction of the pipeline. BG expressed its willingness to re-engage in the pipeline tender process but with one condition. BG made its re-entry into the process conditional on the company also becoming a gas supplier to IEC including from the Gaza Marine field. BG was looking to take advantage of the Israeli government's need to construct the pipeline to re-insert itself into the gas supply process. Supplying gas was likely to be the more lucrative business opportunity and it provided an opportunity to gain approval for the development of the Gaza Marine field.

The substitution of BG for Tractebel was not straightforward. If BG was also to become a gas supplier then under regulations governing the project, its ownership level in the pipeline consortium was restricted to 26%. Tractebel held a 60% share of the consortium. So, as part of its negotiations to re-join the project, BG demanded a change in the regulations or at least a waiver so there was no 26% cap on its ownership level. It also demanded government guarantees on the volume of gas to be supplied. BG wanted a third share of the gas supply needs i.e. 1 billion cubic metres per year. The government rejected the demand to change the regulations concerning ownership level. Negotiations stretched through June and July 2002. In late July, BG announced that it would join the consortium and that it would drop its demand for change in the regulations. The concession came too late. On 26 July, the government announced that it was cancelling the tender and re-assessing its options. The government had run out of patience. It had extended the project several times to give BG and its potential partners a chance to come to an agreement. Also, priorities had changed. The priority was now to connect Yam Tethys' Mari-B field to a gas receiving terminal at Ashdod on the Israeli coast and ensure there was market for the gas when the field was due to come online in early 2004. The end of the pipeline tender closed one avenue for BG to pursue gas sales to Israel and allow the development of Gaza Marine. It was not the only avenue that BG was pursuing. BG was looking at other opportunities to find customers for Gaza Marine gas. BG was also receiving positive signals from the Israeli government despite the worsening security situation and worsening relations between Israel and the PNA.

Meanwhile, IEC and Yam Tethys inched closer to finalising the agreement for the consortium to supply gas to Israel from its Mari-B field. Having announced an agreement in principle in December 2001, the government announced in March 2002 that IEC and Yam Tethys had signed an agreement for the supply of gas for 11 years. In that period, Yam Tethys agreed to supply 18 billion cubic metres in total at a cost to IEC of $1.5 billion. This represented an annual supply of 1.6 billion cubic metres per year, a little less than IEC's plan to source 1.7 bcm/y from Yam Tethys. The agreement called for the gas supply to start on 1 January 2004. It was nearly two years since IEC had launched the process to secure long term gas supplies. It had now secured a portion of that supply but there were still serious challenges to surmount. An agreement with EMG remained a distant prospect. IEC also faced legal action over construction of the pipeline to connect the Mari-B field to the gas receiving terminal in Ashdod. IEC separated this pipeline from the larger pipeline project and had awarded it separately to Yam Tethys. This made sense as unlike the transmission network, this pipeline would only serve Yam Tethys. However, without a second gas supplier, Israel now faced a situation that it had tried to avoid: it would rely on one gas supplier from one field along one pipeline.

Concern over monopoly control over Israel's future gas supply and opposition to Egyptian gas imports created an opportunity for BG to press Gaza Marine's case. There was support for Israel buying Palestinian gas despite the Intifada and deteriorating relations between the Israeli government and the PNA. The government (as did many ordinary Israelis) distinguished between most Palestinians and those responsible for the violence. Particular hostility was directed towards Arafat. Very few in Israel, particularly in government trusted him and accused him of (at least) not doing enough to prevent Hamas and other militant groups staging attacks and (at worst) directly ordering attacks. Articles appeared in the press making the case for Israel buying Gaza Marine gas. Some of these were the result of BG efforts but others stemmed from opposition to Egyptian imports. As 2003 dawned, BG and the Palestinians could be optimistic about the chances of reaching an agreement over Gaza Marine. Concerns over Yam Tethys' monopoly position and Egyptian supplies were growing as was support for Gaza Marine. Also, in June 2002, Arafat had appointed Salam Fayyad as PNA finance minister. Fayyad was a former IMF official and enjoyed a high level of trust with the Israeli government, the US administration and other governments and international institutions.

Independent Power Producers

With its failure to secure a gas supply contract in the IEC tender process, BG turned to another route to secure a market in Israel for Gaza's gas. The Israeli government was committed to liberalising the power generation market and ending IEC's monopoly. To this end, the Israeli government encouraged independent private power (IPP) producers to compete with IEC. By 2002, a number of private Israeli companies were examining this opportunity and putting together projects to build gas-fired power plants. An essential part of these projects was securing a gas supply. Mari B was dedicated to IEC and the same would be the case for the first tranche of Egyptian gas. Gaza Marine and any subsequent phases of Egyptian gas were, at the time, the only options for these would-be independent power producers.

BG spent much of the next two years (2002 and 2003) pursuing opportunities in the Israeli power generation sector but without success. At the time, there were three main sticking points. The first was practical. The construction of the high pressure national transmission pipelines which would deliver gas to proposed IPP sites was now behind schedule and with little immediate prospect of being built after the cancellation of the tender process. There was no certainty that a pipeline would be available to transport the gas on the day Gaza Marine started production. The second was commercial. IEC's monopoly position and the gas price it had agreed with Yam Tethys and EMG set a benchmark for the IPPs. It was not a price that made commercial sense for BG given the relatively small volumes of gas involved and the higher degree of uncertainty. Also, none of the IPP project developers were willing to pay a higher price than IEC. None of the companies that BG spoke to had a project that was "*bankable*" i.e. was robust enough that a bank would lend money to it. The third factor was political. Relations between Israel and the PNA deteriorated as the second Intifada raged and provoked some of the worst violence seen in the conflict. Hamas and other extremist groups launched suicide attacks against Israeli civilians and Israel responded with military strikes on Palestinian militant targets, some of which caused large numbers of civilian casualties.

Despite the unpromising environment, BG persisted with its efforts to find a market for the Gaza Marine gas. The company held extensive discussions with Israel Chemicals Ltd (ICL) which was one of several large Israeli companies looking to secure its energy requirements. ICL wanted a gas supply to generate power for its chemical works near the Dead Sea and in northern Israel. While ICL was a potential customer for Gaza Marine gas, it alone would not have sufficient demand to underpin the development of the field. So, BG also sought other potential customers. The other large company that seemed to provide good prospects was the Ofer Group. This family owned business is best known for its shipping business but also has interests in oil and gas. Sammy Ofer had founded the company in the 1960s having served in Britain's Royal Navy during the Second World War. At this time, it was also an investor in ICL. Ofer, at this time, was considering developing power stations in Israel to take advantage of the opportunities created by the government's attempts to liberalise the country's energy generation market. BG also held discussions with Dorad, which was also trying to develop an IPP project. In the end, BG could not agree terms with ICL, Ofer, Dorad or any other potential customers at a price that made economic sense. BG could therefore not aggregate enough gas demand to justify the development of Gaza Marine.

BG was facing not only specific difficulties in aggregating sufficient demand in the Israeli market to underpin Gaza Marine's development, but also the political and security situation was going from bad to worse. The second Intifada showed no signs of abating in the West Bank and Gaza Strip. In March 2001, Ariel Sharon became prime minister following his win in the February 2001 general election. Sharon took a hard-line stance towards the Palestinians, the peace process and the concept of a Palestinian state. Gaining Israeli approval for development of the Gaza Marine field would be more difficult under his premiership. BG would need Sharon's specific approval for the project to go ahead and he was unlikely to give this without stringent conditions. In the early months of his premiership, he appeared ambivalent towards Gaza Marine, expressing neither strong support nor hostility. Although as leader of opposition he had spoken against gas imports from both Egypt and Gaza Marine. At this stage though, BG did not require a specific decision from Sharon. It had lost out on the IEC tender and was struggling to find other Israeli customers for the gas. However, in 2001, the British government had obtained a commitment from Sharon to support the Gaza Marine project.[15] That commitment had come in a meeting between Sharon and British Prime Minister Tony Blair.

In parallel to securing customers for Gaza Marine gas, BG also sought to reinforce Israeli government support. In March 2002, BG's Tim Forbes met with the Ministry of Finance and officials

---

15 Financial Times, "BG still hopes to supply Israel gas", 20 August 2003

in the Prime Minister's Office (but not the PM). The meeting seemed to make a breakthrough with an apparent change in Israeli government policy. Ronen Wolfman, the ministry's deputy director for budget finance stated, "*The Ministry of Finance supports the entry of a third energy supplier, which would be very positive for the natural gas economy.*"[16] The door was ajar for BG to enter as a gas supplier. The PM's Office made a proposal that IEC undertake to purchase gas from BG in its next buying round. This was not a watertight commitment, but it did mark progress. There was further good news two months later when Sharon gave support "*in principle*" to buying Palestinian gas during a meeting with a visiting delegation of British business executives. This did not mark any strengthening of his 2001 commitment to Blair but demonstrated that it was still in place and Sharon was not having second thoughts despite the violence of the Intifada and Israel's military response.

Sharon and his team enjoyed good relations with Blair and his advisors, especially Nigel Sheinwald and the British ambassador to Israel Simon McDonald. Blair, who had been present at the signing of the Gaza Marine agreements with Yasser Arafat in London in November 1999, had pressed BG's case. Sharon and his advisors, such as the head of his office, Dov Weissglas, viewed BG as affiliated to British government interests. They saw the company as more than a private company with commercial interests. To Sharon and his team, BG was a semi-official part of British interests. If Blair asked for help, Sharon was willing to help as part of maintaining good relations with the UK, at least in the early days of his premiership.

A little over a year into his premiership, the security situation deteriorated and hardened Sharon's attitude even further. On 27 March 2002, the Palestinian militant group Hamas staged a suicide bomb attack in the Israeli coastal city of Netanya, killing 30, mostly elderly, Israeli holidaymakers. Sharon responded by launching

---

16 Globes, "British Gas pressing to sell", 25 March 2002

Operation Defensive Shield in the West Bank. Israeli forces entered Ramallah, besieging Arafat in his headquarters in the city. Israeli also staged military incursions in other West Bank cities in an attempt to end attacks in Israel. Military operations ended in May 2002, but Israeli forces maintained a cordon around the West Bank. Following the end of Operation Defensive Shield, Sharon and his cabinet took the decision to approve the construction of the first sections of a separation wall between the West Bank and Israel. Under Barak's premiership, the government had taken the first steps to investigate the feasibility of such a wall and undertook some preparations. Sharon now put those plans into effect and actual construction got underway. This was a popular move in Israel, where the population was reeling from multiple suicide bombings which had caused considerable number of deaths and disrupted normal life.

The construction of the separation wall (frequently referred to by Palestinians as the apartheid wall) also provoked changes in Sharon's attitude towards a Palestinian state and how to achieve it. During his long career in the military (he fought in the 1948 War of Independence and in the 1967 war) and in politics (since the 1980s), his attitude to a Palestinian state had evolved. He is often painted as an implacable opponent of a Palestinian state. A close study of his approach over the decades shows a more nuanced position.[17] He has not denied that a Palestinian state should exist, but he has often placed constraints and conditions on it. For much of his military career and his early political career, he believed that Jordan should be the Palestinian state. Following the Oslo Accords, he slowly changed his position after coming to accept the Accords and accepted the concept of a two state solution with a Palestinian state in the West Bank and the Gaza Strip but without dismantling the settlements and with limits on any Palestinian security forces. He also accepted that this should be negotiated with the Palestinians. When he served

---

17 Landau (2014)

in Netanyahu's 1996-99 government, he took part in some of those negotiations. With the start of work on a separation wall, Sharon woke up to the possibilities of a unilateral approach to securing Israel and separating the country from the Palestinians. He would force a Palestinian state into being by physically separating Israel from the Palestinians. He would follow this thinking through to make one of the most dramatic moves of his premiership, the unilateral withdrawal from the Gaza Strip.

One element of Sharon's attitude to the Palestinians did not change and that was his hostility towards Arafat. He viewed Arafat as the enemy, did not trust him and would not reach any agreement with him. During peace talks in 1996-99 he was reluctant to deal directly with Arafat and refused to shake his hands. He believed that any money that flowed to Arafat would, at the least, be put to corrupt purposes and in many cases would go to fund terrorist attacks against Israel. He would not allow any development of Gaza Marine. He characterised this as money for terrorists. Although it was Hamas and its allies launching suicide attacks against Israelis, Sharon saw Arafat as ultimately responsible. Sharon's view of Arafat was formed in the battles against the PLO in the 1970s and 1980s. He had missed the opportunity to eradicate the PLO in Beirut in the 1980s. Instead, the PLO had been allowed to relocate to Tunis and Arafat had survived the Israeli siege of Beirut, during which Sharon was held responsible for the massacre of Palestinian refugees in Sabra and Shatila camps. Sharon's attitude towards Arafat was not replicated towards other senior Palestinians. He was happy to meet with Mahmoud Abbas, Salam Fayyad and other senior Palestinians outside Arafat's immediate circle. He would invite them to his ranch in the Negev desert. He was prepared to deal with them and reach agreements with them.

CHAPTER 5

MONEY FOR TERRORISTS
(2002-2004)

" *Money for terrorists*" was a sound bite that appealed to Prime Minister Sharon's supporters and was easily understood by the Israeli public. It was also a red herring to some extent. Any future revenue from Gaza Marine would flow to the PNA, not to Hamas or other militant groups. It would flow into the same accounts that the Israeli government paid customs revenues that it collected on behalf of the PNA. The Israeli government continued to pay these during this period. It was only a red herring in part. There were genuine concerns in many quarters about the transparency of revenue flows to the PNA under Arafat's leadership. There was a great deal of opacity surrounding the PNA's finances and how much ended up in the personal accounts of Arafat and other senior officials. In 2003, international donors would force Arafat to make wide ranging reforms to improve transparency.

The Arab Peace Initiative
On the international stage, there was a positive development that held out hope for the future. In another juxtaposition of timing, on 28 March 2002, the day after the Netanya attack, the Arab League at its annual summit in Beirut published its plan for ending the Israeli/Palestinian conflict, the Arab Peace Initiative (API). This plan represented a huge policy change for the organisation, which

often failed to agree a unified position on major issues confronting the region. Several years later the veteran Israeli politician Shimon Peres would term it a "*U-turn*" and mean it positively. The API was deceptively simple (it has only 10 statements at its core). It offered a comprehensive peace agreement between the Arab League member states and Israel, including full diplomatic recognition. In return, it demanded a sovereign Palestinian state in the West Bank and Gaza Strip, an equitable resolution of the Palestinian refugee situation and the return of the Golan Heights to Syria. This was a momentous shift in the Arab position. It tacitly recognised Israel's right to exist within secure borders and did not insist on the right of return of Palestinian refugees to Israel. Prior to the March 2002 Beirut summit, the Arab League's official position was based on three "*no's*" that had been first articulated in the aftermath of the 1967 war i.e. no peace, no diplomatic recognition and no negotiations.

The Arab Peace Initiative did not get a good start. Sharon rejected it immediately on the pretext that it did not meet UN resolutions that called for bilateral negations between Israel and its neighbours. In reality, Sharon was not prepared to make the compromises that the API called for and he was not prepared to contemplate a Palestinian state in the West Bank and Gaza. Also, the apparent unified Arab approach was not as rock solid as it may first have appeared. While the API was launched by Saudi Arabia, which gave it a great deal of authority (and so it is also referred to as the "*Saudi initiative*"), a number of Arab leaders were absent from the summit and had sent foreign ministers in their place. This undermined the credibility of the plan. Among those absent were Yasser Arafat, Hosni Mubarak of Egypt and King Abdullah of Jordan, all of whom had already made peace with Israel. Also, both Lebanon and Syria expressed some reservations, especially about the future fate of the large Palestinian refugee population in their countries. They were concerned that "*an equitable solution*" may involve financial compensation to the refugees but their remaining in situ in Lebanon and Syria.

Despite the difficult start, the API proved to have longevity. It remains the Arab League's stated position. It has been amended slightly at subsequent summits but in 2017 was re-affirmed as the Arab League's basis for ending the conflict. While Sharon may have rejected it outright, subsequent Israeli prime ministers have been less hostile but have stopped short of accepting it is a basis for negotiation. Ehud Olmert gave it a cautious welcome as did Shimon Peres. Benjamin Netanyahu has also given it a tentative welcome. However, it remains on the shelf and did not make any immediate contribution to improving the political environment for the Gaza Marine project.

Sharon's rejection of a potentially historic opportunity to negotiate a peace deal underlined the difficulty in getting him to agree to anything that helped the Palestinians. For the development of Gaza Marine to proceed, a change in Israeli policy and in particular Sharon's position was needed. Throughout the second half of 2002 and early 2003, BG managers embarked on extensive rounds of meetings with Israeli officials to promote the merits of the Gaza Marine project and gain political support for the project. BG did find support within the Israeli government. The then national infrastructure minister (whose responsibilities included energy), Joseph Paritzky was an enthusiastic supporter. He believed it was in Israel's national interest to use Palestinian gas rather than Egyptian gas. This would create linkages between Israeli and Palestinian economies that could underpin any peace process. He also expressed concerns about the long term reliability of Egyptian gas supply (rightly as it turned out). Then finance minister, Benjamin Netanyahu, was also supportive and recognised the economic and political case for supporting development of the Gaza Marine gas field.

A US Peace Initiative

Meanwhile, another peace initiative was launched, this time by the US. On 24 June 2002, US President George Bush expressed support for an independent Palestinian state and called for a roadmap for peace. The US published a draft version of the roadmap in November 2002. It called for a staged process leading to a Palestinian state. The first stage would be an end to violence on the Palestinian side and a freeze on Israeli settlement building. Stage 2 would be provisional agreement on a Palestinian state and the third stage would be a final agreement and the creation of an independent Palestinian state. Progress to the next stage would depend on the performance of both sides and the meeting of specific goals. While the US created the roadmap, responsibility for nurturing it would rest with four powers: the US, Russia, the UN and the EU. This group was known as *"The Quartet"*. It would have its own staff (drawn from all four members but with a budget largely provided by the US). It would also eventually appoint its own Special Representative and create a new institution, the Office of the Quartet Representative (OQR). The most prominent holder would be Tony Blair but that was still to come.

Like the Arab initiative, the US roadmap also had a difficult birth. While Sharon did not reject it outright, as he was not in a position to reject an initiative from his strongest ally, the US. Some of the more right wing ministers in his government did want to reject it outright. Instead the Israeli cabinet reached compromise, where they accepted the *"steps in the roadmap"* rather than the document itself. The cabinet also stated 14 reservations and pre-conditions with the roadmap. Sharon also made it clear that he would only accept a Palestinian entity that consisted of no more than 42% of the land area of the West Bank and 70% of the Gaza Strip and that any entity would be under full Israeli control. Nevertheless, the roadmap became the framework within which the Quartet attempted to bring about an end to the conflict. Real implementation of the roadmap would not start until spring 2003.

"Making a Meal of it"

My own introduction to the Gaza Marine project came in January

2003. I had joined BG Group a year earlier on 23 January 2002 as a government relations manager. I was recruited to join the BG team in Cairo. My focus was Egypt and my role was to help BG Egypt understand and manage the political risks to its business. At the time, Egypt was the jewel in the crown of the BG portfolio and was set to become a major contributor to the company's profits. In January 2003, BG's government relations team at head office in the UK had organised for four British MPs (all from the Labour Party) to visit Cairo as part of the company's efforts to build relations with parliamentarians. The four MPs were, Bob Blizzard, Michael Connarty, Ashok Kumar and Frank Doran. While the visit was intended to focus on BG's activities in Egypt, BG's regional vice-president Martin Houston also wanted to use this opportunity to get the Egyptian petroleum minister to express support for the supply of Palestinian gas to Israel before Egypt supplied gas to Israel. A slide on Gaza Marine was inserted into the briefing pack for the parliamentary delegation.

The four MPs followed the script and duly asked the then Egyptian petroleum minister Sameh Fahmy whether he supported the supply of Palestinian gas ahead of Egyptian gas to Israel. BG got the semi-public expression of support that it wanted. Fahmy told the four that he had no objection to Gazan gas being supplied to Israel despite Egypt also hoping to supply gas to Israel. Fahmy did though express reluctance to say as much to his Israeli counterparts. The four MPs asked him to be more direct in his support of Gaza Marine to the Israelis. During a meeting with the then British Ambassador John Sawers (who later become head of the Secret Intelligence Service, MI6), the MPs heard Sawers suggest that BG *"were making a meal of it"*. His implication was that BG did not need any signal from the Egyptian government but should just push harder with the Israelis. However, Sawers was prevented by the arrival of Baroness Symons, then British trade minister, from expanding on his comments. She struck a more realistic tone, expressing doubt that any progress could be made without some form of peace process in place. The four MPs offered to write to Tony Blair asking him to renew his intervention in the project. BG decided at this time to decline this offer although they did recognise some potential advantages for this type of support from MPs at some point in the future.

Sharon Changes his Mind – Twice

In April 2003, BG was receiving mixed messages from the Israeli government. The Ministry of Infrastructure was talking positively in public about an imminent deal with BG to allow the supply of Gaza Marine gas to the Israeli market. The Israeli side placed one significant condition on any deal: Salam Fayyad is in charge of the project on the Palestinian side. Arafat and his cronies could have no involvement. This was a condition that BG could accept. Fayyad also accepted this condition. He wrote to the Israeli government to provide the necessary assurances. His letter contained the assurance that,

> *"the Palestinian Investment Fund would be responsible for the PNA (Palestinian National Authority) share from the Gaza gas project and that all Palestinian revenues from this project would be transferred to the Finance Ministry fund - the same account into which the Israeli government transfers its financial dues to the PNA".*

This appeared to satisfy the Ministry of National Infrastructure. While BG seemed to be getting closer to an agreement with the Ministry of Infrastructure and Salam Fayyad was providing the necessary assurances, the Gaza Marine project received another setback. Sharon expressed unequivocal support for EMG and the supply of Egyptian gas to Israel as well as total opposition to the supply of Palestinian gas to Israel. BG approached the British government and asked it to intervene again on its behalf with Sharon. The Israeli prime minister was scheduled to visit London in July 2003 for meetings with his British counterpart, Tony Blair. BG requested that Blair raise Gaza Marine during his meeting and attempt to persuade

Sharon to reverse his position. Blair was believed to have a good relationship with Sharon. He had been part of the effort in 2001 to persuade Sharon to support Gaza Marine then. Blair did indeed raise Gaza Marine with Sharon during their meeting in London in July 2003. BG did not have high hopes that Blair would succeed this time with Sharon. The political situation was different this time round. Against expectations, the intervention was successful. Blair obtained an undertaking from Sharon that he would support the development of the Gaza Marine field. A major political obstacle appeared to have been removed. Although, there was still a great deal of work to complete, BG was now more hopeful that the project could proceed.

Blair may not have been the only means that some in BG were prepared to use to persuade Sharon to change his position. The British prime minister may have had some assistance without his knowledge. A BG senior manager is alleged to have approached Sharon privately, without telling his BG bosses, and offered him a deal. This senior manager allegedly offered to pay Sharon in order to allow the Gaza Marine project to go ahead. According to the allegations, a contract was drawn up but never signed. The senior manager is also alleged to have approached Avigdor Lieberman with a similar offer when he was Minister for National Infrastructure in Sharon's administration in 2001-02 and responsible for energy matters. However, when Lieberman was moved to the Ministry of Transportation, he no longer had responsibility for gas issues and so the offer was withdrawn. If such payments were offered, they were never paid. The lack of payment may have influenced Sharon's later decisions on Gaza Marine. These allegations of offering payments were also not addressed in BG's 2008 investigation of the project. As BG's executives and its lawyers were probably unaware of the allegations at the time, they could not have included them in the investigation's scope. The senior manager and the small number of BG employees who knew about the offers to Sharon and Lieberman would also have been able to withhold any documents and keep the matter hidden.

BG also appeared to be exploring other channels to secure access for Gaza Marine gas to the Israeli market. In mid-June, the largest Israeli newspaper Yediot Ahronot reported that BG was talking to Yossi Maiman and his Merhav Group about joining the Gaza Marine project and assisting in securing a market for the gas in Israel. Any talks that were going on behind the scenes soon came to an abrupt end. On 15 June, BG issued a strong statement that it was severing all contacts with Maiman. BG claimed that Maiman had demanded a 30% stake in the project but was not prepared to pay for it but to use his connections and influence to persuade the government to approve Gaza Marine gas sales to Israel. BG also claimed that Maiman's interest in joining Gaza Marine showed there was no prospect of EMG supplying gas to Israel.

Maiman responded by launching a war of words against BG. On 18 June, he wrote to the Knesset's economic committee, ostensibly to provide assurances that the EMG project was still alive and the prospects for importing Egyptian gas to Israel had actually improved. He also used the opportunity to throw mud at BG. He claimed that he had contacted the PNA to obtain assurances about how funds would be used and further that he had been informed that Muhammad Rashid and Arafat were still in charge of the Gaza Marine project. The implication was that the assurances that Fayyad provided in April were false. Maiman was fuelling the perception that Gaza Marine development would mean money for terrorists. BG replied with its own letter to the Knesset's economic committee the following week. In the letter, BG's country manager in Israel John Field rebutted Maiman's claims by asserting that Gaza Marine would not pose a threat to Israel. He stated that BG would retain control over the field from the plant in Ashkelon where the gas would end in Israel. On the question of "*money for terrorists*", Field pointed out that revenue from Gaza Marine would not necessarily mean additional funds for the PNA. This revenue was likely to displace funds that the PNA received from donors, so overall the PNA would not be better off. He wrote, "*The sale of gas to Israel will only increase Israeli control over where the money goes*". He continued, "*The PA also regards as important a guaranteed source of gas for operating its Gaza power station and for other future projects in power production and water desalination.*"[18] This dispute between BG and Maiman would simmer for years. Both sides would continue to use the arguments and themes in these letters as well as add to them. Maiman would persist in claims that Gaza Marine's development threatened Israeli security and that the PNA could not be trusted. He would also make allegations of corruption against BG. For its part, BG would stress the lack of threat to Israel as well as the benefits of Gaza Marine to both Israel and the Palestinians.

BG Examines Options for Gaza Marine
While Maiman and BG were arguing, a separate discussion about Gaza Marine was occurring. In late June, Israeli infrastructure minister Joseph Paritzky met with Fayyad to discuss Israel buying Palestinian gas. Both ministers may well have been acting in good faith, but their meeting also highlighted the lack of co-ordination in both governments over Gaza Marine. Neither minister had a mandate from their political bosses: Sharon in the case of Paritzky; Arafat for Fayyad. In both cases, the political leaders would have the final say and would not necessarily give the go ahead for whatever Paritzky and Fayyad agreed. Sharon already seemed to have changed his mind, while Arafat was well known for not delegating decisions or powers. He would want to ensure maximum benefit to him and his cronies. This lack of co-ordination was behind the mixed messages BG was receiving and frustrating the company's efforts to make progress on Gaza Marine.

Prior to Blair's meeting with Sharon, BG Group management

---

18 Globes, "British Gas: Gas supply from PA will only increase", 24 June 2003

had started the process of considering its options with regard to Gaza Marine. BG's Board was due to discuss at its July meeting the option of withdrawal from the Gaza Marine licence. The prospects for developing the field were looking increasingly bleak. There was no apparent route to market for the gas, the Intifada continued to rage and the political environment in Israel was growing hostile. In early June 2003, Martin Houston attended a meeting of the British Palestine Business Council (BPBC) where he received a gloomy assessment of the prospects for developing the field. He did not hold out much hope for the forthcoming Blair-Sharon meeting, commenting that Blair was likely to be "*sowing seed on stony ground*". As it turned out, Blair's efforts did bear fruit, but it proved to be short-lived. In anticipation of a lack of breakthrough with Sharon, Houston set in motion a process to examine the options for Gaza Marine. This process marked the start of my substantive involvement in the Gaza Marine project which would continue off and on for almost eleven years. Houston set out three options for Gaza Marine: first, continue lobbying politicians as BG was doing; second, conduct an intensive campaign in the Israeli media to highlight the benefits to Israel of developing Palestinian gas and third look into selling the gas to Egypt. Houston tasked me with writing a paper setting out the options in detail and the implications for BG for consideration by BG's Group Executive Committee in July 2003.

My paper looked at the risks for each of the three options and what BG would need to do to make each succeed if it chose that particular option. For all three options, there was a high risk of failure and so there would be a negative impact on BG's reputation, especially in Egypt which was an important country for BG. For option one, intensifying the lobbying effort to persuade Sharon, the prime focus needed to be showing the prime minister that he had more to gain from allowing Gaza Marine to go ahead than rejecting it. For the second option, an Israeli media campaign, as well as the risk of failing to influence Sharon, such a campaign was likely to provoke a counter-campaign by the project's opponents. The third option seemed the least likely to succeed at this time. Israel had no incentive to co-operate with this scheme and the Egyptian government could also prove reluctant. There was also uncertainty about what the market would be for Gaza Marine gas. Would it be supplied into the domestic market or be exported to world markets using the export facilities then under construction on Egypt's Mediterranean coast? To my mind, the political obstacles, lack of Israeli co-operation and Egyptian reluctance, were the key obstacles. In a discussion with one of the project team, I voiced my doubts about the feasibility of the Egypt option. At the time, I had no indication that I would become deeply involved in this option and that it would emerge as BG's preferred option. All that will be examined later.

A Roasting
In the summer of 2003, BG's head office asked the Egypt office to undertake a review of the Gaza Marine project. Having failed to secure a sales contract under the IEC tender, the project was now at a crossroads. It was pursuing other Israeli customers and seemed to have removed a roadblock with Sharon's response to Blair's intervention. Such peer reviews were an established part of the BG process. Typically, they would cover the technical and commercial aspects of a project. This one would be more far reaching and cover the political aspects as well. I was invited to be part of the review. The review took place in Cairo at a hotel in the suburb of Sixth October City. The irony of the location was not lost on the attendees from the Israel office. The suburb's name commemorates Egypt's "*victory*" against Israel in the 1973 war, known in Israel as the Yom Kippur war. On 6 October 1973, Egypt launched a surprise attack across the Suez Canal on Israeli forces occupying Sinai since the June 1967 Six Day War. The meeting attendees from the Gaza Marine project were Tim Forbes and his team from both head office and Israel. From BG Egypt, I was part of the team consisting also of technical and

commercial experts, who were taking time out from their day jobs working on projects in Egypt to conduct this peer review.

The project team seemed to be over optimistic about their chances of success and the amount of progress they were making. John Fields, BG's country manager in Israel, wrote in an e-mail that, "*In Everest terms we have climbed the Khumbu ice falls and are at the South Col preparing to push for the summit.*" Tim Forbes and his team set out their case, which was essentially that they were approaching the point of making a final investment decision on Gaza Marine and would be ready to press the green button on developing the field. The Egypt team questioned them closely on this claim, particularly on the technical aspects. The BG Egypt team ripped the case to shreds. One of those attending from the Israel office would later describe it as a "*roasting*". The conclusion of the meeting was that the Gaza Marine team still had considerable work to do, both on the technical and commercial fronts before it would be ready to make that final investment decision. My conclusion was that the team did not possess sufficiently strong relations with either the Israeli or Palestinian administrations to underpin the final investment decision. In a follow up paper to the regional executive vice president, Martin Houston, entitled "*Who are you going to talk to?*" I set out my concerns. That final investment decision was not taken.

A New Palestinian Partner

There were, though, positive developments on the Palestinian front. In April 2003, the final version of the US roadmap was published. As the first steps in its implementation, the Palestinian leadership and key institutions were re-organised. The main aim was to place limits on Arafat's power and control over Palestinian institutions and more importantly, finance. The reforms included the appointment of a prime minister for the first time. This was Mahmoud Abbas, who had signed the original Oslo Accord and was a close ally of Arafat. Also, as part of the reforms, Salam Fayyad was reconfirmed as finance minister. Fayyad was a former IMF official who was widely respected, including in Israel, for his integrity. He could be trusted to keep Arafat in check and stem corruption in the PNA.

Arafat was also forced to accept reforms to the PNA's finances and to increase transparency. Part of this reform was the establishment of the Palestinian Investment Fund (the PIF) and the abolition of the PCSC. The PIF would be subject to external audit, which the PCSC was not. Another central reform was the establishment of a new "*single treasury account*" into which the Israeli government, international donors and others could pay funds to the PNA. This account would be subject to stringent governance with the aim of preventing the misappropriation of funds. The payment of future revenues from Gaza Marine into this single treasury account would become a central part of BG's efforts to overcome the suspicion that Gaza Marine would provide money for terrorism. Also, the PIF was given oversight of the Gaza Marine project and would hold the PNA's stake in the project after development started. One of Fayyad's assurances had been put in place.

Implementation of the roadmap soon lost momentum. There was no end to the violence. Whilst a ceasefire by all the main armed Palestinian groups was announced on 29 June 2003, it lasted only a few days and was followed by a series of attacks. Even before that, Sharon had torn a hole in the roadmap with a declaration that a freeze on settlement building was impossible as homes were needed for growing settler families.

Payment in Kind

Paritzky attempted to strike a deal with his Palestinian opposite number at the time, Azzam Shawwa. Paritzky proposed that Israel would exchange Palestinian gas for electricity rather than pay for the gas. While Gaza has its own power station, the West Bank is dependent on Israel for supply of electricity. However, the PNA cannot afford to pay for this electricity and has built up a considerable debt with Israel's state-owned electricity provider the Israel Electric Corporation (IEC). Paritzky's proposal was that Israel would take the gas and offset it against the PNA's debt to IEC. When the debt was paid or at least reduced to a more manageable level, Israel would construct a sub-station on the border with Gaza and supply electricity to the territory. Shawwa and the Palestinians appeared willing to agree to this deal. On 23 July 2003 in Brussels, Shawwa and Paritzky along with the EU signed a memorandum of under-standing on energy co-operation. On the EU side, the signatories were Loyola de Palacio, the European Commission vice-president with responsibility for energy and Italian industry minister Antonio Marzano (Italy held the presidency of the European Council at that time).

The Paritzky-Shawwa gas for electricity deal did not go any further. The deal got almost no support. Prime Minister Sharon was opposed to it. BG was also against it. Although the Paritzky-Shawwa deal did not involve paying any money to the PNA and therefore could not be classed as "*money for terrorists*", Sharon was opposed to any deal with the Palestinians. He did not trust the Palestinians and viewed them as an implacable enemy. BG also found it hard to support such a deal as the risks were too high. If there was no funds flowing from the Israelis to the Palestinians to pay for the gas, how was it going to get paid? BG would have to rely on the PNA paying for its share of the gas. Israel was effectively transferring its Palestinian credit risk to BG (and its partner CCC). BG would take on the risk of not being paid by the Palestinians. BG would have to find an institution, such as the EU, to guarantee payment from the PNA. This would be a tall order and add an extra layer of complexity to an already difficult project. At the same time, BG was starting to lose interest in the Gaza Marine project. It was not a core part of the company's plans for the future. It was too small to matter.

While Paritzky did not have the support of his boss, Ariel Sharon, he was not isolated in government. He had the support of leading members of Sharon's own party, Likud. Ehud Olmert, trade and industry minister (who would succeed Sharon as prime minister) and finance minister Benjamin Netanyahu (also later prime minister) supported Paritzky's approach. These two influential politicians recognised the economic and political rationale of reaching an agreement with the Palestinians to secure the gas for Israel's energy needs. Paritzky also had support from the Israeli security services. They appreciated the strategic benefits that it would give Israel. It would provide *"excellent leverage"*[19] over the Palestinians in the West Bank and would be less expensive than military options.

Sharon's Decision

Later in the summer, BG's efforts to make progress on developing Gaza Marine received a severe blow. On 17 August 2003, Ariel Sharon told his cabinet that he preferred buying gas from Egypt rather than from Gaza Marine. In making this decision, Sharon overrode Paritzky. At first glance, a preference for Egypt made strategic sense for Israel. Egypt was already a mature gas producer and at a government level, was a security partner for Israel in the region. While there was great deal of popular mistrust of Israel in Egypt, at the senior levels of government and the security services, there was strong co-operation with Israel, especially over the Gaza Strip. Sharon appreciated the need to maintain that co-operation and even strengthen it.

There were also financial interests at stake. Senior officials in the Mubarak regime in Egypt (possibly including Mubarak himself) were set to gain personally from Egyptian gas exports to Israel via the EMG pipeline. The British Embassy told me at the time that it believed that Mubarak would gain personally from the EMG deal. Sharon was undoubtedly aware of this and saw benefit in ensuring that Mubarak and his cronies continued to benefit financially from relations with Israel. On the Israeli side, allies of Sharon, not least

---

19 Author interview with Joseph Paritzky

Yossi Maiman, were also set to gain personal financial benefit from the EMG deal. In making the decision in favour of Egypt, over Gaza Marine, Sharon was ensuring that both Israel's security interests and the personal financial interests of his allies gained advantage. Sharon indicated that he would give Egypt up to four weeks to confirm its intention to supply gas to Israel.

The reaction of Egypt's Ministry of Petroleum and its state-owned oil company EGPC suggested that Mubarak was calling the shots on gas exports to Israel and that the ministry and EGPC had been kept in the dark. On 3 September, the Ministry of Petroleum denied to the Egyptian parliament, the People's Assembly, that there were any plans to sell gas to Israel. This denial followed critical questions from parliamentarians who reflected popular mistrust of any contact with Israel. The ministry denied both that any negotiations with Israel were underway and that there were any plans to sell gas to Israel. On the first part of the denial, the ministry was technically correct as at that point, there were no formal negotiations underway. On the second part, Egypt had written to Israel back in 2000 stating a willingness to export gas to Israel and there had been government level discussions on gas since 1994. This denial showed poor political judgement on the part of the ministry and EGPC and it was soon put in its place. The British Embassy commented to BG that

> *"It's a bit silly for the Petroleum Ministry to mislead the People's Assembly in this way, as these things always leak out in the end and turn into a political row".*

While it did not turn into a row and the minister and officials kept their jobs, it soon became clear that Egypt did intend to negotiate with Israel to export gas.

On 10 September 2003, EGPC Chairman Ibrahim Saleh wrote to his counterpart at IEC, Eli Landau to confirm that EGPC would guarantee the supply of gas to Israel under a contract between EMG and IEC. This supply would be 7 billion cubic metres per year for 20 years via an offshore pipeline from the North Sinai city of El-Arish.

In his letter, Saleh stated that he wanted to *"reiterate and revalidate"*, EGPC's decision on the matter which had been *"conveyed in our letter of 24 May 2000"*. The letter was not intended for publication but was leaked to the financial news organisation Bloomberg which published extracts on 11 September.[20] Bloomberg's Jerusalem bureau reported the story, perhaps an indication that the Israelis had leaked the letter. The Israeli press picked up on the story. Egypt's state-owned and heavily censored press did not, possibly an indication of Egypt's desire not to draw attention to the political tensions the issue was causing.

BG believed that Mubarak or his officials had slapped down the ministry and that this could have repercussions for BG's position in the country. BG also recognised that supplying gas to Israel would cause not only political problems but also threaten its energy security. Egypt would not have sufficient gas to meet supply obligations to Israel. A senior BG Egypt executive commented at the time, referring to EGPC's 10 September letter,

> *"it indicates that Mubarak has reached down into EGPC, in complete disregard of the reality of the medium term demand/ supply situation. Egypt does not have the gas to supply Israel and won't for some years to come, it really is as simple as that. However, this is not something that BG can or should say publicly, it would cause serious affront to Egypt. EGPC sending any letter, no matter how bland/carefully couched, implies there has been a strong rebuke of the Petroleum Minister by Mubarak. Although it is not BG's "fault" that this matter has arisen, to some extent I believe the Petroleum Minister's statement to Parliament was probably made in recognition of BG's position - hopefully we will not be "blamed" if he has felt any pain in the run-up to the EGPC retraction."*

The executive continued:

---

20 Bloomberg, "Egypt Says It's Committed to Supplying Israel With Natural Gas", 11 September 2003.

"I am at a loss on how to suggest you proceed in the face of this irrational behaviour on Egypt's part - the simplest thing is probably to wait the Egyptians out, because I can't believe they will actually sign up for additional supply obligations. Down the track though, this could see BG Israel urging Israel Inc to time Egypt out, and this is not a position we would want to be in."

Egypt would go on to sign up for *"additional supply obligations"*. Undeterred by the challenges facing the Gaza Marine project, BG, with the support of the British government continued to lobby for change in Israeli policy and in particular, Sharon's position. These efforts were focussed on those in the Israeli government who remained supportive, particularly Paritzky. FCO documents released under the UK's Freedom of Information Act report this support and provide insight into the efforts to change Sharon's position. A memo from the British Embassy in Tel Aviv dated 2 October 2003 reports on a dinner hosted by Baroness Symons who was visiting Israel in her role as junior FCO minister. Paritzky attended the dinner and the British Ambassador Simon McDonald reports on Paritzky,

"He remained enthusiastic about the prospects for BG's bid. Nothing irrevocable had happened with this Egyptian option: although there had been an exchange of letters, this did not amount to a Memorandum of Understanding. EMG (the Israeli-Egyptian consortium) had not undertaken to supply gas by a date certain. As it was now six weeks since Sharon had given EMG "about one month" to prove the seriousness of its commitment, Paritzky suggested that we consider renewed Prime Ministerial intervention."

In the same memo, McDonald goes on to note that Sharon owes the PM (Tony Blair) a reply but is cautious about mobilising Blair once more. One of the two reasons for this caution is redacted from the version of the memo released. This is because it probably refers to a sensitive aspect of the Anglo-Israeli relationship. McDonald does not want to expend precious political capital on Gaza Marine once more. The second reason he describes as *"problems with the structure of BG's bid"* that have come to light over the previous week. The next line of the memo is redacted so the precise problem is unclear. McDonald may have become aware of the BG senior manager's alleged offer to pay Sharon. The problem may also have related to BG's partner CCC. McDonald adds that,

> *"Moreover, it seems that CCC's interest is being supervised by Martin Schlaff, whose other business interests include the Jericho Casino and ventures with Mohammed Rashid, Arafat's financial advisor. Sharon would put himself at some personal political risk if he were to endorse a deal that benefited Schlaff, particularly as Dov Weissglas, Sharon's Chief of Staff, has acted as Schlaff's legal advisor."*

The next line is redacted. Sharon's links with Schlaff would come under scrutiny in years to come but not in connection with Gaza Marine.

McDonald was right to be cautious in the light of the alleged involvement of Schlaff. The references to the Jericho Casino and Rashid point to two of the controversies concerning Schlaff. He had taken advantage of the establishment of self-rule in the West Bank to build close relations with the PNA and particularly Rashid. This effort would also have brought him into contact with CCC. Schlaff, an Austrian banker who shuns publicity, had financed the Jericho Casino. Gambling is illegal in Israel (but not in the PNA-administered areas) and hoped to provide an opportunity for Israeli citizens to gamble. He also proposed a scheme for a casino on a ship which would sail to outside Israeli waters to allow Israelis to gamble legally. It was this scheme that would later bring scrutiny on his connections to Sharon and Sharon's family.

McDonald was also right about Paritzky's enthusiasm for Israel buying gas from Gaza Marine. Paritzky was the chief advocate in the cabinet for buying Palestinian gas and argued against relying on Egyptian gas. He was not alone. Other cabinet ministers, including

Netanyahu supported his position. This set Paritzky in direct opposition to his boss, Prime Minister Sharon, who was adamant in his support for Egyptian gas and rejection of Palestinian gas. Paritzky's advocacy for Gaza Marine gas kept the issue on the cabinet's agenda. In mid-March 2004, the Director-General of the Prime Minister's office Avigdor Yitzhaki told the Knesset economics committee that the cabinet was considering Gaza Marine as a third supplier to Israel in addition to Yam Tethys and Egypt. Yitzhaki proposed this as a possible solution to the Sharon/Paritzky dispute. In remarks to the same committee, Paritzky pressed his case based on two arguments. The first was the risk of Egypt halting supply and the second was the impact it would have on exploration activity in Israeli waters. Paritzky argued that relying on Egyptian gas supply would reduce the incentive to explore for gas. No Egyptian gas would force Israel to rely to a greater extent on its own resources and therefore provide an incentive for exploration activity to find resources to meet demand and replace those being exploited.

"Political and Business Skulduggery"
Paritzky's concerns about the risk of Egyptians not meeting any future supply commitments had some basis. The talks with Egypt were not going well. In May 2004, IEC executives and Ministry of National Infrastructure officials proposed suspending talks with Egypt and returning to negotiations with BG for buying Gaza Marine gas. As well as disagreements inside cabinet on buying Egyptian gas, there was also a lack of agreement amongst the members of the IEC board. IEC's Chairman Eli Landau, who supported buying Egyptian gas, was forced to postpone a discussion at the May 2004 board meeting of the potential terms of an agreement with Egypt as it became clear there were deep differences between board members. This talk of suspending talks and re-engaging with BG could just be a government and IEC tactic to put pressure on Egypt in the negotiations and create some competitive tension. The reaction of some of those

with a stake in the Egyptian option suggested that they took seriously the risk of collapse in talks with Egypt. In particular Yossi Maiman resorted to tactics to discredit those who supported the Gaza Marine option.

In mid-July, press reports revealed that Maiman had hired a private detective to investigate Paritzky and find compromising information on him and his support for the Gaza Marine option. Maiman's investigator unearthed two-year old tapes on which Paritzky was heard plotting to discredit a political rival, Avraham Poraz, interior minister in the Sharon government. This was enough for Sharon to sack Paritzky from the government. Maiman had succeeded in removing one source of opposition to his plans to import Egyptian gas. He was not the only one undertaking investigations. In the wake of Paritzky's dismissal, the police opened an investigation into the decision to buy Egyptian gas and Paritzky's support for Gaza Marine. The police interviewed many of the key figures including Maiman, two of his senior lieutenants, Paritzky and Landau. Suspicions about *"political and business skulduggery"* as the Financial Times called it,[21] grew when IEC made an extraordinary revelation in late July. It had received an offer from BG to supply gas that was cheaper than Egypt's offer. According to IEC, BG had first made the offer in 2000 after the tender process that had resulted in the selection of Yam Tethys and Egypt. BG had repeated the offer in 2003. Supporters of the Egypt option could no longer claim that it was the cheapest option. In the end, the police closed the investigation without bringing charges against any of those involved.

Maiman also directly targeted BG in his efforts to undermine the Gaza Marine option and staged a smear campaign against BG Group. He and his associates, including Shabtai Shavit (former head of Mossad), accused BG's partners CCC of being *"shady"* Palestinian businessmen who directly funded anti-Israeli and anti-US terrorism.

---

21 Financial Times, "Israeli police probe events surrounding energy", 22 July 2004

Maiman also made allegations of corruption in the awarding of the Gaza Marine licence and that the PNA held secret controlling stakes in BG. Despite the second allegation being clearly nonsense and easily rebutted, it gained remarkable traction and was oft repeated. As noted above, throughout the time BG held the Gaza Marine licence, it was a publicly listed company and no institution held more than a 3% share. BG did very little to challenge the allegation of secret shareholders and very rarely engaged with journalists who repeated the allegation to point them at BG's ownership structure. BG seemed to rely on the information already being publicly available and that key interlocutors in the government would not peddle in conspiracy theories. Hence, the allegation continued to have traction. When I gave the facts on shareholders to an Israeli journalist in 2007, he asked, "*why did you not give this information before?*"

Maiman's allegation of corruption in the licence award process was more serious and more difficult to refute. Even so, BG did little to attempt serious rebuttal in public, especially from 2001-2006. After that, it did conduct internal investigations to examine whether there was any unethical behaviour. The overall conclusion was a qualified no (see chapter 7, below). By that time, many of the people involved both inside BG and in other organisations had either moved on or in some cases had died. Also, documents had been lost or were incomplete. These investigations could not escape the conclusion that the licence award was shrouded in mist and it was not surprising that these allegations had emerged. Over time, these allegations against Gaza Marine became entangled with other conspiracy theories surrounding the involvement of the Israeli government, the British government (especially former Prime Minister Tony Blair both in office and after he left office). This is all examined in more detail below (see below, Chapter 8, 'Blood gas').

The process to award the Gaza Marine licence was not transparent. The PNA did not hold a tender but instead held bilateral negotiations with BG, facilitated by CCC. There are also allegations that a number of consultants were used by the parties involved, including BG, the Israeli government and the PNA. A number of these consultants were working on a success fee basis. In this age of more stringent governance requirements, much of this activity would not be tolerated and agreements would be more tightly constructed, if signed at all. In 2006-7, BG went through a period of tidying up some of these loose ends and ending any agreements still in force. Although some had already finished, the end date of some was ambiguous. One reason is that in some cases the success fee depended on the actual development of the Gaza Marine field, which has yet to occur. One agreement was unclear whether the success fee of £250,000 was dependent on the entire field being developed or was per well. With a development plan calling for four wells, the fee was, theoretically, £1 million.

A cursory look back at the circumstances and environment leading up to the award of the Gaza Marine contract showed the scope for allegations of unethical behaviour. There is no suggestion that BG or any of the parties involved did actually engage in such behaviour, especially that CCC funded terrorism. There is enough material though for those who have other agendas to throw mud. Some of that mud stuck and tainted Gaza Marine's reputation in Israel and the Palestinian territories.

Cold Feet in Egypt
Concern in Israeli circles that the talks with Egypt were unravelling seemed justified. BG received indications that tensions within the Egyptian government persisted over gas exports to Israel. In November, the British Ambassador reported to BG that the Egyptian PM had told him that Egypt had no intention of supplying gas in the near future. BG took this as a sign that Egypt was waiting for the political dust to settle and that the government now recognised the difficulties of meeting additional supply obligations. Egypt were also looking for ways to make any supply deal with Israel more politically

palatable. Egypt proposed supplying gas to the Gaza power station to demonstrate that it was helping the Palestinians as well. IEC, who would be the buyer of Egyptian gas, took this as a positive sign that Egypt was moving closer to reaching a deal. IEC were keen to move forward and visited Cairo at least twice in late 2004 in attempts to engage in serious negotiations. There was concern in Israel that Egypt was getting cold feet on the deal and that Israel would be left without sufficient gas supply. BG's country manager in Israel, John Field reported,

"they [IEC] became aware of the potential sale/delivery of Egyptian gas to Gaza which they see as a strategic move by Egypt (more specifically HS [Hussein Salem]) to overcome public sentiment towards the Palestinians, and against the supply of gas to Israel . . . Specifically with this information the buyers feel that Egypt is one step closer to reality though whether it will translate into a firm delivery timetable remains to be seen".

The prospect of Egypt supplying gas to the Gaza power station posed more competition to BG as it believed it had rights to supply gas to this power station. In the suite of agreements signed with the PNA in 1999, was a "Downstream Agreement". This covered the marketing of gas supply in the Gaza Strip. Under this agreement, BG and its partner CCC had first refusal on supply of gas to Gaza, including the power station. In the event that an alternative provider emerged, in this case, Egypt, BG and CCC had rights to match the offer and gain the supply contract. CCC now had potentially conflicting interests. They were (and still are) the majority shareholder in the power station. The prospect of Egyptian gas supply offered the prospect of securing a reliable fuel supply and improving the plant's economic returns. It appeared that Egyptian gas would be able to reach the power station before gas from Gaza Marine. In early November, CCC contacted BG asking them to consider waiving their rights to match a competing offer under the Downstream Agreement. Field described CCC as scoring an own goal as it was potentially jeopardising Gaza Marine development. The overall economic returns from Gaza Marine development would almost certainly far outweigh the profits from the power station.

The prospect of competing gas supplies was not the only commercial pressure facing the Gaza Marine project in late 2003. The cost of developing offshore fields was escalating as contractors providing subsea equipment and services raised their prices. The industry was experiencing a boom on the back of rising oil and gas prices. In the light of escalating costs, John Field reviewed the development plans for Gaza Marine to identify savings by finding alternative methods of undertaking the field development. This was not a wholesale review. The basic concept of a subsea development connected to the shore by pipeline and cables remained. The review's objective was to shave off some of the costs. Despite the political and commercial challenges facing the project, major contractors remained interested in participating in the project but would probably price the risks surrounding the project into their cost estimates.

As well as examining the threat of competition and rising costs, BG was also putting more thought into options for finding a market for the gas. Building on the options that Martin Houston had set out in mid 2003, BG took a deeper look at its options in 2004. While the political engagement continued to seek a change in Sharon's position, BG studied its options towards the development of Gaza Marine. What are the alternatives to selling the gas to Israeli customers? How feasible are those options? What would need to be in place for any of those options to succeed? By late 2004, BG had initial answers to those questions and was ready to embark on a new strategy for Gaza Marine.

A New Palestinian President

As BG was preparing its new strategy, external events intervened once again to create a new layer of uncertainty. This time on the Palestinian side. On 11 November 2004, Yasser Arafat died in a military hospital in a Paris suburb. There had been rumours about the state of his health for some time, but his illness became apparent in October 2004 when he fell ill during a cabinet meeting. After his death, his body was flown first to Cairo and then to Ramallah, where he was buried in the grounds of his headquarters. Israel had refused permission for him to be buried at Al-Aqsa mosque in East Jerusalem. Arafat's death marked the end of an era. He had dominated Palestinian politics since the early 1970s and became the embodiment of the Palestinian struggle for recognition and then statehood. Arafat was succeeded as head of the PNA by Mahmoud Abbas. Abbas, also known as Abu Mazen, was formally elected President of the PNA on 9 January 2005.

Although Mahmoud Abbas had served under Arafat for many years and had long been groomed as his successor, his appointment did mark a break with the past. He represented a new generation of Palestinian leaders who were not wedded to violent struggle but appeared committed to a negotiated settlement with Israel. As well as a change in approach, there was also a change in personnel. Abbas brought in his own cohort of senior officials and many of the Arafat era officials retired from office. For the Gaza Marine project, the most significant of his appointments was Mohammad Mustafa as economic advisor to the president and head of the PIF. In this position, Mustafa became the main contact for BG and CCC with the PNA. This is a position he retains. He has at times also served as deputy prime minister and on 31 March 2024 was appointed prime minister. As a result of Mustafa's appointment as head of PIF, Abbas brought the PIF under the direct control of his office. This move was against the spirit of the terms under which it had been established. The intention was to separate the PNA's political and commercial interests for the sake of greater transparency. While Abbas did not have the same reputation as Arafat for lining his own pocket, he and his family have probably used their position for personal gain. His son Yasser Abbas has built an extensive business empire on the back of his political connections.

The new Palestinian political leadership also marked a disruption in the relationship between the Gaza Marine partners, BG and CCC, and the PNA. This was a more serious issue for CCC than for BG. CCC had more extensive business interests in the Palestinian territories and by this stage, BG was losing interest in Gaza Marine. CCC and particularly its owners, the Khoury family, had enjoyed very close relations with Arafat and his close circles. The Khourys did not enjoy the same level of trust with Abbas and his circle.

Indeed, Abbas appeared to act with caution towards the Khoury family due to its past closeness to Arafat. However, he was closer to the Khourys than the other major Palestinian family and Khoury rivals, the Masris. The two families would become locked in a legal battle in the English courts that would drag in Gaza Marine.

CHAPTER 6

THE EGYPT OPTION
(2004-2006)

In late 2004 and early 2005, with little prospect of securing Israel as a market, BG turned its attention to the opportunity offered by Egypt. As the handover to a new Palestinian leadership was taking place in Ramallah, next door in Egypt, BG and its partners were approaching the end of construction of the first phase of a multi-billion dollar gas export facility. This was the Egyptian Liquefied Natural Gas (ELNG) plant at Idku on Egypt's Mediterranean coast, located between Alexandria and Rosetta. Liquefying natural gas involves cooling it to -162°C and keeping it insulated in purpose-built storage tanks or ships. As a liquid, natural gas is then easier to transport over long distances to a re-liquefaction plant. ELNG's first phase consisted of a processing plant to liquefy the natural gas, storage tanks, a jetty and associated facilities and utilities. The processing plant is usually referred to as a "*train*" as the modules that make up the plant are linked together like train carriages. ELNG train 1 had a production capacity of 3.6 million tonnes per year and was designed to take gas from fields in the Mediterranean, liquefy it and load it onto LNG tankers for export to world markets. If Gaza Marine gas could be delivered to ELNG, then it could also be liquefied and exported to world markets. This would form the basis for BG's new strategy for marketing Gaza Marine gas.

This option, first raised in mid 2003, had remained theoretical to this point but was about to become a realistic possibility and BG's publicly stated preferred option. In early 2005, operations were about to start at ELNG train 1 in which BG had a 35% share. The ELNG facility provided a route for Egyptian gas to reach world markets. In the case of train 1, the bulk of the output was destined for France. At the same time, work was continuing on train 2 (with output earmarked for the US) and BG aspired to build train 3. Indeed, BG had acquired sufficient land at Idku for six trains. Train 2 started production before the end of 2005. BG switched its attention to plans to develop Gaza Marine for supplying gas to ELNG through a dedicated pipeline from the field and exporting the gas to world markets. As the distance from the field to the Egyptian shore was approximately the same as to Israel, the capital expenditure for this was roughly the same. In the spring of 2005, Egypt and the PNA signed a memorandum of understanding on energy co-operation, including working towards the export of Palestinian gas to Egypt. This MoU, although very high level, supported BG's efforts to market Gaza Marine gas via Egypt.

New Project Management Team
As well as a change in BG's strategy for Gaza Marine, there was also a change in the project's leadership. A re-organisation of the regional structure at BG had seen Middle Eastern projects and opportunities (with the exception of Egypt) moved under the responsibility of the regional vice-president for Asia, Dave Roberts, an American. He wanted to inject new life into the search for business development opportunities in the region and the efforts to bring them to fruition. Roberts made two new appointments to the Middle East group in BG. He appointed a new head, Nigel Shaw to replace Tim Forbes. He also appointed me to the management team with responsibility for managing political risk and government relations. I moved from Cairo to head office in Reading to take up my new role in June 2005. Nigel arrived about a month later. He was an accountant by

background and had worked for BG for most of his career, joining the company when it was still state-owned. He had moved beyond purely financial roles to commercial roles and managing individual units of the business. Nigel was relocating from heading BG's business in India, where he had just resolved a complex issue with the government and the state-owned oil company. This experience would prove very relevant for managing the political complexities of the Gaza Marine project. There would be a long transition from Tim to Nigel on the Gaza Marine project. Tim would continue to remain active on the project for most of the rest of 2005 until retiring at the end of the year. As he held the relations with all the key players, this made sense and would allow an orderly transition to Nigel. During that period, I would also become fully familiar with the project since my contact with the project had been minimal since that meeting in Cairo in 2003. The team would not be focussing solely on Gaza Marine. Its remit also included other opportunities in the region. At the time, BG was also looking at potential projects in Oman and Pakistan.

There were also other changes in the BG team. In October 2004, the BG Israel country manager John Field was replaced by Erik Ludtke, a US national. Two days after Ludtke started, one of the senior Israelis in the BG office, Gina Cohen, who was responsible for external relations left the company suddenly. The official reason given was "*personal reasons*". There were allegations of inappropriate conduct by both her and Field. The two were having a relationship. Field had promoted her and recently awarded her a large salary increase. Although Cohen was dismissed from the company, Field was retained but was posted to Nigeria, the company's equivalent at the time of being sent to Siberia.

A Third Gaza Marine Well

One reason for keeping Forbes in place until late 2005 was that BG was preparing to drill its third well in the Gaza Marine licence area

- Gaza Marine-3 (GM-3). Drilling this well would complete BG's exploration commitments. The Gaza Marine team viewed drilling the well as vital for ensuring that BG could retain the Gaza Marine licence. BG moved drilling experts to the Tel Aviv office, now under Ludtke's leadership. A contract to secure a rig was signed and the rig was moved to Gazan waters. However, the rig needed considerable remedial work to bring it up to BG's health and safety standards. The costs of drilling the well were rising and undermining the initial positive economic evaluation of the well. Before giving the final go ahead to drilling GM-3, the project team needed to gain approval from BG's investment committee. The team obtained sign off from the technical and commercial experts in BG. The paper making the case for drilling the well was submitted, as process required, a week before the investment committee meeting date. By that time, the economics were not looking as robust as they had at the start of the planning process. It was Ludtke's role to present the paper to the committee. He expected Forbes, as the main sponsor of the paper, to be present as well. Forbes was not present at that investment committee. BG's chief executive Frank Chapman tore into Ludtke and the committee denied approval to drill the well. Ludtke felt he had been "*hung out to dry*". He left the company shortly afterwards.

Before leaving BG, Ludtke had to explain to CCC and PNA the reasons why it was not going to drill the well. Both CCC and PNA were angry with BG for pulling out at the last minute. BG had lost some of the trust it had enjoyed with both and its commitment to the project was now under scrutiny. While BG's reputation with its partner and the host government, the PNA, was damaged, the company did not suffer significant financial consequences. Under the terms of the Upstream Agreement and the various amendments that had occurred since 1999, there was no financial penalty on BG for failing to meet its exploration commitments. Contrary to the project team's expectations, the PNA did not revoke the licence and did not threaten to do so. There were good reasons for the PNA to avoid revoking the licence. It would have lost a blue chip investor and given the political uncertainty surrounding the project and the wider situation facing the PNA, would have found it difficult to find a replacement investor. Also, any withdrawal of the licence would also have affected CCC.

More Change

The uncertain political situation in Israel caused by the Intifada and Sharon's vehement opposition to buying Gaza Marine gas drove, in part, BG's switch to prefer Egypt as a market for the gas. As BG was making this switch, the political cards were once again being reshuffled. Arafat's death and Mahmoud Abbas' succession as president created an opportunity for a change in Israeli approach to the PNA. On 8 February, Sharon and Abbas signed an agreement bringing an end to the Intifada. A week later, rumours emerged that Sharon had changed his mind on buying Palestinian gas. His office denied the rumours, but they persisted, in part, as the successors to Paritzky as infrastructure minister expressed support. Both Sandberg who replaced Paritzky and then Ben-Eliezer who followed Sandberg both revealed that they had discussed the possibility of buying Gaza Marine gas with Sharon. Ben-Eliezer made direct reference to the changing situation in the region and proposed a way of avoiding revenue being used to fund terrorism. He proposed that Israel pay for Gaza Marine gas in kind. Instead of direct payment, Israel would supply electricity, goods and other services to the Palestinians of equal value. This proposal did not make any progress as any imperative to buy Gaza Marine gas was disappearing. Both Israel and BG were focussing on Egypt. In mid-June, IEC and EMG reached an agreement on the supply of Egyptian gas to Israel. This was followed at the end of June with the signature of a government level agreement to provide an umbrella for the commercial agreement. Ben-Eliezer travelled to Cairo to sign the agreement with the Egyptian petroleum minister Sameh Fahmy.

The option of sending Gaza Marine gas to Egypt had formed part of BG's thinking since 2003 but it had kept these plans under wraps and there had been little, if any, publicity about them. This option was still in its early days and there was a great deal of work to do, including gaining support and approval from the Egyptian government. In the summer of 2005, BG stepped up its focus on Egypt and this became its preferred option for Gaza Marine. BG representatives started to refer to the option in public and in interviews with the press.

There were also changes occurring on the global stage. In the spring of 2005, BG also found itself engaging with a new stakeholder, the Office of the Quartet Representative (OQR). The first incumbent was James Wolfensohn, a US lawyer of Australian origin, who until the start of the year headed the World Bank. In April 2005, he was appointed the Quartet's special envoy for Gaza disengagement, following Sharon's announcement of Israel's unilateral withdrawal from Gaza (see below). The Quartet (the US, Russia, EU and UN) had come together in 2002 when then US President George W Bush launched his roadmap for Middle East peace. However, until this point, the Quartet did not have any distinct identity or organisation. With Wolfensohn's appointment, it gained a separate organisational structure with a small secretariat which would grow over time, especially under the next office holder, Tony Blair. Although Wolfensohn was nominally representing all four parts of the Quartet, in reality he was a US government appointee. The US government paid his salary and that of his staff, who were largely seconded from the US State Department.

"Flim flam"

A BG delegation consisting of Steve Larcombe, Erik Ludtke and Kit Bethell travelled to Washington DC in May 2005 to brief Wolfensohn, State Department officials and the US Senator from California Dianne Feinstein, who was taking an interest in Palestinian affairs. The trip's purpose was to brief Wolfensohn on the Gaza Marine project. He was a potentially influential voice and could advocate for the project in his interactions with Sharon. For similar reasons it also made sense to keep State Department officials up to date. At that time, the head of the Near East department at State was David Welch. He was familiar with BG from his time in the earlier part of the decade as the US Ambassador in Cairo. In that role, BG representatives had met him several times to brief him on BG's business in Egypt. The US had strong interest in BG's operations in Egypt as the company was a major investor in one of its key allies in the region; BG used several large US companies as contractors on its projects and also BG had ambitions to export Egyptian gas to the US as LNG. This was an ambition that was realised in late 2005 with the start of operations at ELNG train 2, whose output was exported largely to the US, at least in the early months.

Senator Feinstein was also a potentially useful pro-Gaza Marine advocate, but BG squandered the chance to get her total support. A few months earlier, Feinstein had visited Israel and the Palestinian territories. During the visit, Ludtke had briefed her on the Gaza Marine project. She came away from the visit with a strong sense of the benefits that the project could bring to the Palestinian economy. She was already committed to making what contribution she could to building relations between Israelis and Palestinians. However, she also came away from the visit with the strong, but erroneous, understanding that most of the Gaza Marine gas would be supplied to Palestinian consumers either via electricity generated at the Gaza power station or directly. So, when the BG delegation of Larcombe, Ludtke etc briefed her in her Washington office on BG's plans to export most of the gas, she did not react well. She got angry with the BG delegation and accused them of flip flopping and *"flim flam"*. The BG delegation left with their tails between their legs.

T3GM

For around 18 months, until the summer of 2006, the BG team

working on Gaza Marine focussed on this project: development of Gaza Marine for supply to a future ELNG train 3. The project was given the acronym T3GM. At its height, BG had a team of more than 40 people working on this project in Cairo, Tel Aviv, Ramallah and its headquarters in Reading, UK. This team was a mixture of technical and commercial experts. The technical work focussed on the elements needed to bring Gazan gas to the Egyptian shore and feed it into the country's distribution system. While the basic concept of four subsea wells connected to the shore by pipeline and cables had not changed, the route of that pipeline and cables and the site of the processing plant onshore were new. This technical work therefore involved conducting a survey of the pipeline route from the proposed site of the subsea facilities to the Egyptian shore near El-Arish and locating a suitable site for the processing terminal.

The thrust of the commercial work was three-fold. The first part was putting in place the commercial agreements and framework to send Palestinian gas to Egypt, transport it through the Egyptian grid and liquefy it through the ELNG plant at Idku. This would be a series of agreements between the partners, the PNA and Egyptian state-owned companies. The second part of the commercial work was securing a market for the resulting LNG from Gaza Marine gas in international markets at a price which made development of the field economically viable. The third leg of work was securing other sources of gas for ELNG train 3. BG needed to find 4 trillion cubic feet of gas in order to make train 3 viable. The volume of gas that the Gaza Marine field could supply amounted to around 25% of the total volume needed to fill ELNG train 3. Without sufficient gas to fill a third train, its construction would not be feasible and ELNG would not be able to provide an export route for Palestinian gas. BG looked to other potential suppliers in Egypt. There were other international oil and gas companies who might have volumes available to fill train 3. BG signed MoUs with the US company Apache, the German RWE and held negotiations with BP. All these companies were significant investors in Egypt's oil and gas sector. The negotiations with BP proved especially difficult. BP demanded as part of the deal of supplying volumes to a future train 3, an equity stake in the ELNG holding company. This was part of BG's crown jewels and there was a very strong no from the BG chief executive. The talks to supply gas to train 3 never got beyond non-binding MoUs and initial talks. BG itself was losing interest in a future train 3. It was becoming aware that it may not even have enough gas for the two existing trains let alone a third one. Also, its relationship with the ministry and the state oil company EGPC was coming under strain due to the economics of ELNG. Since the original agreements on ELNG had been signed in 2001 and 2002, the price of LNG in global markets was rising. BG was doing very well out of the deal, but Egypt was not seeing any of this upside. EGPC were demanding a renegotiation of the agreements to give them a slice of the higher prices.

The basic plan for exporting Gaza Marine gas to Egypt was to use Egypt's facilities for onward export to global market. The Gaza Marine field would still be developed using the same concept as outlined above: sub-surface wells and gas gathering facilities operated remotely from the shore. However, the offshore facilities would be connected by pipeline and control cables to an onshore receiving terminal located on Egypt's north Sinai coast and the gas would enter Egypt's gas transmission system. Gas required to fuel the Gaza City power station would be supplied by a new build pipeline from Sinai to the power station while the bulk of the gas would be supplied to the ELNG plant where it would be liquefied, loaded onto an LNG tanker and supplied to one of BG's LNG customers such as France, US or Japan. Molecules from the Gaza Marine field would not necessarily be physically supplied to ELNG, but an equal volume of gas would be supplied from the Egyptian gas grid under commercial arrangements.

This scheme had many advantages for the PNA, BG and Egypt. It provided a route to market and would ensure that the Palestinians received the best possible price for its gas based on international benchmarks. For BG, it secured sufficient market to underpin Gaza Marine development, created increased demand for its ELNG plant and access to more LNG cargoes. Egypt would earn revenues from transit fees and the government's equity share in ELNG. Furthermore, the government could point to the arrangement as evidence for its practical support of the Palestinians.

The one stakeholder who did not gain any direct benefit from this scheme was Israel. This was one of several challenges that the project faced. Israel's co-operation was required to allow the project to go ahead as it still had security control over the Gaza offshore area, the K, L and M zones. However, there was little political or economic incentive for Israel to give this co-operation and allow the project to proceed. Successful implementation of this project would give the PNA a revenue source over which Israel had no control. Israel would also lose control over the fuel supply to the Gaza City power station. Co-operation with the Israeli security forces is required in order to undertake any offshore work on the Gaza Marine field such as surveys of the seabed, drilling wells, laying pipeline and cables as well as for ongoing maintenance work after the field started operations.

Unilateral Gaza Withdrawal

The work to advance the Egypt option for Gaza Marine took place against the backdrop of dramatic political events once again. In the spring of 2005, Israeli Prime Minister Ariel Sharon announced a unilateral withdrawal of Israeli forces from the Gaza Strip and the evacuation of all Israeli settlers in the territory. The Gaza Strip would be handed over to the Palestinians. At first this seemed to signal a new start for Gaza and the chance to rebuild its economy including developing its largest natural resource, the Gaza Marine gas field. Sharon, in making this bold political move, was motivated entirely by security considerations and was not trying to restart the peace process or instigate closer co-operation between the PNA and Israel.

His motivation was to separate Gaza from Israel and make the PNA entirely responsible for maintaining order in the Strip. Any economic motive for the unilateral withdrawal was simply to save money. The cost of protecting each of the eight thousand Israeli settlers in the Gaza Strip far outweighed the equivalent cost in the West Bank and there was almost no strategic rationale for maintaining a settler presence. The Israeli government's preparations for the withdrawal of its forces and settlers was made with almost no co-ordination with the PNA for the handover. The Quartet, which at this time was represented by former World Bank chief James Wolfensohn, attempted to put together a plan for the greenhouses and other settler infrastructure to be used for the benefit of the Palestinian economy. Wolfensohn even invested some of his own money in the project. However, the Israelis left nothing behind except piles of rubble. All settler buildings including factories, workshops and greenhouses were bulldozed before the final member of the Israeli army left the territory. Wolfensohn resigned his post in March 2006, disillusioned by the failure of the Israelis to leave anything behind that could benefit the Palestinian economy and also due to the approach of the US government towards his office. The State Department ended the secondment of many of his staff and reduced his operating budget. From the outside, it appeared that the US had only appointed him to give international legitimacy to Sharon's withdrawal from Gaza and give it the appearance of contributing to implementation of the roadmap. While Gaza's residents at first celebrated the departure of the Israelis and Hamas claimed it as a victory for resistance, it was to prove the start of a stranglehold on the Strip which Sharon's successors tightened, and which was still in place more than a decade later.

Sharon's unilateral disengagement from Gaza was part of his strategy towards the Palestinians to separate them from Israel. In addition to withdrawing all settlements from Gaza, he also withdrew from four small settlements in the West Bank. He envisaged a separate Palestinian entity (which may or may not eventually become a fully sovereign state). This would include the Palestinians gaining access to their own facilities and resources, including a port and airport in Gaza. He held discussions with Abbas on these issues. Now that Arafat was dead and he was separating the Palestinians, Sharon appears to have changed his mind on buying Gaza Marine gas. In late September as the withdrawal from Gaza was ending, he was reported to have changed his mind. Sharon would now support development of Gaza Marine and the supply of gas to Israel. This would form part of a package of measures to support a separated Palestinian economy. Sharon never got the chance to reveal this package and implement it. Less than four months after the completion of the Gaza withdrawal in September 2005, Sharon suffered a massive stroke on 4 January 2006, leaving him in a coma. Ehud Olmert, a former mayor of Jerusalem, who was finance minister and deputy prime minister, took over as acting prime minister. In April 2006, Olmert was confirmed as prime minister when it was clear that Sharon would not recover from the stroke and the subsequent coma. Sharon would remain in a coma until his death in January 2014. The end of Sharon's premiership created an opportunity to build on Sharon's apparent change of mind and lobby for an official change in the Israeli position. While Olmert was a Sharon ally and came from the same right wing political stable, he was less hard-line than Sharon and was perhaps more open to persuasion on the merits of developing Gaza Marine and allowing export of the gas to Egypt. If Sharon had really been planning to allow Gaza Marine to go ahead, then Olmert may have been aware and willing to implement his predecessor's plan.

A Turning Point
From the first conversations with Israeli officials on the idea of Gaza Marine gas to Egypt, it was clear that the Israeli government, at best had serious reservations and more likely opposed it completely. There was no direct expression of opposition but a clear message that Israel wanted to be certain that its security would be protected. There was a

great deal of focus on how the revenues from the project would flow to the PNA for the lifetime of Gaza Marine production, at least 15 years. At the time, Salam Fayyad was the Palestinian finance minister. A former World Bank official, He was widely trusted by the Israelis and other governments. He had been appointed as part of reforms demanded by international donors to bring greater transparency to the PNA's finances. However, it was recognised that he would not be in power for ever. Israel wanted arrangements put in place that would survive any change of administration in Ramallah. There was a potential route for BG to supply Gaza Marine gas to Egypt and for Israel to benefit (and have a level of control). In mid-September, Yam Tethys revealed that it was in talks to buy Gaza Marine gas and sell it into the Israeli market. Yam Tethys was looking to access additional resources in addition to its Mari-B field. The gas would still flow to Egypt in the first place but then travel back to Israel in the pipeline that would bring Egyptian gas to Israel. This was a convoluted plan shaped by the region's politics. BG did not take it seriously and the proposal did not make any progress.

Fears for the longevity of Fayyad's time in office and indeed the survival of the PNA seemed justified. The popularity of the PNA and its ruling party Fatah was suffering at the expense of Hamas. The group was performing well in the multi-round local elections held during the course of 2005. It was winning control of local councils in both the West Bank and the Gaza Strip. Hamas was emerging as a political force as parliamentary elections scheduled for January 2006 approached. Hamas was capitalising on its reputation as both an effective resistance movement to the Israeli occupation, its integrity (compared to the corruption-beset PNA) and its provision of social services which were often the only option in the face of ineffective provision by the PNA.

While many in Israel and outside were sounding the alarm about the rise of Hamas and the risk this posed to political stability in the Palestinian territories, BG were not heeding this alarm. BG's partner

CCC, which was closely tied to the PNA and Fatah, were giving out a different message. CCC representatives were dismissive of Hamas and convinced that Fatah would win the January 2006 election. Senior CCC executives made sure that their BG counterparts received this message. BG's senior executives were happy to hear this message. This is what they wanted to hear. My colleagues and I in the project team were not so convinced. I could see that Hamas were going to be a more significant political force and that BG may eventually have to engage with them. Any engagement would have to be handled carefully. Hamas were a proscribed organisation under UK and EU law. Direct engagement with them would be illegal. The team's efforts to alert our bosses of the potential political shock coming were not successful. There was no appetite for bad news.

So, when in January 2006, Hamas won elections and were invited into the PNA government, senior BG and CCC executives were in shock. Gaza Marine, an already politically complex project had just become even more complicated. The Hamas victory in the Palestinian legislative elections was also a turning point in Israel's attitude towards the Gaza Marine project. The Israeli government's determination to have control over both the destination of gas and the flow of revenue from the project redoubled. The government could not countenance a scheme under which both the gas and revenues would by-pass Israeli control and in which Hamas would have an element of control. Exporting Gaza Marine gas to Egypt would severely weaken Israeli control and could give Hamas access to a revenue stream. The idea that Gaza Marine represented "*money for terrorism*" was back on the agenda.

In reality, the Hamas victory did not have the immediate impact on the political situation in the PNA as many had feared. Over the months that followed the election win, there were several attempts to form a PNA government of national unity involving a mixture of Hamas, Fatah and technocratic appointees as ministers. All these attempts foundered on the inability of either Fatah or Hamas to make compromises. Hamas would not accept conditions (largely imposed by Israel and the international community) including an end to violence, recognition of Israel's right to exist and adherence to the Oslo Accords. Fatah would not let go of key positions in the government and relinquish control of some areas to Hamas. The outcome was that Hamas were shut out of the PNA administration, but this set the scene for an even more serious development in Palestinian politics, the Hamas takeover of the Gaza Strip.

Following the Hamas election victory, there was a definite hardening in the Israeli position. While Israeli officials continued to meet with BG and to be cordial, there was a change of tone. There was no significant attempt to obstruct progress on the Gaza Marine project but at the same time, there was no willingness to co-operate. Looking back at this period, one BG manager involved in the commercial negotiations at the time, remarked, "*I suspect that was the point when the Israelis stopped negotiating.*" However, BG did not give up and continued to plug away at the ELNG train 3 option for Gaza Marine.

Lack of Israeli co-operation was just one of several potential show-stopping obstacles that gas to Egypt faced. The project also required co-operation with the Egyptian government who would have to expend political capital with Israel in order for the project to proceed and secure Israeli co-operation. Egypt would also have to agree to the use of its gas transmission infrastructure, including setting a fair tariff for its use. There were two factors that made Egyptian support uncertain. The first was the need to intervene with Israel and put in play another factor in what was already a complex and fraught relationship. The other was that the project would draw Egypt and Gaza closer together. The Egyptian government did not want this. Anything that risked pulling Gaza back into Cairo's orbit was seen as letting Israel off the hook and making Cairo responsible for the situation in the territory. Cairo did not want to import Gaza's political and security challenges along with its gas.

At the time (2005-07), there were also considerable commercial challenges to overcome. As well as securing an international buyer for the resulting LNG, there was the need to expand ELNG by constructing a third train. Gaza Marine gas would be insufficient to fill a whole train and therefore other sources of gas would be required. The Egyptian government was waking up to the looming gas shortage it faced and would not sanction any further exports of Egyptian gas. Without a commercially viable third train, Gaza Marine gas would remain stranded.

Olmert's Intervention

In the end, the idea of Gaza gas to Egypt did not go any further. In early 2006, the Israeli government intervened in dramatic fashion. Olmert, who had retained the post of finance minister as well as assuming the premiership, wrote in January 2006 to his British counterpart as finance minister, Chancellor of the Exchequer Gordon Brown, demanding that the British government intervene and persuade BG Group to return to the negotiating table with the Israeli government. Olmert's letter followed a conversation with Brown in which he had raised the Gaza Marine project. Before Brown replied to Olmert, his officials met with BG representatives on 30 January. The BG delegation briefed the Treasury officials on the project and made it clear that Egypt remained their preferred option. They told the Treasury officials that they were working with the Egyptian state-owned gas company, EGAS, to finalise a contract for EGAS to buy the gas. On 21 January BG and EGAS signed a memorandum of understanding which provided a framework for the deal and a basis for negotiations. BG hoped to conclude these negotiations in early 2007 and start construction on the facilities, allowing gas to flow in 2009. EGAS had a strong interest in buying the gas, were offering a good price and already had the necessary infrastructure in place, the BG representatives informed the Treasury officials. The BG delegation went on to explain that the Egypt option not only made commercial sense to BG and the Egyptians but was also in the Palestinians' best interests. BG stated that the Egypt option would lead to the PNA receiving revenues of $100 million per year compared to $30-40 million per year under the Israel option. BG also noted there was the possibility of the PNA's equity share in the project rising from the proposed 10% to 20%.

Brown replied to Olmert on 7 February 2006. In his letter, Brown makes clear his support for the Gaza Marine project, says that BG is willing to discuss an Israeli offer and urges Israel to make early contact with BG. Brown wrote,

> *"Let me say at the outset that I think this is an extremely important project that goes to the heart of the vision that you, Salaam Fayyad [Palestinian finance minister] and I discussed in Tel Aviv in November: a viable Palestinian economy with reliable and predictable public finances and upholding the rule of law."* [22]

Olmert followed up this exchange of letters by requesting a meeting with Brown during a visit to London on 12 and 13 June 2006 specifically to discuss Gaza Marine. In briefing notes for Brown, his officials cautioned that this was, *"a sensitive commercial issue . . . which would require careful handling, and Mr Olmert may make requests which it will not be possible to fulfil."* [23] The officials do not specify what those requests might be but could have included the British government exerting pressure on BG to meet Israel's terms or some kind of political quid pro quo for allowing the Gaza Marine project to go ahead. Olmert and the Israeli government appeared to be under the impression that the British government had more influence over BG than it actually did. In Israel, BG was universally known as *"British Gas"*, a misnomer that often went uncorrected by

---

22 Copy of Chancellor Brown letter to PM Olmert dated 7 February obtained under UK Freedom of Information request.

23 Copy of Meeting proposition to Chancellor Brown dated 1 June 2006 obtained under UK Freedom of Information request.

BG staff. This impression seemed to originate from BG's time as a state-owned company. The British government no longer had any stake in BG.

Olmert and Brown did meet during the Israeli prime minister's visit to London on 13 June 2006. In a briefing note for the Chancellor before the meeting, his officials emphasised the British government's position that, *"all decisions concerning the project are taken on a commercial basis."* The officials went on to advise that the lines to take were, *"This is a commercial decision for BG . . . A successful project run by a reputable international company like BG is vital for the Palestinian economy. A strong Palestinian economy is in Israel's interest, and should help the prospects for peace in the region."* [24]

Olmert in his exchanges with Brown did not make any requests that would prove difficult to fulfil but he did make undertakings that he would be unable to meet. Olmert undertook that the negotiations would last no more than three months and Israel would offer terms that matched those that BG and the PNA would receive from exporting the gas to world markets via Egypt. In their brief meeting on 13 June, Brown stated that he understood the issue was one of price. Olmert in turn stated his serious intention to make a commercial offer. Brown promised to pass on the message and advised that Israel needed to act quickly.[25] The British government had always been clear in its private and public pronouncements that while it stood by to help if needed, BG's decisions were driven by the company's commercial imperatives and not by British government policy. The British government did pass on Olmert's message. It did not apply any pressure on BG to heed Olmert's demands. It did not need to. It was clear to BG that gas to Egypt would have to be put

---

24 Copy of BG Background brief dated 9 June 2006 obtained under UK Freedom of Information request.

25 Copy of Email readout of Chancellor Brown-PM Olmert meeting dated 14 June 2006 obtained under UK Freedom of Information request.

on the back burner.

While Egypt as a route to lucrative world markets was, at least temporarily, off the table, the country was set to become a potential market in its own right. The country was moving from a position of natural gas self-sufficiency to deficit and the need to import gas. The reasons for this are complex and beyond the scope of this book. Over-promising on gas exports was among the reasons. This included the construction of the EMG pipeline to Israel to supply gas. The emergence of demand in Egypt and the existence of a physical transport route could enable Palestinian gas exports to Egypt. However, like other plans to develop Gaza Marine, this has yet to come to anything.

CHAPTER 7

"NEVER IN A BULL'S ROAR" (2006-2008)

Olmert's intervention marked the end of BG's strategy to develop Gaza Marine for supply to a future third train at ELNG and export the gas to world markets. The strategy had not though ended in total failure. BG had demonstrated that there was an alternative (at least in theory) to exporting the gas to Israel. From now on, BG would continue to cite the Egypt option to create competitive tensions with the Israel option. The Egypt option provided a useful reminder to Israeli interlocutors that they were not the only game in town. The strategy had also succeeded in one important aspect. It had brought Israel back to the negotiating table and that had been a secondary aim all along. From the outset of the strategy to develop Gaza Marine to supply ELNG, BG had recognised that the chances of success were not high. BG had calculated that if it did not succeed in exporting the gas to Egypt, it would probably force Israel back to the negotiating table and so it was. The British government had played a part in reinforcing the impression that BG had options beyond Israel. The briefing that BG had given Treasury officials in January 2006 had convinced the government that Egypt was a viable option and in the commercial interests of BG, the Egyptians and the Palestinians. The message to the Israeli government that they had to act quickly, gave the impression that a window of opportunity was closing.

BG returned to negotiations with Israel. The first meeting following the Olmert-Brown exchange of letters took place on 22 February.

This time, rather than talking to potential customers for the gas such as IEC or private companies, BG dealt directly with the Prime Minister's Office. One of Olmert's undertakings in his dealings with Brown proved wildly optimistic. The talks lasted much longer than three months. At that first meeting, the Israeli team seemed ready to comply with Olmert's second major undertaking, that any deal with Israel would match the Egypt option gas price. The Israelis seemed ready to talk about a gas price that would meet BG's demands. BG also made demands that went beyond price. BG also asked for a safety net in the form of a government guarantee of the volume of gas that Israel would buy. The Israeli side seemed ready to negotiate but there was though a sting in the tail. Israel would extract value by other means.

The Israeli government lawyer, who was a close aide to Olmert, made an outrageous demand. He was also aggressive in making this demand. In return for agreeing a gas price acceptable to BG, Israel would provide *"political risk insurance"* and indeed only the Israeli government could provide this *"insurance"*. BG would have to pay millions of dollars to the Israeli government for this *"insurance"*. This was nothing less than a shake-down. The Israeli government lawyer was in effect demanding a bribe in return for allowing the project to go ahead. The BG team could not quite believe what they were hearing. This was completely unacceptable. BG could not agree to such a deal. In private, BG made clear to Israeli government representatives that the lawyer's demand was unacceptable and if Israel insisted on this, then the talks would be over. BG also complained about the lawyer's aggressive manner. This was not the spirit in which BG wanted to conduct these talks. BG could always return to the Egypt option. The conversation had the desired effect. The lawyer was never seen again at discussions and the demand to buy *"political risk insurance"* was never repeated.

While the negotiations between BG and the Israeli government started with the wrong tone, both sides demonstrated a willingness to continue. In late April, the Israeli government wrote to BG CEO Frank Chapman and Nigel Shaw to make an offer on price. The letter suggested that the government was united in its desire to reach an agreement with BG to become a third gas supplier to Israel. The letter was signed by Prime Minister's Office director general Ilan Cohen, Ministry of Finance budget director Kobi Haber, Ministry of Finance Accountant General Yaron Zalika and Ministry of National Infrastructures director-general Eli Ronen. The letter asserted that a third supplier was in line with government policy and that it wanted supply to start in 2009. The letter offered a price of $3.10 per mBtu for 1.5 billion cubic metres per year. This price was above that agreed with Yam Tethys and Egypt. However, the government officials refused to offer a guarantee on the volume of gas and stated that BG would have to rely on the strength of consumer demand for gas. This was a serious offer and BG took it seriously. Two weeks later a BG delegation visited Israel to hold further discussions with government representatives.

Subsequent rounds of talks focussed on the key commercial issues. The gas price was at the core of the negotiations. Without agreement on a gas price that made the development of Gaza Marine economic, there would be no development and no gas flowing to Israel. Nigel Shaw and his team were demanding a gas price that was higher than Israel was paying for its own production. The BG team were using the gas price from the Egypt option as the benchmark. BG could get $7.10 per mBtu for gas exported as LNG from Egypt. This price was based on the price that the gas could eventually receive in the US market. At the time, the US was the largest importer of natural gas and LNG prices at the time were at historic highs and climbing. Israel could not afford to pay such prices without risking economic damage through higher energy prices. The higher cost of gas would be passed through to both gas and electricity consumers as gas was largely used for power generation. Also, as it would be the Israeli government buying the gas, they would have to be seen to get the best deal in the public interest. The government's united front at the start of the negotiation process did not last until the end of the year. In November, signs of disunity were evident. The Ministry of Infrastructure made it clear that they did not support the structure of the talks with BG. This was a turf war. The infrastructure ministry believed it should be leading the talks rather than the finance ministry. It also claimed that the government's purchase of Gaza Marine gas would harm competition. Lack of agreement in government and questions over the government's role in the gas market would continue into 2007.

As well as convincing the government on the merits of buying Gaza Marine gas, BG also faced a public relations battle in Israel. The attacks against BG had become more subtle than allegations of funding terrorism or engaging in corrupt practice. For example, in July, reports appeared in the Israeli press claiming that the Gaza Marine licence was no longer valid. The reports claimed that the licence had expired in 2004. The reports cited "*senior sources*" who stated that, "*British Gas was acting like a gangster, as if the British Mandate for Palestine was still in existence, whereas it actually had no legal standing. Energy market officials expressed astonishment that the company was sitting at the negotiating table when it had no formal permit*".[26] If the anonymous briefing was intended to disrupt the talks between the government and BG, it did not succeed. In any case, the article was misleading. While BG's rights to conduct exploration activities in the Gaza Marine licence area had expired, it retained the right to develop the discovered resources under the compromise reached with the PNA in 2002. The use of half-truths and misleading claims about Gaza Marine, including casting doubt on the validity of the licence, would persist as talks continued. BG's approach was to ignore these articles and resist the urge to rebut every claim and falsehood. The result was the spread of myths and conspiracy theories about Gaza Marine. This made it harder to influence opinion in both

---

26 Globes, "British gas operating off Gaza without license", 4 July 2006

Israel and the Palestinian territories in favour of a deal to develop Gaza Marine and market the gas. BG was usually on the back foot in the public relations battle.

In mid 2006, the Gaza Marine project had a new overseer in BG. While Nigel Shaw was in day-to-day charge of the project, he now reported to a new regional executive vice president, Stuart Fysh, an Australian who had worked at BG since 1999 and was the general manager in Egypt when I first joined BG. Indeed, Fysh had interviewed me for the role. Fysh was blunt speaking and commercially very astute. He saw the opportunity in developing Gaza Marine but did not have a mandate from the BG Board to do a deal. The BG Chairman, Sir Robert Wilson made it clear to Fysh and to BG CEO Frank Chapman that the Board had no interest in investing in Gaza Marine and that BG should sell its interest. In the meantime, Fysh should spend the minimum time necessary on the project. At the same time, Fysh and his colleagues were under pressure to secure more gas reserves. One of the key measures by which oil and gas companies are measured by City investors is the volume of reserves on their books and their reserve replacement ratio i.e. the rate at which they are replacing production with new reserves for future production. There are strict accounting rules about when reserves can be "*booked*" i.e. officially included in the accounts. An oil and gas company can only book reserves when it has formally sanctioned development of those reserves i.e. the board has approved the expenditure on the development project. BG in 2006 was facing a dearth of projects to sanction and therefore difficulty in booking new reserves. It had gained a reputation with City investors for a strong record of converting exploration success into development projects and therefore had a good track record of reserves booking. Fysh and other senior executives in BG were therefore under pressure to find bookable reserves.

While, he did not have a mandate from the BG board to do a deal on Gaza Marine, this was not the message that Fysh gave the project team in 2006. He told the team that Gaza Marine was one of the most sanction-able projects in the company's portfolio. If sanction of Gaza Marine development could be achieved in 2006 then 90% of its 1 tcf of reserves could be added to BG's books, contributing to maintaining its strong reputation with the City. To achieve project sanction in 2006, the team would have to reach a deal with the government of Israel to show the Board that there was an economically viable project. The official BG position was that Gaza Marine would make a contribution to its future growth. Each year around August time, BG issued a databook that gave details on all its operations and projects on a country by country basis. Both the 2006 and 2007 Databooks listed Gaza Marine under long term opportunities. The 2007 Databook gave a timeframe of 2010-12 when the contribution would come to fruition.

Despite the instruction from Chapman and the Board to spend minimal effort on Gaza Marine, Fysh did devote some effort to finding a deal. Fysh visited Israel in late June 2006 to meet representatives of both the Israeli government and the PNA. He also met with Salam Fayyad in London in early 2007 before he became Palestinian prime minister and again later in the year in Ramallah after he had taken office. During that trip to Ramallah, Fysh came to understand the full complexity of the Gaza Marine project and was dubious that a deal would ever be achieved. There were too many different people to keep happy: BG, CCC, the Israelis and the Palestinians. He also came to appreciate that BG had definitely sided with one Palestinian faction when it had joined with CCC to acquire the Gaza Marine licence. There were other powerful families in the Palestinian territories (some of whom Fysh met) and from these meetings he gained the perception that perhaps BG had chosen the wrong side, and this could have severe repercussions at a later date. Nevertheless, Fysh found the Palestinians and particularly Fayyad easy to deal with and described him as *"fantastic"*.[27] Fayyad clearly wanted to do a deal but at the same time get the best possible deal for the Palestinians and not a deal at any price. Fysh could understand that approach by a government. However, in his meeting with the Palestinian President, Mahmoud Abbas, Fysh found less enthusiasm for a deal.

Fysh also met with representatives of the Israeli government in an attempt to make progress on Gaza Marine but found their approach hard to understand or tolerate. These meetings took place in both Jerusalem and London. In some ways, Fysh found the Israeli government easier to deal with than many other governments he encountered in his job. They were more straightforward and less nationalistic than many of their counterparts, partly because they were not wedded to their posts. Many Israeli officials, especially at senior levels, only serve for relatively short periods and then move on. However, in one important aspect, Fysh found the Israeli government representatives some of the worst he had ever dealt with and left a very bad taste behind. Fysh described their attitude towards the Palestinians as *"disgusting"*. He reported that they treat the Palestinians *"beneath contempt"*. Israeli officials told him that whatever commercial construct BG and Israel agreed, they (the Israeli government) could get the Palestinians to agree also. An official in the Prime Minister's office told Fysh, *"We can put pressure on the Palestinians to sign anything. . . All of these people want passes, there is no one that we can't touch."* This approach was *"anathema"* to Fysh and refused to proceed on this basis. In any case, it was clear to him that the two sides were, *"never in a bull's roar"* of agreement.

Planning for Success
While discussions continued with the Israelis, it was not just time that Stuart Fysh, Nigel Shaw and the rest of the BG project team were spending on Gaza Marine. They were also spending money

---

27 Author interview with Stuart Fysh

on technical work. The re-organisation of the project team that had brought Nigel and me on to the project, also included a new technical manager for the project, Ian Howard. He was a very experienced project manager who had worked in Tunisia, one of BG's most important operations at the time and was now based in Egypt. He remained in Egypt but was dedicated full time to the Gaza Marine project. His role was to oversee all the engineering work on the project. A considerable amount of planning, design, surveying and engineering tasks needed completion to get to a point before BG was even ready to sanction the project in the event of a successful outcome of the gas price discussion and agreement of other terms with the Israeli government and with the PNA.

The first substantive task that Ian undertook was to plan and commission a survey of the seabed along the route the gas pipeline would take from the field around 30 kilometres from the coast to landfall near Ashkelon in Israel. The purpose of the survey was to obtain a detailed picture of the topography of the seabed, identify any obstacles and understand the stability of the seabed. The survey was conducted in early 2007 with a vessel mobilised from Israel. The survey was for the whole route of the pipeline including the 1.5 kilometres that fell within the K zone (the no-sail zone). As before with the exploration activities carried out in the early years of the project, undertaking the survey required co-operation with the Israeli navy and gaining explicit approval to operate in the no-sail zone. BG sought and obtained permission from the Israeli military to sail in this zone for the survey. In the end, it was decided that the survey vessel did not need to enter the K zone. The Israeli navy took a pragmatic approach. They wanted to know the full scope of activities. Where there were potential problems, they sought solutions rather than trying to block activities. One issue that the Israeli navy were very concerned about was how much noise the gas flowing through the pipeline would make. The naval officers that Ian and others at BG dealt with would not explain why they were so concerned with the noise that a pipeline on the seabed would make. The most likely explanation was that the military had installed microphones on the seabed to listen for boats and possibly even submarines infiltrating from the Gaza Strip or further afield. The Israeli naval officers gave Ian and his team a maximum decibel level allowed for the pipeline. The team then did some work to make sure that the pipeline noise would stay below that level. The Israeli navy made clear that BG would be responsible for any breach of that noise level.

Screaming in the Desert

As well as surveying the route of the pipeline from the field to the Israeli coast, BG also commissioned a survey of the potential pipeline route from the field to the Sinai coast in Egypt. This was part of the strategy of keeping the Egypt option alive and demonstrating to the Israeli government that it remained a real option and an alternative to taking the gas to Ashkelon. This survey was conducted by a different vessel mobilised from an Egyptian port. As the vessel approached Gazan waters (but remained within Egyptian waters), it was contacted by the Israeli navy wanting to know its purpose. It was not just the pipeline route that BG surveyed, it also undertook a reconnaissance of potential sites on the Sinai coast for a processing terminal for the gas. BG looked at two potential sites. One near El-Arish, the capital of the North Sinai Governorate and one further along the coast close to the border with Gaza. The whole area was sensitive for the Egyptian authorities, who maintain a heavy police presence in the area. A group of British nationals travelling around remote areas of the coast in four wheel drive vehicles, taking photos and making notes aroused the suspicions of the local police. At one point the BG team were detained in a police station in El-Arish. They were held for several hours while BG's security liaison in Cairo explained the purpose of the trip to the authorities and secured their release. During their detention, the BG team were treated with respect but not everyone held in that police station seemed to be getting the same level of respect. During their detention, the BG team heard prolonged screams coming from elsewhere in the building which sounded as though someone or perhaps several people were being tortured.

Following the seabed survey, BG then needed to undertake further investigations into the geography of the field area. The next major task on Ian's to do list was to undertake a survey known as a geotech survey. This would require shallow drilling of the seabed to understand the composition of the seabed and whether it would be able to support the weight of the equipment that would be installed on the seabed. The budget for the survey was more than one hundred thousand dollars and Ian negotiated a contract with a leading provider of this service. The technical work on the project was making considerable progress. Ian and his colleagues were planning for the next significant milestone. This was activities that would prepare for the first stage in the actual development of the field after BG sanctioned the project. This stage is known as front-end engineering and design (FEED). The FEED stage involves the spending of considerable amounts of money, totalling tens, if not hundreds of millions of dollars.

Knesset Committee Debate

In a sign that a deal between BG and the Israeli government was a real possibility, the Knesset's economic committee held a meeting on the potential agreement. A search of the Knesset's records suggests this was the only debate that the parliament held on buying Palestinian gas. The discussion took place on 26 December 2006. The committee's chair was Moshe Kahlon, a Likud MK who would later become Israel's finance minister. He opened proceedings by noting that the committee, "*would be discussing the agreement that is being finalised to purchase natural gas from British Gas*".[28] Kahlon also noted the importance of Israel having sufficient gas supply including an

---

28 https://oknesset.org/meetings/1/8/183228.html as translated

emergency backup. He told the committee, "*I would like to take this opportunity and call for all the leaders of the gas field to do everything they can so that Israel will have emergency gas reserves.*" In holding the debate, Kahlon was responding to a request by fellow Likud MK and committee member Gilad Erdan. In his opening remarks, Erdan agreed on the importance of the subject and lamented the poor attendance of fellow MKs with only six MKs attending the committee. Erdan preferred to focus on the security implications of buying Palestinian gas and he echoed Sharon's accusation that the Palestinians would use the revenues to fund terrorism. Erdan appeared to misunderstand the ownership structure of BG, claiming that CCC owned 10% of BG and that in any case the identity of the Palestinian partners was unclear. He told the committee,

> "*It should be noted that BG is British owned (90%) and CCC owned (10%) and to this day, no one, including the people running the negotiation, unless I am told otherwise, do not know for sure who the Palestinian partners of CCC are and any other partners for that matter. What is clear is that if the deal is signed, the PA will have 10% of it and we know that the PA, currently led by Hamas, will receive from this deal some $200, 250 or 300 million if we are talking only about 10% because CCC's part should increase by 30% if I remember correctly, if the deal is carried out.*"

BG was not represented at the committee and so could not correct this misinformation. The committee invited BG but due to the Christmas period, BG had declined to attend. While expatriate members of the BG team in Israel were unavailable due to Christmas, there were Israeli BG staff members who could have represented and put across BG's position. An Israeli consultant who BG used for government affairs advice, Gal Blau, was present but did not participate in the discussion. CCC was represented by former BG employee Gina Cohen. During the committee's discussion, she attempted to give more information on CCC's owners and the company's relationship with both BG and PIF. Erdan does not appear to have been convinced by her explanation, which was factually accurate. Erdan also raised the question of whether Barak had been right to allow the PNA to award the licence and the involvement of figures such as Genossar. He noted, *"For those who are not aware of it, the same place where BG discovered the gas was given (to the Palestinians) by then PM Barak, in 1999, and there have been some questions about the involvement of Barak's confidants, such as Yossi Genossar RIP and others in giving that area to the PA."* He goes on to state his belief that the Ministry of Justice has prepared a note on this question. However, the ministry is not represented at the committee to confirm his belief.

As well as Erdan's security concerns, two other issues dominated the debate: concern over the security of supply of gas to Israel and over the government's apparent intervention in the country's natural gas market. Two committee members, Ronit Tirosh and Israel Hasson raised concerns that Israel will not have sufficient gas to meet its future requirements as the Yam Tethys field will be depleted in five to six years' time and there is still uncertainty when Egyptian gas will arrive. There is support for buying Palestinian gas from the Ministry of National Infrastructure (MNI) Director-general Hezi Kugler, from the IEC representative Shimshon Bruckman and from Israeli companies looking to build private power stations. Representatives of the Israeli partner in EMG, Merhav, also participated in the discussion and not surprisingly insisted that Egyptian gas would arrive and opposed buying Palestinian gas. The Merhav representative, Nimrod Novik, repeated the assertion that there was division in the PNA, and that Arafat had warned off Salam Fayyad from intervening in the project. Novik suggested that BG had approached EMG to join forces and stated, *"It was not also Salam Fayyad. I met with Fayyad after BG approached us and wanted to make a joint deal. Fayyad said that Arafat instructed them to not touch this project."*

Novik and the CEO of Delek (one of the Yam Tethys partners)

Gideon Tadmor both raised the question of whether it is appropriate for the state to intervene in the natural gas market and act as a gas buyer. Both men questioned why the government is not holding a tender process for gas purchases. Tadmor claimed that purchasing gas from other sources such as the Palestinians will discourage exploration in Israeli waters. This was of direct interest to him as at that time the Yam Tethys partners were preparing for an exploration campaign. Also, for both Merhav and Yam Tethys, the entry of Palestinian gas or gas from other sources (Turkey and Russia are both mentioned during the discussion) presents a competitive threat. Kugler from the MNI explained that state intervention is necessary due to the underdeveloped nature of the natural gas market in Israel. He pointed out that the state has intervened previously when private companies failed to provide what the market required, citing the example of the state setting up a company to build the gas transmission system. He also held out the possibility that the government will hold a tender at a future date.

The committee did not come to any conclusions, make any decisions or call for further action such as demanding input from specific ministries or officials. It was not an evidence gathering session and so does not seem to have had any impact on government policy or subsequent actions by Kugler or any of his colleagues. It does though appear to be the only time that a Knesset committee discussed the issue of buying Palestinian gas.

A Sense of Optimism

All the time and money spent on the Gaza Marine project looked as though it would pay dividends. At the start of 2007, there was a sense of optimism that a breakthrough was coming. The Israeli government representatives were talking up the chance of an agreement. The BG side were more cautious in their diagnosis of success. The cause for optimism was a narrowing of the price range in the negotiations. The two sides were now discussing a gas price in the range of $3.80 and $4.10 per mBtu. This represented a compromise by both sides. The price marked an improvement on the original Israeli government offer of $3.10 per mBtu. While for BG, this was considerably lower than the price it could achieve by exporting Palestinian gas to world markets via Egypt. A price in this range would still represent an economic proposition that would allow BG a profit and a healthy return on its investment. The costs of getting the gas from the Gaza Marine field to Israel were less than getting it to world markets. To get the gas to world markets, the gas price would have to cover the cost of getting it to Egypt, liquefying the gas, shipping the gas, re-gasifying it and then transporting it to the end user.

In late March, the Israeli government representatives sought cabinet approval of the outline of an agreement with BG to purchase Palestinian gas. This was a deal that the powerful Ministry of Finance, the Prime Minister's Office and the Ministry of National Infrastructure negotiated at the behest of Prime Minister Olmert who supported in principle buying Palestinian gas. The outline agreement faced questions from heavyweight ministers in the cabinet. The Minister of Strategic Affairs Avigdor Lieberman raised the issue of revenues funding terrorism. The Minister of Defence Amir Peretz wanted to understand the defence and security implications of any agreement. The Minister of Foreign Affairs, Tzipi Livni called for understanding of the diplomatic consequences of buying Palestinian gas and the impact on relations with the British government of not reaching a deal with a British company. The Israeli government negotiators had neglected to make their case and persuade other important parts of the government before bringing the issue to cabinet. While none of the ministers, except perhaps Lieberman, opposed the purchase of Palestinian gas in principle, they could not at this time give approval. The cabinet decided to postpone a decision.

In the meantime, BG briefed the PNA during early April on the outline agreement reached with the Israelis. Subsequently, the PNA offered to provide guarantees over the supply of gas to Israel.

In a sign that the Israeli government supported the principle of buying Palestinian gas, a month later, the cabinet voted to lift the Sharon-imposed ban on buying Palestinian gas. This marked a small but significant step forward for an eventual agreement. While BG was winning the political battle, it was still facing difficulties in the public relations war. Maiman reacted to news of the cabinet lifting the ban by repeating allegations of shady dealings in the Gaza Marine project. He alleged that Martin Schlaff and Muhammad Rashid were secret partners with BG. The Gaza Marine project was about to face much more serious challenges.

First there were signs of a lack of an agreed strategy on gas in other parts of the government system, not just at cabinet level. In mid-May, the government-owned IEC announced a tender for long term gas supply. Israel was experiencing a higher than expected increase in energy demand and IEC's current contracts with Yam Tethys and Egypt for supply would not be sufficient. From 2012, Israel would need more gas. IEC criticised the government strategy of negotiating with BG without holding a tender for gas supply. IEC stated that it was legally obliged under government procurement regulations to conduct a tender for future gas supply. The government countered by talking up the prospect of a deal with BG. The normally cautious BG also stated in public that it was making progress towards a deal.

Hamas Seize Control of Gaza but not Gaza Marine
That optimism soon evaporated as external forces once again caused the brakes to be applied to any progress towards developing the Gaza Marine field. In June 2007, Hamas seized control of the Gaza Strip and established a rival administration to the PNA. This development marked the end of any form of unity government under President Abbas. In Israel, attitudes towards the Gaza Strip and all things Gazan hardened. Over the months that followed, the Israeli government under Olmert's direction imposed increasingly restrictive measures on Gaza. These measures included restrictions on the types of goods

that could be imported into the Strip, including basic foodstuffs. The ability of Gaza's residents to leave the Strip was also severely curtailed. Israel imposed a blockade on the Gaza Strip that continues to this day. The sanctions against Gaza also included restrictions on electricity supply and reductions in fuel imports. As the weeks passed, anything connected with Gaza became politically toxic in Israel. It was politically untenable for the government to conclude any deal which would appear to grant any benefit to Gaza and its Hamas overlords. The Israeli government continued to meet with BG but briefed journalists that a deal was now several months away at the earliest. To keep the negotiations on the rails, BG proposed an arrangement to bring greater transparency to the funds flow and safeguard against the revenues being diverted for terrorism or other illicit purposes. It proposed that the revenues would be paid into an escrow account and a neutral third party would distribute the funds as per the contractual terms and would report on payments disbursed. The proposal was not enough to overcome the growing hostility towards Gaza from the Israeli government.

While Hamas had gained control over Gaza, it had not gained control over the Gaza Marine project. Nor had the organisation gained any direct stake in the project. The original Gaza Marine licence had been signed with the Ramallah-based PNA. The PNA remained in power and remained the recognised self-rule authority by Israel and other governments such as the British and the US. Israel continued to deal with the PNA under the terms of the Oslo Accords. There was no question of the Oslo Accords being torn up and Israel re-imposing itself in the West Bank and Gaza Strip. So, BG (and its partner CCC) continued to deal with the PNA regarding Gaza Marine. It would still be the PNA that would have to grant approvals under the agreement signed back in November 1999. There was also still no question of BG engaging directly with Hamas as it remained a proscribed organisation by the EU, the US and others. In any case, there was little need to talk to Hamas about Gaza Marine. The only activity on the project was the discussion of commercial terms with the PNA and with the Israeli government. The project was still a long way from development and having any physical impact on the Gaza Strip or its waters.

Hamas did though express its views on the project but did not seem to have an agreed position on the project. The initial reaction to the project following its takeover of Gaza came from the economy minister in the newly formed Hamas administration, Ziad Al-Zaza. He described BG as *"an embarrassment to the Palestinian people"* and the Gaza Marine project as an *"act of theft"*. This rhetoric uttered in the heat of excitement of taking power was followed by more considered commentary from Hamas. Other Hamas officials indicated that they would be willing to negotiate with BG on project terms that would be more acceptable to Hamas and provide an increased share of the revenues to the Palestinian people and especially those in Gaza. No negotiations of any kind took place with Hamas on the project. BG did though find a channel to send and receive occasional messages from Hamas. BG retained Alastair Crooke as a consultant. Crooke was a former British intelligence officer who had played a role in negotiating with Hamas during Israel's besieging of the West Bank in 2003. In particular he had helped negotiate the end of a hostage situation in Bethlehem's Church of the Nativity. After leaving government service, Crooke started his own consultancy and maintained his contacts with Hamas. Crooke's role for BG was more than just passing the occasional message to Hamas. He also gave advice on the overall political situation.

Political Reshuffle

To acknowledge the new political landscape, the PNA president, Mahmoud Abbas, reshuffled the government. He tasked Salam Fayyad, previously finance minister and the Palestinian politician most trusted by the outside world, with forming a new government on 15 June 2007. Fayyad would go on to serve as prime minister for nearly five years and became a key interlocutor on Gaza Marine. He appreciated the benefits that Gaza Marine could bring to the Palestinian economy but also saw the need to gain the best possible deal for the Palestinians. He understood that any deal which seemed to sell the Palestinian territories short would attract a political backlash from Hamas and other opponents of the PNA. Fayyad could not afford to be seen to give Palestine's largest natural resource away to foreign interests. During his time as premier, Fayyad's central demand on Gaza Marine was that the PNA's equity share in the project increase from 10% to 20% after project sanction. This demand placed another obstacle in the way of making any progress on the project. CCC were totally opposed to giving up more equity to the PNA. They had lost equity in the arrangements that had been agreed in the post licence signing period over the issue of the *"surplus interest"*. CCC did not want to give up any more equity. BG was also not minded to give up any of its equity share. It did not want to reduce the value that it would gain from the project, if it ever generated revenue. However, BG did understand the political agenda behind Fayyad's demand and appreciated the need to ensure the political perception of the project was conducive. BG understood the need to build strong support for the project amongst Palestinian society. Without this support, development and future operation of the project would likely to be beset with difficulty and face strong opposition.

The need to ensure widespread support for the Gaza Marine project in Palestinian society came from the very top in BG. It was one of three demands that BG's Board made of the project team. These demands were set as conditions that the project would have to meet before the Board would consider granting a final investment decision. There was no time limit on meeting these conditions and in any case, the project was still some distance from a final investment decision. The BG Board was growing increasingly sceptical about the Gaza Marine project and concerned about the risks to BG's reputation. The project team would have to demonstrate that the project enjoyed widespread support, this would include amongst pro-Hamas sections of society. The Board's other two conditions were robust legally binding agreements to govern the project and guarantees from Israel.

In late June 2007, there was another appointment that would have an impact on Gaza Marine. On 27 June 2007, Tony Blair was appointed to the Office of the Quartet's Representative (OQR). The appointment came the day after he ended his term as British Prime Minister after ten years in office. The appointment, largely at the instigation of the US government, marked an attempt to enhance the credibility of the Quartet's efforts to implement the roadmap and find a peaceful solution to the Israeli/Palestinian conflict. However, Blair's appointment was controversial from the outset and he was given a limited remit. The controversy initially centred on Blair's role in the Iraq war and the removal of Saddam Hussein from power. For many in the Arab world, including many Palestinians, this was another example of Western colonialism. Also, the Iraq war had left a chaotic situation in its wake and arguably undermined rather than buttressed stability in the region. The controversy around Blair's appointment would grow as the extent of his business interests that he also pursued as a former Prime Minister became apparent. This would come to include allegations of a conflict of interest directly related to Gaza Marine due to his business interests and his role as Quartet Representative.[29] Blair's role as Quartet Representative was not to find a lasting peaceful solution to the conflict. His role was limited to building economic relations between Israelis and Palestinians.

The International Angle

The new circumstances for the project created by Olmert's intervention, the appointment of Fayyad as Palestinian prime minister and

---

29 For example, see Murphy (2013), Chapter 6

Blair as Quartet Representative took place while I was absent from the project. In August 2006, I had relocated to Muscat in Oman as part of a BG team to start operations following the winning of an onshore block in the Sultanate. In March 2007, my boss, the BG Oman asset general manager informed me that my job was being localised and an Omani would fill the position. I would be leaving Oman in July 2007. Forced to find a new job, my first thought was to ask Nigel Shaw for a job on the Gaza Marine project. Fortunately, he said yes. There was a role for me on the project management team as the government relations manager. My re-introduction to the project took the form of participation in a project workshop in East Jerusalem in July 2007. After the workshop, I would need to return to Muscat to pack up my house and move my family back to the UK. To attend this workshop required convoluted travel arrangements. Oman did not recognise Israel and there were no direct flights. Furthermore, Oman did not allow entry to those who had Israeli stamps in their passport. I could not risk getting an Israeli stamp in the same passport that held my Omani residence visa. I did though have a second passport which I had used for travel to Israel previously, but this was in the UK. So, I flew from Muscat to London, picked up my second passport and left my first in the UK. The next day I flew to Israel and spent the next two days participating in the workshop. I then flew back to London, swapped passports again and the next day flew back to Muscat.

The purpose of the workshop in Jerusalem was to take stock. At that point, Nigel and the team had been negotiating with the Israelis for around a year since Olmert's intervention with his letter to Brown. There were a number of issues that were blocking progress in the negotiations that had gone on far longer than the three months Olmert committed to in his letter. The main point of disagreement was the price that Israel would pay for the gas. The Israeli government was proposing that it would buy the gas rather than IEC, the state electricity generator, being the customer. IEC would have to hold a tender for the gas. The Israeli government would then sell the gas to IEC or other customers such as industrial users or independent private producers. The transparency of the revenue flows from Gaza Marine and the prevention of the revenues being used to support terrorism also remained an issue. There was now increased focus on Gaza and the threat posed to Israeli security from militants in the Strip following the Hamas election win and Gaza takeover. At the workshop, my predecessor on the project team, Nicole McMahon presented the findings of research that BG commissioned in Israel on perceptions of the Gaza Marine project. This research was based on survey findings and focus groups. Against expectations, the research found that there was still overall positive perception of Gaza Marine and the contribution that the gas would make to meeting Israel's energy needs. Even more surprising, the name "*Gaza Marine*" was viewed more positively than the term "*Palestinian gas*". This seemed to reflect the perception of "*Palestinian*" as the enemy and the threat. "*Gaza*" had yet, in these early days of Hamas dominance, to acquire any specific negative connotations in the minds of many Israelis. The outcome of the workshop was an agreement to push on with efforts to reach a deal for the supply of Gaza Marine gas to Israel. With such a deal, a final investment decision could be taken on developing the field.

The extensive travel I undertook to attend the workshop set the tone for the rest of the year. Along with the rest of the project team, I spent most of the remaining months of 2007 travelling on project business. Most of the trips were to Israel and the West Bank to talk to officials and other stakeholders. There was also one trip to Washington DC to talk to the State Department, the World Bank and its sister organisation, the International Financial Corporation (IFC). During this trip, we returned to the hotel one afternoon, to find a stage had been set up in the square opposite in preparation for a potential candidate in the 2008 presidential election to address a rally. The candidate's name was Barack Obama. I and other members of the team took the opportunity to listen to him and although he was only a distant speck, I was impressed by what I heard.

The World Bank and IFC were included on the Washington trip as they were important stakeholders in the project. The World Bank was a major donor to the PNA. Moreover, the World Bank Group had the potential to reduce the political risks facing the project. BG engaged with the IFC to examine the potential for it to take a minor stake (up to 10%) in the project. The IFC's involvement could reduce the likelihood of either the Israeli government or the PNA interfering in the project. The World Bank also undertook research which highlighted the benefits to the Palestinian economy switching to gas. Its 2005 Report demonstrated the benefit of switching the Gaza power station to gas. The report also provided a benchmark for a gas price which was helpful to BG in the negotiations with the Israeli government. This is not to suggest that BG colluded with the World Bank but showed that BG's position was based on a rational analysis of the regional gas market.

The IFC was not the only international financial institution that BG was talking to about taking a stake in the project. One other trip undertaken during the second half of 2007 was to Luxembourg to visit the European Investment Bank (EIB). The EIB, which is the investment arm of the European Union, was also a potential investor in the Gaza Marine project. As with the IFC, EIB investment could contribute to reducing political risk to the project and align with wider EU policy. The EU was also a major donor to the PNA and also a major trading partner with both Israel and the PNA. The EIB's office is near Luxembourg airport so this was a day trip, involving an early flight and a late return to Heathrow.

A New Legal Challenge
During all this travel and activity to advance the project, a new issue emerged that would once again throw into doubt any chance of developing Gaza Marine. The negotiations with the Israeli government

were proceeding on the basis that the government itself would be the buyer of the gas. Some of the other participants in Israel's gas market objected to this concept. They saw this as government interference in what was supposed to be a liberalised market. On 25 June, Yam Tethys petitioned the High Court to request an injunction to stop the negotiations between the government and BG. Yam Tethys argued that the government's role gave Gaza Marine gas unfair access to the market. The court agreed. The legislation governing the natural gas market in Israel did not contain any provision for the government to act directly as a gas seller. The government could buy Gaza Marine gas but then would not be able to sell it on. This was a severe blow to the project. The negotiations, which had last for nearly 18 months, had come to nothing and had been based on a false premise. The discovery of this legal obstacle was a shock to the project team. It seemed an obvious aspect that should have been confirmed early on. Could the Israeli government act as a gas seller? The BG lawyers do not seem to have checked this fact. Also, the Israeli government's own lawyers do not seem to have checked. Some on the project team suspected that the government had known all along and had just played along with BG. One BG manager closely involved in the negotiations had detected a change in Israeli government tone ever since Hamas won the election. Since that point, the manager felt that the Israeli government was just going through the motions and was not committed to reaching an agreement.

Game Theory

By mid 2007, the Gaza Marine project team which I had re-joined became increasingly aware that the prospects for a deal were fading. Gaza Marine did not get to the FEED stage. The geotech survey and the pre-FEED activities did not take place. BG was losing interest in the Gaza Marine project due to lack of progress in the commercial negotiations and external factors. Israel was clearly not prepared to do a deal and potentially hand a reward to the Palestinians. At the same time, the BG Board's appetite in developing Gaza Marine had all but disappeared. BG was no longer in a desperate search for success and sanctionable projects. In September 2006, it had made a major oil discovery offshore Brazil. This opportunity dwarfed Gaza Marine and was in a much more stable political and commercial environment. Also, BG had operated successfully in Brazil for many years and so knew the country well. BG also had other significant opportunities in other stable countries, such as in Oman, where I had just left.

In the autumn of 2007, another factor entered BG's thinking. An objective assessment suggested that there was no path towards success. There was no set of circumstances that would allow Gaza Marine to be developed. BG arrived at this conclusion using game theory, the branch of mathematics and economics that deals with the interactions between multiple players. The US mathematician John Nash, depicted in the film "*A Beautiful Mind*", made significant contributions to the mathematics underpinning the theory for which he was jointly awarded the Nobel prize in economics. Nash's work has been developed by others and one practical application is to assist decision-making for companies facing complex business situations. BG commissioned the Canadian consultancy Open Options to help them. Open Options was founded in September 1996 by Dr Niall Fraser who has developed practical applications through his research on game theory. BG had used Open Options and its proprietary process and software in other complex commercial situations and had been able to develop successful solutions. The Gaza Marine project was an ideal candidate for the use of game theory to find a solution.

Open Options has developed a five step process. The first step is a careful definition of the issue. In the case of Gaza Marine, this was a carefully worded question which the project team was seeking to answer and identifying the key players in the "*game*", such as the Israeli government, the PNA, CCC and of course BG itself. Also, at this stage, we identified the BG members of staff who could provide insight into the project. This included current members of the project team as well as past members and other colleagues who had a high degree of familiarity with the project. Step two involved asking this *"issue team"* to identify for each player, the five actions that each was most likely to take and the five least likely actions. Step three was a workshop attended by most of the issue team and facilitated by two consultants from Open Options. At this workshop, the insights gathered in step two were discussed and combined lists (most likely and least likely actions) were agreed for each player. For the fourth step, the Open Options consultants took the output from the workshop and fed it into their proprietary software. At the fifth and final step, the consultants fed back to the team the results of their analysis using the software. The output was a range of models for the Gaza Marine project ranging from the most likely to the least likely. The analysis showed that a path to successful development of the Gaza Marine field was highly unlikely.

The Open Options analysis made a significant contribution to BG coming to its next decision. BG came to the conclusion in early December 2007 that there was no prospect of reaching agreement on commercial terms. Furthermore, it decided to make the break decisive. BG would close its office in Israel, making the eight staff in the office redundant. Also, BG would hand back to the Israeli government, its remaining licences offshore Israel. BG would, however, retain its stake in the Gaza Marine licence and maintain its offices in Ramallah and Gaza City. News of this decision was kept confidential amongst a small team at head office in Reading. If the staff in the Israeli office got wind of the decision, it was assessed there was a risk of information and company property going missing based on past experience with other office closures. An initial decision, to send a team to Tel Aviv to close the office abruptly and dismiss the staff immediately, what became known as the *"black bag"* option, was quickly discarded as too arbitrary and difficult to achieve. The Israeli office staff and the knowledge they possessed would be needed for a smooth and complete closure of the office.

Instead, a team was sent to Tel Aviv in early January 2008 to inform the staff of the decision, explain the process and secure their co-operation in closing down the office. In return, they would get a generous severance package including access to external support for finding new roles. As well as informing the staff, a number of other stakeholders needed to be informed, not least the Israeli government and also the British government through the British Embassy in Tel Aviv. A detailed plan was put in place with precise timings of meetings to ensure co-ordination and that the news did not leak. About a week before the team arrived, the staff in the Tel Aviv office were told to expect them but not the reason for the visit. The team consisted of the project manager Nigel Shaw, me, a representative of BG's human resources department, a finance representative and someone from IT. On the day, the staff were told first thing. This included having one member of staff on the phone as she was receiving chemotherapy in hospital. A great deal of effort was made to ensure that she was treated sympathetically, and her medical treatment would continue under the company's health insurance policy. Once the staff were informed, the project manager left for a series of pre-arranged meetings with the government, petroleum commissioner and the British Embassy. In the meantime, I undertook a round of interviews with the press. The news did not come as a shock to the staff. There did not seem to be a great deal of surprise more widely that BG was leaving. It took approximately a month to close the office. The majority of the staff co-operated fully which is a great credit to them. All of them went onto to find other roles. Sadly, the lady undergoing chemotherapy died about a year later.

Corruption Investigation
One other piece of work had been carried out during most of 2007 and was concluded in August 2008. This was an internal BG investigation into the circumstances surrounding BG's acquisition of the

Gaza Marine licence and the corruption allegations that had dogged the project. In particular, BG's lawyers wanted to know the extent of any risk of prosecution under the US Foreign Corrupt Practices Act as BG at that time had a secondary listing on the New York Stock Exchange. The BG lawyer in the regional management team, Neil Murphy, launched the investigation in May 2007. At that point, BG was fully engaged in negotiations with the Israeli government and was planning on making a final investment decision in due course. Murphy wanted to assure himself and the BG executive that there was minimal risk of such a decision provoking an investigation from the US or other authorities. In May 2007, he asked the US-based law firm Vinson and Elkins (V&E) to investigate the circumstances surrounding BG's acquisition of the Gaza Marine licence. The V&E investigation included interviews with BG employees and a review of relevant documents. V&E also sought interviews with CCC employees but were rebuffed. CCC did eventually agree to a telephone interview with one of its staff which Neil Murphy conducted. The V&E lawyers interviewed BG employees who had been involved in the early days of the Gaza Marine including Tim Forbes, Steve Larcombe, Daniel Silver, Amos Kreiner (BG's lawyer in Tel Aviv), Sam Dunkley (a BG lawyer) and John Field. The documents reviewed by V&E included board minutes and papers, memos and other documents held in the Tel Aviv office and notes made by the employees interviewed. The investigation lasted nearly 18 months but produced an interim report in August 2007. That interim report identified several "*red flag*" issues that required further investigation including repeated allegations of corruption, the nature of CCC's rights to acquire extra equity in the project, the overall relationship with CCC and its role in acquiring the licence and the prospect of substantial revenues for all participants.

In the investigation's second stage from September 2007, V&E undertook a second round of interviews with those BG employees identified above and a re-examination of available documents.

Murphy, on behalf of BG, also commissioned an investigation from another external organisation. He asked Control Risks Group (CRG) to conduct due diligence enquiries into the reputation of CCC and the Khoury family in the Palestine territories as well as key individuals involved in the licence award such as Muhammad Rashid. CRG submitted their initial report in September 2007 but later withdrew that report, calling it *"unreliable"*. CRG then submitted updates in April and May 2008 before sending their final report. CRG's report was based on interviews with numerous Palestinian sources in Jerusalem and Ramallah as well as a review of publicly available documents. To the surprise of many in BG, the CRG report was generally favourable towards CCC. CRG's main conclusion was that the partnership with CCC did not present a substantial risk to BG. The report noted that CCC enjoyed a positive reputation in the Palestinian territories and had good relations with the PNA. The current CCC leadership did not though have the same strength of relations with President Abbas as the previous generation had enjoyed with Arafat. CRG's report was not entirely positive on Gaza Marine. The report described a *"cloud of secrecy"* surrounding the Gaza Marine project and that there was a speculation that some individuals involved (particularly Rashid and Genossar) had received large commissions for their role in the licence negotiation and award. However, the report did not offer any concrete evidence to support the speculation about large commissions. The report provided detailed background on many of the individuals allegedly involved in the early days of the Gaza Marine project. CRG also did not provide any direct evidence of bribes or other corrupt activity as part of the licence award process. It did though report rumour and speculation from its sources and quoted others who had previously made such allegations.

The V&E lawyers also submitted their final report in August 2008. Their main conclusion was that BG had not undertaken any specific act related to the licence award or to granting CCC additional equity that could result in prosecution under the US FCPA. V&E did though point out that BG's documentation of the Gaza Marine project was incomplete, and that BG had failed to conduct adequate due diligence into CCC or the PNA at the time of licence negotiation and award. V&E concluded that if the US or other authorities undertook a rigorous investigation of the circumstances, then BG would find it difficult to defend some allegations. V&E also concluded that it was highly unlikely that anyone in BG had paid a bribe (and certainly not $40 million) to acquire the licence. The V&E report provided a detailed examination of the events of the licence negotiation, award and the surplus interest issue. The report also contained a detailed examination of the corruption allegations including a note that BG put effort into refuting the allegations at the time but criticising BG for not examining the basis of the allegations. BG staged a PR campaign but did not look to see if there was any substance to the allegations. Forbes told V&E during his interview that Israeli government officials had accused him of paying $40 million but according to Forbes relied on material related to BG's business in Brazil. The V&E report served to highlight the weaknesses in any defence BG might need against corruption charges and investigation. However, by the time the final reports from both CRG and V&E were submitted, BG's interest had waned and there was no looming deal that might have focussed the attention of the US authorities on the project's circumstances and background. The allegations of corruption and unethical collusion between BG and others were not going to go away. Rather than a business deal focusing attention on Gaza Marine, Israeli military action would focus attention on Gaza. The focus would come from journalists, commentators and activists and make links between Israel's military action, the siege against the Gaza Strip and attempts to seize control of the Gaza Marine gas

CHAPTER 8

BLOOD GAS
(2006-2009)

While the negotiations between BG and Israel were making progress in 2006 and into early 2007, there was little let up in the conflict and the security situation was deteriorating. Israel's unilateral withdrawal from the Gaza Strip completed in September 2005 had not stopped the threat of attacks. The Israeli authorities reported that between September 2005 and June 2006, 757 missiles were fired from Gaza into neighbouring areas of Israel. The small militant group Islamic Jihad were responsible for many of these attacks. Hamas largely observed the ceasefire that had ended the second Intifada in February 2005. However in June 2006, four incidents occurred that escalated the level of violence.

Stormy Weather
On 8 June 2006, Israeli forces killed Hamas leader Jamal Abu Samhadana in the first such targeted killing since the February 2005 ceasefire. Hamas responded by launching two rockets at the Israeli town of Sderot. The second incident was the Israeli response to these rockets. The Israeli navy shelled locations near to the coast that had been used as rocket launch sites. At least two of the shells landed on the beach killing seven members of the same family (including children) and one other person. The attack was captured on mobile phone footage and caused outrage around the world. The third

incident also caught the world's attention. On 25 June 2006, Hamas members crossed by tunnel from the Gaza Strip into Israel and kidnapped Gilad Shalit, a private in the Israeli Defence Force. The kidnap brought home to many Israelis the extent of the threat from Hamas. In response to the kidnap, the fourth development occurred: Israeli forces launched Operation *"Summer Rains"* with ground forces invading the Gaza Strip to search for Shalit and to attack Hamas. The operation ended in July.

Hamas and other militant groups continued to stage rocket attacks against Israel. On 31 October 2006, Israeli forces launched another assault on Gaza, named Operation *"Autumn Clouds"*. The operation lasted just over a week, with Israeli forces withdrawing on 7 November but the last artillery attack occurred on 8 November. The operation, like *Summer Rains*, did not stop rocket attacks but the intensity lessened in 2007 despite a rise in political temperature. On 14 June 2007, Hamas seized power from the PNA in the Gaza Strip and set up their own administration. Hamas had long presented a security threat to Israel, staging suicide bomb attacks inside Israel, launching rocket attacks and kidnapping Israeli soldiers. With its takeover of Gaza, the perception of that threat was magnified many times over. Hamas now had control of territory from which it could launch operations against Israel. Moreover, it demonstrated a readiness to do so, launching missile attacks into Israeli towns and villages close to Gaza.

As we saw in the previous chapter, the Israeli government responded to the takeover with a series of increasingly restrictive measures designed to isolate Hamas. Eventually, these measures included military action in the Gaza Strip. While the blockade against Hamas did succeed in isolating Hamas to an extent from the outside world, it also had other consequences with direct implications for the Gaza Marine project. The Hamas takeover and the Israeli response focussed international attention on Gaza. The Strip was now under greater scrutiny than it had been for many years. The conflict between Hamas and Israel made headlines around the world, provoked responses from governments such as the UK anxious to defuse tensions and fostered renewed sympathy for the plight of the Palestinian people from humanitarian and human rights organisations and their supporters. NGO activists and politicians lined up to condemn the Israeli blockade as collective punishment of Gazan residents and contrary to international humanitarian law.

Operation "Cast Lead"

The 2007 and 2008 rocket attacks from Gaza on neighbouring Israeli towns, such as Sderot, persisted but did not immediately lead to any significant escalations. In June 2008, Egypt brokered a ceasefire between Israel and Hamas and its allies in Gaza. The ceasefire largely held until 4 November, when Israeli paratroopers conducted a raid in the town of Dayr Al-Balah to close a tunnel that Israel suspected Hamas would use to infiltrate into Israel. Hamas resumed rocket attacks in response. At the same time Egypt-mediated ceasefire talks restarted with both sides expressing a wish to resume the ceasefire.

On 27 December 2008, Israel launched a massive military offensive against Hamas in the Gaza Strip. On that day, Israel conducted air-raids against Hamas targets in the Gaza Strip, including a police training college in which at least 40 people were killed. For at least six months, Israeli intelligence had been collecting information on Hamas targets inside the Gaza Strip. That information formed the basis for planning the 27 December air raids and the many that followed until Israel declared a ceasefire on 18 January 2009. During the 23 day conflict between 1,100 and 1,400 Palestinians were killed and many thousands more were injured. Many of those killed were non-combatants including 288 children and more than 100 women. Israel launched the first air raids at school finishing time. Israeli casualties during the conflict were 3 civilians and 10 soldiers (4 of whom were killed by *"friendly fire"*). The conflict weakened Hamas but did not defeat the organisation. Hamas lost approximately 700 fighters, including several leaders, and suffered considerable damage to its infrastructure and equipment, including weapons. In the aftermath of the conflict, it continued to launch rockets into southern Israel but at a much reduced rate, around 10% of the pre-conflict level. Israel called the offensive, Operation "*Cast Lead*". Many Palestinians referred to it simply as the Gaza War or the Gaza Massacre. Hamas named it the "*Battle of Al-Furqan*".[30]

Conspiracy Theories

The Gaza Marine project was caught in this spotlight of attention. The project was viewed by some as an important factor in the conflict and a driver behind Israeli policy towards the Gaza Strip and Palestinians more generally. Commentators both within Israel and outside were soon making claims about the role the project was playing in the conflict and setting forth a series of conspiracy theories. Many of these theories were based on incomplete or even totally erroneous information while others demonstrated an ill-informed understanding of the project. The starting point of these claims was the concern that revenue from Gaza Marine would fund terrorism. This claim had been around for several years and had gained currency under Sharon, when the fear was that the PNA would use the revenue to finance violence against Israel. This claim now evolved to express fear that revenue from Gaza Marine would find its way to Hamas' coffers and fund its attacks and kidnappings. The claims would evolve further and expand to encompass conspiracy theories that control of the gas reserves in the Gaza Marine field was the prime motivation behind Israeli military operations against Hamas in Gaza.

At BG, we came to refer to articles espousing these claims and conspiracy theories as "*blood gas*" material. This was a reference to the mining sector where the term "*blood diamonds*" was used to signify

---

30 Quran, chapter 25, "The Criterion", a reference to the battle between good and evil

the trade in diamonds that had been mined in conflict areas and were therefore seen as funding conflict. We were using the term *"blood gas"* ironically as we did not believe for one minute that the Gaza Marine project was funding the conflict in the Strip nor was control over the project an objective of Israeli military campaigns in Gaza. The Gaza Marine project could not be funding terrorism. There was no revenue flowing from the project to fund anything. In the future, revenue would flow to the PNA through the same channels used by Israel and not to Hamas. At the time, we did not give any credence to these articles as they were either wildly factually inaccurate or showed a complete misunderstanding of the project's dynamics and many were by known conspiracy theorists. However, we also did little to correct the factual inaccuracies or engage with the more reasonable commentators. The result is that myths and misinformation about the project grew, damaging its reputation in Israel and in the long term making political approval for the project more difficult.

$4 Billion

A central theme in all the *"blood gas"* articles is the large sums of money at stake. A frequently cited figure was that the Gaza Marine gas reserves were worth $4 billion. This is not a figure that BG ever used or recognised. It is not clear how the figure of $4 billion was calculated or what it referred to. Was it the total value of the gas or was it the profit expected from selling the gas after the costs of developing and operating the field were deducted? Another often cited figure was that the PNA would receive $1 billion in tax revenue from the project. Again, there was no explanation for the calculation of the figure and whether it referred to annual revenue or the total revenue over the lifetime of the field's production. A third statistic often used was that the PNA would earmark 10% of the revenue it earned (so 10% of $1 billion, hence $100 million) to Gaza. The implication drawn from this statistic was that either there was potentially a large sum of money heading towards Hamas or conversely, Gaza would see relatively little benefit from the development of Gaza Marine. Gaza's population was more than 10% of the total Palestinian population in the Occupied Territories and Gaza's economy accounted for more than 10% of the Palestinian economy.

BG was very reluctant to state publicly any numbers concerning the Gaza Marine field in line with its general policy of the time regarding publication of data. BG carefully managed the release of all information. This was in part due to legal and regulatory obligations it was under as a listed company on the London Stock Exchange. These obligations included ensuring that information was accurate and that nobody received the information before the whole market did e.g. no offering exclusives to one news outlet. There were also concerns about commercial confidentiality and undermining its negotiating position. In the case of Gaza Marine, BG had yet to agree a price for the gas. Publication of a number for the value of gas, such as $4 billion, would reveal BG's price assumption and could establish a benchmark, limiting its ability to negotiate. To add to the complexity, there would also be the need to make assumptions on the cost of developing the field and annual operating costs.

That said, the $4 billion figure was probably a reasonable ballpark estimate for the total likely profits over the lifetime of the field's production. Based on that figure, the figure for $1 billion in tax revenue for the PNA was probably based on the corporate tax rate of 25%. Again, the situation was more complex than that. The PNA would receive revenue from the Gaza Marine from three sources. The first would be the 12.5% royalty rate on total production. The second would be the 25% corporate tax on profits and the third would be from the 10% equity share it would receive on sanctioning the field's development. Like the other shareholders it would receive a dividend. Given these factors, a sum of $1 billion for total PNA revenues over the lifetime of the field's production was probably an underestimate.

The Gaza Marine project team, led by Nigel Shaw and including me, came to the decision that we would need to publish a figure to manage expectations, especially around the financial benefit the PNA would receive. Based on our own internal assessment of the project's economics, including our assumptions on price and other factors, we gained approval for stating that PNA tax revenues would average around $100 million annually for the production life of the field. We expected 15 years of production and so total PNA tax revenues over the field's lifetime could be $1.5 billion.

British Foreign Policy Goal

One of the first *"blood gas"* articles was published on 19 October 2007 by the former chief of the defence staff Moshe Yaalon, who would later serve as defence minister. This followed an open letter that Yaalon had published in July 2007 to Tony Blair who had recently been appointed the Quartet's Middle East envoy. In this letter, which reflected Yaalon's right wing views, he accused BG of pressurising Blair to talk to Hamas (this was untrue). Yaalon wrote a paper for the Jerusalem Center of Public Affairs, posing the question: *"Does the Prospective Purchase of British Gas from Gaza Threaten Israel's National Security?"*[31] Yaalon's answer was that it undoubtedly would. In the paper, he alleges that funds from Gaza Marine would fund Hamas. This builds on existing allegations, made by Sharon and others, that revenue from Gaza Marine would fund militant groups in the Palestinian territories. Yaalon goes further though and draws a direct link between Israeli government policy and Gaza Marine. He also makes a direct link between British foreign policy and Gaza Marine. These direct links between government policy (especially Israeli policy) and Gaza Marine would become a thread that would run through *"blood gas"* articles. Yaalon alleges that Israeli Prime Minister Ehud Olmert

---

31   http://jcpa.org/article/does-the-prospective-purchase-of-british-gas-from-gaza-threaten-israel's- national-security/

avoided direct military conflict with Hamas in June 2007 so as not to jeopardise a deal with BG on Gaza Marine. While BG and Israel were negotiating in June 2007 when the Hamas takeover occurred, a deal was still some way off and it was not certain that Israeli government representatives were negotiating seriously, if they ever were. Yaalon's letter and paper reflected his opposition to Sharon's 2005 unilateral withdrawal from Gaza. His three year term as chief of staff ended just before the Gaza withdrawal was implemented and was not extended for another year as had become traditional.

Yaalon's claim that the Gaza Marine deal was a key goal of British foreign policy was even more speculative. One sub-section of his paper is entitled, "*Selling British Gas to Israel: A Key British Foreign Policy Goal Since 2000*". In this section, he describes much of the British government's Middle East policy being "*pinned*" on a successful outcome for Gaza Marine. To support his case, Yaalon points to Blair's past interventions in the project and to Gaza Marine being placed at the heart of an "*economic road map*" for the Palestinian territories. Yaalon seems to be exaggerating to make his point. At this stage there was no real "*economic road map*" for the Palestinian territories. The British government's policy towards the Middle East since 2000 (and before) has been broader than the Israeli/Palestinian conflict. It has encompassed Iraq, Iran and its important relations with the Gulf countries, especially Saudi Arabia. While the British government would certainly have welcomed success in Gaza Marine, it was never a "*key goal*" of foreign policy. Despite some wild claims and allegations, Yaalon's paper is moderate in tone. This was not the case with many articles that followed from other commentators.

"*Blood gas*" articles were not limited to Israeli commentators. The apparent link between Israeli policy and Gaza Marine was also picked up by pro-Palestinian commentators. On 22 January 2008, the Electronic Intifada website published an article by Mark Turner, entitled, *"Gaza siege intensified after collapse of natural gas deal"*.[32] In this article, Turner suggests that the Israel military campaign underway at that time against Hamas in Gaza was in part motivated by the collapse of talks between Israel and BG that had occurred in December 2007 and become public knowledge earlier in January 2008. He offers almost no evidence to support this claim and indeed does not state the claim with a great deal of certainty. He writes that the reasons for the Israeli military conflict, *"may include motivations with roots back in 2000, when the British firm British Gas Group (BG) discovered proven natural gas reserves of at least 1.3 trillion cubic feet beneath Gazan territorial waters worth nearly $4 billion."* Turner goes on to allege that the end of BG-Israel negotiations prompted Israel to *"radically expanded its sanctions."* Like many articles of this type at this time, it makes the assumption that Hamas would have some control over the Gaza Marine project and would benefit from the revenues. Any kind of deal on Gaza Marine at this time was a distant prospect and even if it went ahead, Hamas was unlikely to have a direct stake.

Despite the Israeli military campaign and the imposition of a blockade on Gaza, Hamas remained in control of the Strip and consolidated their hold on the territory. The tone of *"blood gas"* articles became more conspiratorial and wilder in their allegations. On 16 July 2008, the right wing Israeli politician Moshe Feiglin published an article on the jewishpress.com website, entitled *"British Gas: A Deadly Deal"*.[33] The central allegation in the article is that BG has a long-standing corrupt relationship with the Israeli government and is preventing the government moving decisively against Hamas. He states that there is a 60 page report, *"The British Gas Government"*

---

32 https://electronicIntifada.net/content/gaza-siege-intensified-after-collapse-natural-gas-deal/7312 121

33 http://www.jewishpress.com/indepth/columns/british-gas-a-deadly-deal/2008/07/16/? src=ataglance

that ties Israeli leaders including Sharon to BG. However, the article is full of errors, one of the clearest is his claim that Martin Schlaff is the owner of BG and so demonstrates a misunderstanding of BG's ownership. In my research, I have been unable to locate the 60 page report and Feiglin does not provide a link. Also, I have not been able to find any other reference to this report.

On 8 January 2009, Canadian academic Professor Michel Chossudovsky published an article on the GlobalResearch.com website that marked a more serious evolution of the "*blood gas*" allegations. The article entitled, "*War and Natural Gas: The Israeli Invasion and Gaza's Offshore Gas Fields*" makes a direct link between Israel's military campaign Operation Cast Lead and the Gaza Marine project. Chossudovsky's central contention is that this is a "*war of conquest*" to seize control of the Gaza Marine gas field. Like the other articles mentioned in this chapter, the Professor offers little evidence but appears to rely on apparent coincidences in timing. He also bases his case on a misunderstanding of the nature of negotiations between BG and Israel. Chossudovsky claims that Israel and BG resumed negotiations in June 2008 at the same time that the Israeli government started planning for Operation Cast Lead. In this apparent coincidence, the Professor sees conspiracy. He also characterises these and previous negotiations between BG and Israel as being about ownership of the field and an attempt to by-pass the Hamas administration in Gaza. Chossudovsky is mistaken on both counts. By June 2008, there were no substantive contacts between BG and Israel. BG had closed its Israel office and all but ceased contact with the Israeli government. On the nature of the negotiations, they were always about finding a market for the gas, not about ownership of the field. Both BG and the Israeli government were always clear, the PNA remained the owners of the field and would have to approve any deal to sell the gas to Israel.

The themes and accusations of Chossudovsky's article were reflected in an article published in the Palestine Chronicle by Palestinian writer

Mohannad El-Khairy on 22 January. This article makes the same link between the Israeli military reportedly planning for Operation Cast Lead in June 2008 and the (erroneous) assumption that Israeli-BG talks were still going on at that time. El-Khairy expands the conspiracy theory to allege that Israel and BG were colluding to deny the Palestinians access to the gas and revenue from the field's eventual development. He cites BG's decision to retain its interest in the Gaza Marine licence and the resumption of contacts between Israel and BG in August 2008 as evidence of this collusion. El-Khairy writes,

> *". . . by August 2008, talks officially resumed between BG and the Israeli state. British Gas' willingness to retain the Gaza Marine license is thus revealed, as its partnership with the Apartheid State [as El-Khairy refers to Israel] had been arranged a whole six months prior to the attacks."*

He goes on:

> *"The ultimate goal of the Israeli military onslaught is to incorporate Gaza's offshore natural gas fields into her own, to form a continuous linkage that ultimately settles in the Turkish port city of Ceyhan, and to satisfy the corporate profits of a multinational corporation. This move also bypasses Palestine's rights to these gas reserves, and continues the traditional Israeli policies of theft, lies, and more appallingly, the killing of thousands of innocent civilians.*
>
> *How ironic, isn't it? That whilst Gaza suffered an 18-month blockade, of which natural gas was no longer available amongst many other basic necessities, 1.4 trillion cubic feet of the thing was sitting there right underneath their feet, confiscated by the corprotocracy of British Gas and the Apartheid State of Israel."*[34]

This article, like other *"blood gas"* articles was a mixture of selected facts, misunderstandings and wild speculation. A version of this article was re-printed in Lebanon's English language newspaper, the Daily Star in April 2010. This time, El-Khairy boldly states that

---

34 The Palestine Chronicle, 22 January 2009

Gaza's natural gas resources were the motive behind Operation Cast Lead but this time, references to Israel as "*the Apartheid State*" were removed.

El-Khairy was right on one matter. Talks between Israel and BG had resumed in August 2008. However, BG was unaware of any military planning that Israel was undertaking and there was certainly no collusion to deprive the Palestinians of their rights to the gas resources or the revenue that would flow from Gaza Marine's development. One of the reasons for the resumption of talks was that BG had received indications from the Israeli side that it had changed its mind on the issue of a supply guarantee and a new price range was on the table. The Israeli team, now consisting of Ministry of Finance director general Yarom Ariav and Ministry of National Infrastructures director Hezi Kugler, expressed a willingness for Israel to guarantee to buy all the volumes that Gaza Marine could produce. The gas price range now being discussed had once again increased and had narrowed. The price range was now $4.50-4.60 per mBtu. There also appeared to be a new willingness by IEC to consider a deal with BG, so that it rather than the government would be the gas buyer. There was a large gap though between IEC expressing a willingness to discuss a gas purchase agreement and actually signing and implementing such an agreement. One of the gaps was the volume of gas that IEC wanted to buy. It was seeking supply of 800 million cubic metres per year, which was about half of what Gaza Marine could supply. This did not make the field's development economically viable, even when taking into account the supply of gas to the Gaza power station in addition. The Israel-BG discussions continued in a desultory manner until mid-December 2008, when they broke down over the issue of volume.

All of the authors of these "*blood gas*" articles had a wider political agenda, whether it was opposing Gaza withdrawal, a more extreme right wing agenda, a hard-line Palestinian nationalist position or spreading conspiracy theories. Some, perhaps most, could be dismissed as poorly informed. All these articles contained serious errors and misstatements. None had approached BG for interview or to check facts. Due to their seeming marginal importance, BG made a decision not to issue any rebuttal but to ignore the articles. Many of the allegations and claims made were highly speculative and BG had a long standing policy of not commenting on speculation. There was also a concern that taking such articles seriously would only provoke further articles and replying to them would become a time consuming activity. At this time, BG was attempting to minimise the amount of time and money spent on the project. The company had no interest in provoking publicity for Gaza Marine.

The Gaza Marine project continued to attract publicity and comment despite BG's lack of effort. The central themes of these articles were picked by more mainstream commentators. In early 2011, the renowned intellectual Noam Chomsky in a lecture at University of London's School for Oriental and African Studies (SOAS) used Gaza Marine as an example of the connection between exploitation of energy resources and political power. His wider point is certainly valid and was well argued, as expected from one of the world's foremost academics. However, his use of the Gaza Marine example was based on a misunderstanding and demonstrated a surprising lack of research. He claimed that BG was acting contrary to international law in dealing with Israel and that it was involved in Israeli theft of natural gas from Gaza. An important aspect of international law concerning occupied territories, such as the Gaza Strip, is that its resources are developed for the benefit of the occupied population. BG acted to uphold that principle. Its negotiation to obtain the best possible price for the Palestinians for their gas and supply of gas to the Gaza power station was an important element of the project. The breakdowns in the negotiations with Israel over the years were typically caused by lack of agreement on price and terms acceptable to both BG and the Palestinians.

The "*blood gas*" themes were also reflected in Palestinian reporting on the project. In June, a Palestinian news service ran an article about Noble (one of the partners in Yam Tethys) exploiting gas resources off the Gaza Strip. This seems to refer to the small gas deposits close to the Israel-Gaza maritime border. The article erroneously conflates these with the Gaza Marine resources. The article refers to Professor Chossudovsky's claim that the Gaza Marine resources are much larger than BG have reported and could make the Palestinians as rich as the Kuwaitis. Chossudovsky is a known conspiracy theorist and would probably not have had access to enough information to make such a claim about the size of the Gaza Marine field. The claim is false. The Gaza Marine resources are not larger than reported.

The "*blood gas*" articles continued to appear occasionally such as the one that appeared on the salem-new.com website on 22 August 2013 or on revolution-news.com almost a year later or on the Mother Jones website in March 2015 headlined, "*The Often Overlooked Role of Natural Gas in the Israel-Palestine Conflict*".[35] While many of these articles could be dismissed as ill-informed conspiracy theories and so BG was right to ignore them, they did have an impact as they entered mainstream reporting on Gaza Marine. For example, on 9 July 2014, the British daily newspaper The Guardian published an article that recycled Yaalon's allegations.[36] Yaalon was now serving as Israeli defence minister. The same article also quotes Mark Turner but also respected academic Anais Antreasyan of the University of California's Journal of Palestine Studies, who makes a more measured contribution and is closer to the reality. She states that Operation Protective Edge is designed to make, "*Palestinian access to the Marine-1 and Marine-2 gas wells impossible. Israel's long-term goal besides preventing the Palestinians from exploiting their own resources, is to integrate the gas fields off Gaza into the adjacent Israeli offshore*

---

35 https://www.motherjones.com/politics/2015/03/how-gazan-natural-gas-be-came-epicenter-international-power-struggle/

36 The Guardian, "IDF's Gaza assault is to control Palestinian gas", 9 July 2014

installations. This is part of a wider strategy of separating the Palestinians from their land and natural resources in order to exploit them, and, as a consequence, blocking Palestinian economic development. Despite all formal agreements to the contrary, Israel continues to manage all the natural resources nominally under the jurisdiction of the PA, from land and water to maritime and hydrocarbon resources."

Later in the month, another mainstream British newspaper, the Independent, published an article making the link between the military campaign and control of natural resources.[37] From the headline, *"Palestinian natural resources lie beneath this terrible conflict"*, the article appears to be another in the *"blood gas"* series but steers away from that vein of reporting. It is written by a representative of the Palestinian human rights organisation Al-Haq, Shawan Jabarin. The article draws attention to Israel's obligation under international humanitarian law in relation to the exploitation of natural resources, not just gas but other resources such as land and water. On gas, Jabarin identifies the crux of the matter, *"And while Israel withdrew its settlers and military from the Gaza Strip in 2005, it continues to occupy the territory in a manner that still allows for exploitation and control of gas reserves off the coast of the territory. The illegal naval blockade imposed by Israel has not only prevented the development of the Gaza Marine Zone, depriving the Palestinian economy of billions in much needed gas revenues, but also forces the Occupied Palestinian Territory to maintain its dependency on Israel for gas supplies, thus bolstering the Israeli economy."*

Blood Gas Broadcasts

Inaccurate reporting on Gaza Marine was not confined to the written word, *"blood gas"* reports also appeared on television channels. There appears to have been less coverage on television, probably because

---

37   The Independent, "Palestinian natural resources lie beneath this terrible conflict", 25 July 2014

the story is not telegenic. For all the money and time spent on the project, there is little to show. Most television reports on the project consist of archive footage of the field's discovery and then interviews with "*experts*" or "*talking heads*" in television jargon. With a few rare exceptions, these "*experts*" rarely are and even rarer are representatives of any of the organisations involved in the project such as BG, CCC, the PNA or the Israeli government. Most of these reports are short news reports on channels that have reputations for peddling conspiracy theories such as the Russian-owned RT or the Iranian-owned Press TV. Like in the written media, these reports focus on the same themes and also as in the written media, these themes have entered mainstream reporting.

The most substantial report on Gaza Marine on television appeared on Al-Jazeera Arabic in April 2019. This was a documentary, almost an hour long, whose Arabic title translates as "*My greatest secret, Gaza Gas*".[38] The Gaza-based Al-Jazeera journalist Tamer Al-Misshal presented the programme. An English language version of the programme, entitled simply "*Gaza Gas*" was released in June 2019.[39] The documentary's central claim was that the Gaza gas deal was a poor one for the Palestinian people and economy. Al-Misshal's fire was directed mainly at the PNA who he accused of negotiating a bad deal with BG. He makes a number of errors including identifying the wrong company as "*British Gas*" but his most significant error is his wrong interpretation of how the deal would work. While he rightly states that the eventual ownership of rights in the field were anticipated to be 60% BG, 30% CCC and 10% PNA, he then interprets this as the Palestinians only getting 10% of any future revenue from the development of the Gaza Marine field. He emphasises that the PNA refused to talk to him for the programme and he tries to contact "*British Gas*" and eventually gets a bland statement from Shell,

---

38 https://www.youtube.com/watch?v=MFGk7WMa61k&t=2s
39 https://www.youtube.com/watch?v=8-QLL6fHIGg

who by then had briefly taken over BG's share and then handed it back to the PNA. Al-Misshal also does not interview anyone from CCC. He does interview a number of real experts, many of whom provide useful commentary on some of the issues surrounding the project such as the potential extent of any future Palestinian exclusive economic zone (EEZ) and Israel's role in the project. He also does not appear to have tried to speak to any former BG employees. However, Al-Misshal has clearly gained access to key documents such as copies of the Upstream Agreement.

The timing of the documentary's broadcast is curious as there is no apparent news hook to inspire the programme. There had been no recent development on the project nor any approaching milestone. The documentary was broadcast shortly before the release of President Trump's *"Peace for Prosperity"* document and it may have been an attempt to highlight the plight of Gaza and the prospect for investment in the natural gas industry. Qatar, Al-Jazeera's owner, has played a leading role in attempting to get economic aid to Gaza, including energy. So, the programme may have reflected Qatar's interest in investing in the Gaza Marine field and bringing it into production. If so, there do not appear to have been any substantial moves in that direction. Qatar has though been providing assistance to the OQR for its *"Gaza for Gaza"* project that involves building a pipeline to supply the Gaza power station (see below). Al-Misshal may also have held a personal motive for making the programme. In the programme, he identifies Ismail Al-Misshal as the person who first alerts Arafat to the potential for gas resources in Gaza's waters. However, Al-Misshal does not state whether he is related to Ismail and does not declare any personal interest Whatever the motivation for the documentary, it misrepresents the Gaza Marine deal in a way that reflects badly on the PNA and acts as a pro-Hamas piece of propaganda.

These *"blood gas"* articles added to the patina of grime and dirt that had accumulated around the Gaza Marine project over more than 10 years. Like an ever-present family heirloom sat on a shelf, the accumulation went unnoticed and unremarked. In the BG team, the changes in leadership and managers involved meant that nobody saw the damage that was being done to the project's integrity and credibility. This grime and dirt made it more difficult for politicians, especially in the PNA, to make decisions as the political costs could be high. The grime would continue to accumulate as more layers were added by accusations of conflicts of interest involving Tony Blair. After leaving office as British prime minister in June 2007 and being appointed the Quartet representative, Blair also took on advisory roles, including for the US investment bank J.P. Morgan. Allegations arose of conflicts of interest between his Quartet role and his private business roles.[40] These allegations persisted and in September 2011 became directly linked to Gaza Marine. Reports in the Daily Telegraph[41] and a Channel 4 Dispatches programme [42]alleged a conflict of interest as Blair was promoting the Gaza Marine deal ostensibly in his role as Quartet representative, but BG Group was also a J.P. Morgan client and so potentially Blair stood to gain personally.[43] While BG was undoubtedly a J.P. Morgan client, BG did not use them as an advisor on the Gaza Marine project.

---

40   See for example, https://www.dailymail.co.uk/news/article-1152311/Blair-Inc-Former-PM-launches-new-business-offering-political-advice-wealthy-clients.html

41   https://www.telegraph.co.uk/news/politics/tony-blair/8784596/On-the-desert-trail-of-Tony-Blairs-millions.html

42   https://www.channel4.com/press/news/blair-role-palestine-contracts-gives-rise-conflicts-interest

43   For an assessment the issues around Blair's alleged conflict of interest, see https://www.palestine-studies.org/en/node/162560

CHAPTER 9

SECOND-HAND GAS FIELD FOR SALE (2008-2012)

Following the closure of its office in Israel, BG placed the Gaza Marine project firmly on the back burner. It lost any remaining interest in efforts to develop the project. It was now pursuing bigger opportunities in Australia and Brazil. The Gaza Marine project team was disbanded, and everyone was re-assigned to other roles. The project leader, Nigel Shaw moved to a role in the Commercial function at head office. Responsibility for Gaza Marine was nominally given to a vice-president in the regional management team, Ian Hewitt. He had been my first line manager at BG when he had been the number two in BG's Cairo office. He had almost no interest in Gaza Marine. There was a strong message coming from the BG Board that Gaza Marine was not to be pursued. Ian was not going to waste any time on a project that would not advance his career. He delegated responsibility to one of his commercial managers, Matt Wilks. Matt was not assigned full time to the project but managed the project as part of a wider portfolio of responsibilities. I was re-assigned to the government relations team at head office. Gaza Marine remained part of my responsibilities, but it was made clear to me that I was to spend minimal time on the project. Spending on the project was cut to the minimum but the offices in Ramallah and Gaza City were maintained but with minimum staff.

While BG had lost interest in pursuing the Gaza Marine

project, it was committed to retaining the licence. This was a conscious decision rather than just an accidental by-product of doing nothing and maintaining the status quo. BG did examine the other options. As well as actively pursuing the project and the option it had chosen of retaining the licence with minimal activity, the other options were selling its interest in the licence or handing back the licence to the PNA. BG's assessment was that selling its licence share was not a viable option as it would have difficulty in finding a buyer. It would be proved wrong on this. Its licence share had value and so simply handing the licence back to the PNA would be giving away value, something that was not in BG's DNA and would have a financial consequence. It would have to write off the asset and this would impact its profits (although this was unlikely to be a material charge to its accounts). More importantly, it would undermine BG's carefully nurtured reputation with City investors for prudence and capability to develop projects. Furthermore, it was not certain that the PNA would accept BG handing back the licence. For the PNA, having a blue chip international gas company as an investor gave credibility to attract further international investment.

The decision to retain its share in the Gaza Marine licence came with implications for BG. These implications included maintenance of good relations with the PNA and the avoidance of any actions that threatened those relations. As part of the process of closing the Israel office, BG had taken pains to ensure that the PNA understood that it remained committed to Gaza Marine. BG was walking a tightrope here. It would have to maintain the pretence of continuing activity on the project whilst at the same time undertaking as little activity as possible. The PNA were not fooled and to an extent went along with the fiction. As long as they could point to BG still holding the licence, they were satisfied. Also, the PNA were not in a position to insist on progress in the project. They were battling internal divisions, the challenge of Hamas in Gaza and were anxious about what Israel would demand in return for giving approval to any deal on Gaza Marine.

The PNA did push ahead with efforts to attract international investment to the territories and particularly the West Bank. In May 2008, it organised the first Palestinian Investment Conference in Bethlehem. This was the first event of its kind with business leaders and politicians from all over the world attending, including representatives of Gulf states who travelled through Israel's Ben Gurion airport. BG was approached to sponsor the conference but declined to do so. CCC did sign up as one of the conference's leading sponsors. BG was attempting to downplay its profile in the Palestinian territories. However, I was tasked with attending the conference to represent BG. It was an uncomfortable experience. This was meant to showcase the Palestine territories as an investment destination and here was I representing one of the largest potential investors who was decidedly lukewarm on the idea. Whenever asked about progress on Gaza Marine, I had to give vague answers that BG was still committed to developing Gaza Marine. The conference itself was well organised and I was made very welcome as were all the participants. Some participants had travelled from countries that did not recognise Israel but were still allowed to transit through Ben Gurion airport. As I travelled back to the airport from Bethlehem, I was passed by a very senior Gulf Sheikh heading the same way. At the airport, I was subject to another uncomfortable experience: a thorough grilling and search from Israeli security. I was catching the British Airways flight back to London with a number of other conference participants. All my fellow passengers who attended the conference were subject to intensive questioning by Israeli security and our luggage thoroughly searched. At one point I was escorted to a separate room and braced myself for a strip search. That did not happen, but I was x-rayed. The Palestinian Investment Conference was repeated in June 2010. This time, the only BG representative was the local office manager Wael Abulaila. BG again turned down the opportunity to sponsor, unlike CCC who were again a high profile sponsor.

Inching Closer

Placing Gaza Marine on the back burner also meant the end of formal negotiations with the Israeli government over purchase of the gas for supply to Israeli customers. The Israeli government seemed keen to maintain a channel of communication. The main point of contact was Hezi Kugler, the Director-General in the infrastructure ministry. Kugler and colleagues in the Israeli government, especially in the security services seemed to believe it remained in Israel's interest to reach a deal on Gaza Marine. Their motivation went beyond ensuring energy supplies for Israelis. Rather they saw an opportunity to create an additional lever to exert pressure over the Palestinians. In their discussions, their language focussed on "*control*" over the Palestinians and the revenue flows from the gas sales. Neither Matt Wilks nor I had a mandate to negotiate and BG management was not going to give us one. However, we did need to maintain contact with the Israeli government (as well as with the PNA and PIF) to maintain the fiction that we were still committed to the project and attempting to find a way forward. Matt and I could justify to BG management the time and effort on these contacts as defending the licence. Also, in the event that there was any breakthrough, it would make BG's 90% more attractive to a potential buyer. As well as not having a mandate, we also had no confidence that Israeli government representatives had any mandate to negotiate as well.

In our contacts with Kugler and other Israeli representatives, the gas price and a mechanism for ensuring that revenue did not fund terrorism remained the main talking points. On gas price, one step at a time we inched towards convergence on an acceptable price. First, both the Israelis and BG compared acceptable price ranges. There was an overlap. This led to more detailed discussions of price. There was also progress on a mechanism to bring transparency to the revenue flows. We managed to sketch out the principles of a revenue mechanism. A trusted third party would be involved, probably a reputable international bank. Israeli payments for gas could be paid into an escrow bank account in say New York. The bank would then make payments to BG, CCC and the PNA along an agreed formula and to appropriate accounts. The whole process would be subject to external audit. This process was acceptable to the Israeli government, the PNA and BG. On price, we were inching tantalisingly close to agreeing a price. There was now less than five cents difference between the price Israel was offering and the minimum price that BG could accept. In a sign that the two sides were getting close to agreement, an outline agreement, known as a *"heads of terms (HoT)"* was drafted and initialled by both sides.

The heads of terms was never turned into a fully-fledged agreement. Both commerce and politics got in the way. The two sides could not quite bridge the five cents divide. The PNA would not accept a price in that range. They wanted a much higher price which would be unacceptable to the Israelis. BG counselled that they are being unrealistic and that this was as good a deal as they would get. Reaching a deal now did not fit with the PNA's agenda and there was no consensus in the PNA for reaching a deal. With Hamas in control in Gaza, there was no appetite within the PNA for taking any action which seemed to benefit Gaza and the Hamas regime. Also, senior figures in the PNA and PIF feared the political price they would have to pay for reaching a deal. That price would include greater control exerted by Israel and a backlash from Hamas and other regime critics that they had sold the gas too cheaply to Israel. At least one of the key figures on the Palestinian side consistently displayed an ambivalent attitude towards reaching a deal. Some on the BG side wondered what his agenda really was and whose interests was he really serving. He did not see to be serving the Palestinians' interests.

Outside Approaches

During this time, BG was approached by a number of different individuals and companies who believed they could help unlock progress in some way. Matt and I would judge each approach to assess whether it merited further attention. Among these approaches, there were three that stood out. One was from a potential Israeli customer for Gaza Marine gas, Clal Industries. Clal planned to construct and operate a private power station in Israel and was looking for a gas supply. They were anxious to meet BG but wanted to do so on neutral ground, so neither London nor Tel Aviv. Two of their senior executives would be in Istanbul on other business so could we meet there? So, Matt and I travelled to Istanbul to meet the Clal representatives. While the meeting was amicable, it was clear that on its own, Clal's gas needs would not provide a sufficient basis for Gaza Marine's development.

The second notable approach was from a company seeking to develop a compressed natural gas (CNG) scheme to transport gas over long distances. The company claimed that this presented a more economic solution than LNG for smaller volumes of gas as the technology was less expensive and required less investment. In particular the company pitched the idea of supplying Gaza Marine gas to Cyprus. The scheme would use a floating facility to compress the gas, load it on to ships which would keep the gas under pressure and transport it to Cyprus where it would supply power stations. While this scheme initially seemed to offer a potential solution for Gaza Marine, there were several challenges. Although the technology for compressing natural gas had long existed, it had yet to be employed on this scale and so was unproven for this scheme. Also, no similar scheme yet existed. For BG, there was also a potential competition issue. BG was committed to developing LNG projects and if it encouraged this CNG scheme, it would be co-operating with a potential competitor.

The third approach was not a potential customer or solution but someone who was offering to act as a middleman between Israel, BG and the Palestinians. This person certainly had all the right political connections and was well known to all those with a stake in the project. He was Dov Weissglas, who had served as Ariel Sharon's right hand man and was known to share his former boss's views. Weissglas had left politics following Olmert becoming prime minister and returned to private practice as a lawyer. At a meeting in BG's London office with me and a member of BG's executive team, Weissglas made his pitch. He had the experience of office and the contacts to help BG overcome opposition within the Israeli system and to persuade the Palestinians to reach a deal. He made a point which many Israelis would make in talking to BG: BG had made many mistakes and did not understand Israel and the ways things were done in Israel. My colleague and I had agreed to the meeting as we were curious to meet such a giant of the Israeli political system. We listened politely to what he had to say. BG had no intention of using Weissglas or indeed any other person as a middleman. While this had been the approach in the past, BG's attitude had changed, partly under the pressure from a growing need to comply with stringent anti-corruption requirements and also to greater confidence in our own ability to deliver our own messages. Using former government figures such as Weissglas was beset with potential traps and opened up BG to accusations of unethical behaviour. The oft made point that BG had *"made mistakes and did not understand how Israel worked"* raised our suspicions. Was this code for *"BG has not paid the right people and needs to grease the wheels in Israel"*? We could never be sure but the accusations of corruption that had long circulated around the project made BG very cautious.

A New Route?
While BG had lost interest in developing Gaza Marine, it did not stop considering its options. The company was aware that circumstances changed and there was also a chance that it would come

under pressure to make progress. That pressure could come from its partner CCC, from the PNA or from an external party such as Tony Blair. One of the main blockages to progress and development of the field was the need for Israeli co-operation, particularly on security issues related to access to the K, L and M zones. One of the questions asked at BG was: is there a development option that does not require Israeli co-operation? Part of the Gaza Marine field lies outside the L zone but still within the licence area agreed with the PNA. BG looked at the viability of developing the field from waters outside the security zones. It was theoretically possible to drill wells close to but outside zone L to gain access to the gas. Once under the seabed, BG could drill horizontal wells to reach the gas that lay under zone L. All the facilities to collect the gas could be placed on the seabed outside zone L. This development concept would have to be based on taking the gas to Egypt. It would be possible to construct a pipeline to the Egyptian coast that circumvented the no-sail zone (zone M). While BG did not undertake detailed work on this option, it realised that it would be a more expensive option. The wells and the pipeline would be more expensive than the development scheme that was the default option. While this option, in theory, by-passed the need for Israeli co-operation, it did not remove the risk of Israeli interference. Israel could put pressure on both the PNA and Egypt to refuse co-operation with this option. Moreover, Israel could intervene directly to prevent vessels operating in waters outside zone L. Israel would demonstrate its willingness to interdict vessels in international waters when it used military force to prevent a flotilla of six civilian Turkish vessels reaching Gaza in May 2010. Turkish and international charities had organised the flotilla to bring relief supplies to Gaza and break the Israeli blockade of the territory. During the raid, which occurred in international waters, nine activists were killed (eight Turkish citizens and one dual Turkish-US citizen). The incident provoked widespread international condemnation of Israel's tactics. In response, Turkey (one of the few Muslim states which recognises Israel) broke off diplomatic relations with Israel. The incident also highlighted the Israeli government's sensitivity to activities related to Gaza and in the maritime area. Gaining Israeli approval for any activities related to the Gaza Marine project was now going to be even more difficult. Furthermore, the repercussions of any challenge to Israel's control over Gazan waters, whether in zone L or not, were now much more severe.

CCC's Power Surge

While BG, the Israeli government and the PNA had no immediate interest in making progress on the project, CCC asserted that it did want to push forward. Gaza Marine and the company's wider interests in the Palestinian territories were more material to its business than the project was to BG's portfolio. CCC had aspirations to construct up to three power stations in the West Bank to address that area's power needs. The West Bank imported all its power needs from Israel. CCC would need a gas supply to fuel these power stations. It approached BG with a plan that it would become the customer for all of the Gaza Marine output and would use this to generate electricity in the West Bank (along with supplying the existing power station at Gaza City). This scheme had a lot of holes in it. The plans for West Bank power stations were not well developed and had no financing. There was a great deal of uncertainty whether Israel would ever allow them to be built and to allow the construction of a gas pipeline across its territory to supply them. As part of the scheme, CCC wanted BG to get the British government behind the scheme and apply pressure on the Israeli government to agree. BG was not convinced by the scheme and in a tense meeting in its London office gave a forthright assessment to CCC. In any case, BG was still not interested in developing Gaza Marine. Any scheme to develop the field would have to be robust enough to overcome the Board's anxieties. CCC's West Bank power scheme was not robust. It was still in the very early days of thinking about these power stations.

There were no detailed plans for the stations, precise sites, capacity or other design specifications. In other words, the projects were far from bankable and were unlikely to ever be, in BG's view. As of the time of writing, the plans for power stations in the West Bank have not progressed far beyond the stage they were in early 2010.

Giant Discoveries

What did change in 2009 and 2010 was the size of Israel's known gas reserves. In March 2009 the Noble-Delek partnership announced the discovery of the Tamar and Dalit fields offshore Israel. The Tamar field was estimated to contain 10 trillion cubic feet of gas and was the largest discovery in Israeli waters at that point. Tamar is located around 83 kilometres (52 miles) off the northern Israeli coast. This was followed by the announcement of the Dalit field discovery. This is a much smaller field and is closer to the Israeli coast. The Tamar discovery was hugely significant for Israel as it gave it substantial energy resources for the first time in its history. The discovery was also significant for BG on two fronts. First, it would alter perceptions about the market for Gaza Marine gas. Israel now had no requirement for Palestinian gas and therefore even less incentive to co-operate with the field's development. The second significance for BG was of lost opportunity. BG had once held the exploration licence for the area that covered Tamar and Dalit but had relinquished the licence. BG's exploration team considered that there was not sufficient prospect of reserves and that any reserves would be high pressure and high temperature. This would make exploration and development expensive. BG's exploration team called this one wrong. There were substantial reserves present and they did not present any significant challenges. The Tamar well was though one of the most expensive wells ever drilled at the time.

There was more to come. In mid 2010, Noble and Delek announced the largest ever discovery in Israeli waters and one of the largest offshore gas fields discovered in more than decade anywhere on the planet. This was the Leviathan field. Noble and Delek estimated that the field contained around 20 trillion cubic feet of natural gas. It is, though, located further from the shore, lying 130 kilometres or around 80 miles from the coast. This distance and the size of the reserves makes development a very expensive proposition. However, the discovery transformed Israel's energy security. It gives the country a long-term energy supply, provided that the reserves could be developed economically. The discovery also seemed to end any prospect of developing the Gaza Marine field for supply to Israel. Gaza Marine was now marginal to Israel's energy needs as Israel's gas resources were now at least thirty times greater than Gaza Marine. Israel now had no need to co-operate with the development of Gaza Marine. It seemed as though Gaza Marine would remain stranded. Or would it?

There was a counter-intuitive argument that Israel's huge offshore discoveries opened the way for Gaza Marine's development. CCC amongst others advanced an argument that went like this: while Israel no longer had any need of Gaza Marine gas, it also had no right to stand in the way of the Palestinians developing their most significant economic resource. International pressure should now be brought to bear on Israel to allow the development of Gaza Marine and not stand in its way. The advantage for Israel would be international goodwill, a more stable Palestinian economy and a confidence boost to the peace process. This argument found favour with Tony Blair and his team. A large part of his remit was to improve the Palestinian economy. This included both short term measures such as improving the transit of Palestinian goods through Israeli checkpoints and long term developments projects. In terms of inward investment and generation of revenue, Gaza Marine could be one of the most significant contributions to the long term development of the Palestinian economy. With little tangible success to show for his efforts since his appointment in June 2007, Blair was preparing for another surge of activity to build economic co-operation between

Israel and the Palestinians. Gaza Marine would be at the core of this strategy.

Also, in mid 2010, IEC published a specific opportunity that could provide a route for the Gaza Marine gas to reach the Israeli market. On 13 July, IEC published a request for proposals to supply gas to its Hadera power station which it was converting to gas-fired. The request revealed that IEC wanted to purchase 2.24 billion cubic metres of gas per year for 15 years. Gaza Marine could supply a large proportion of that (but not all) and was reported in the Israeli press as a potential bidder. The opportunity was not as attractive as it first seemed. IEC were demanding that the gas price be linked to the price of coal. This made sense for IEC as the gas would replace coal to fuel Hadera and it would lead to a low (by global standards) price. For potential bidders, including BG, this made the opportunity economically less lucrative and perhaps even unfeasible. BG would probably not be able to obtain a price that supported the costs of developing Gaza Marine. BG also knew that it would be at a disadvantage as it would not be able to supply all the volume required, whereas the Yam Tethys partnership (Noble-Delek) would be able to do so. For these reasons and in the light of the previous bad experiences with IEC bid rounds and the on/off negotiations over the years, BG decided not to participate in the Hadera tender.

Second-hand Gas Field for Sale

One option that BG considered was selling its interest in Gaza Marine but who would buy a second-hand gas field offshore the Gaza Strip? My colleagues and I did come up with a short list (a very short list) of who might be interested in buying BG's share in the Gaza Marine licence. This list included companies with an interest in the region already e.g. Noble and Delek as well as BG's existing partner, CCC. There was also a small, independent Turkish oil company, Zorlu, that had reportedly expressed interest in the past. We considered that there may be a remote chance that a Russian or

Chinese company might be interested. That was the extent of our list. When we considered what companies would be acceptable to the PNA, the list became shorter. The PNA would be unlikely to accept Noble and Delek as licence holders due to their strong connection to Israel. To test the market for its share in the licence, BG would have to spend money on advisors and putting together an information pack. In the light of BG's desire to minimise spending on the project, BG was not prepared to start a formal process to market its stake but would entertain any serious offer that came along.

To BG's surprise, a serious offer did come along in the autumn of 2011. The Malaysian billionaire Ananda Krishnan approached BG's Chief Executive Frank Chapman with a request to buy BG's Gaza Marine stake. Krishnan headed the Usaha Tegas group which held a diverse range of companies. Among his holdings at the time was an oil and gas exploration company, Pexco and a power station in Egypt. His stated interest in Gaza Marine was partly philanthropic - making a practical contribution to helping the Palestinians - but also hard-headed business. His plan, as outlined by his lieutenants, was to develop Gaza Marine for supply to Egypt to ensure gas for his power station in the country. At first glance, this was a reasonable plan and had some similarities to BG's Egypt plan. At this time, it was becoming apparent that Egypt would run short of gas and so the viability of Krishnan's gas-fired power station in Egypt was under threat. Krishnan was also considering one other option: taking the gas beyond Egypt to Saudi Arabia as there was potential demand in north east Saudi Arabia near the border with Egypt. This was an isolated part of the Kingdom but one which the Saudi government hoped to develop and so would need an energy source. Krishnan hoped to use his connections with members of the Saudi royal family to get the go ahead for this option. This option had some logic as well. BG in the past had looked at the opportunities in that part of the world. BG was aware that under some of the islands close to the Saudi shore there was a potential gas field. When BG bought

Tenneco in the late 1980s, the company held an exploration licence for this area and had undertaken preliminary work. While BG was pleasantly surprised to receive an offer from a credible business leader who clearly had the means to make a serious offer, my colleagues and I were sceptical from the start that we would complete the transaction.

Nevertheless, BG seized the opportunity to rid itself of a non-material and difficult asset. BG put in place a formal process to negotiate the sale agreement. The early stages were signing a confidentiality agreement with the potential buyer, making documents, including the licence agreements available to the would-be buyer and appointing external lawyers to advise on the sale. The specific entity buying the stake would be Pexco, the upstream oil and gas company in the Usaha Tegas group. Pexco was a Netherlands-registered company but headquartered in Kuala Lumpur, Malaysia. It planned to use a subsidiary, named Aquedo, registered in the British Virgin Islands to hold its Gaza Marine stake. Aside from Malaysia, Pexco also had interests offshore Australia and held licences in Ethiopia. While the company did not have the same level of experience or resources as BG, it did have offshore experience and had the backing of a much larger group whose owner had close connections with the Malaysian government. It was also the type of company that was most likely to be interested in Gaza Marine: independent, entrepreneurial and possessing a stronger stomach for risk than BG.

By this stage, there had been another change in responsibility for Gaza Marine within BG. The executive vice president for the region was now Sami Iskander. He is Egyptian and has considerable experience in the oil and gas sector. Before joining BG, he had worked for the international oil services firm Schlumberger. For day-to-day responsibility, Sami had assigned Gas Marine to the member of his team charged with managing new ventures and business development, Paul Warburton. Paul was also very experienced and had worked at BG almost all his career, joining when it was still British Gas. I had first met him in Egypt as he was working there when I joined, and we happened to live in the same block of flats.

My colleagues and I at BG were sceptical about the deal on several fronts. First, we anticipated the initial enthusiasm to purchase Gaza Marine would dissipate when Pexco and its advisors came to understand the extent of the complexities associated with developing Gaza Marine, such as the difficulties of negotiating with both Israel and the PNA. Second, we were concerned that Pexco would not be acceptable to either the PNA or the Israeli government for different reasons. For the PNA, Pexco did not have the same credibility as BG as a partner i.e. it was not a blue chip FTSE 100 company. However, the connection with a Muslim country would be a plus. However, this same factor could be a negative for Israel, which did not have diplomatic relations with Malaysia. For Pexco, securing government support for its efforts to develop Gaza Marine could be hampered by this lack of diplomatic relations. The third area of scepticism concerned Pexco's plan to develop Gaza Marine for supply to a power station in Egypt. We were not sure this made commercial sense as the power station would be unlikely to need sufficient gas to support the cost of developing Gaza Marine, even with some gas also being supplied to the power station in Gaza, as BG had planned to do. There was also the difficulties of persuading Israel to agree to an Egypt export option as BG had discovered. The Saudi option could provide sufficient demand to underpin Gaza Marine development, but this was a more uncertain option as there were not yet the power plants or other facilities available in north east Saudi Arabia to use the gas.

Krishnan appears to have made the decision alone to buy Gaza Marine and did not consult Pexco or other oil and gas experts in his organisation before making the initial approach to BG. He imposed the project on Pexco and instructed them to make it happen. When Pexco executives looked into Gaza Marine, they also grew sceptical about the project. The economics, based on developing the field and taking the gas to Egypt and perhaps Saudi Arabia, did not seem to work. They also realised the political difficulties that surrounded the project, even at a time when relations between Israel and the PNA were relatively good with the efforts to bring about an economic peace. Pexco executives and their legal advisors counselled Krishnan that they needed to get political risk advice from a reputable firm such as Control Risks Group. Indeed, one Pexco executive contacted Control Risks to start the process of obtaining advice. However, Krishnan vetoed the idea of obtaining external risk advice. He believed he understood the situation and his connections with leaders in the region, especially on the Palestinian side made external advice unnecessary. The Pexco team were to proceed with negotiating the purchase of BG's share in Gaza Marine.

BG's scepticism did not stop the company putting its best foot forward in attempting to agree the sale. One of the first actions was to give Pexco access to relevant documents including the text of the licence agreements that BG signed in November 1999, the seismic surveys, the results of the two wells drilled in 2000, agreements with CCC and other supporting technical and financial documents. This process, usually called a "*dataroom*" is now typically conducted through a secure site online. In this case though, BG insisted on a physical dataroom. In preparing all the documentation for the sale process, BG came to appreciate how much was missing. Some original documents could not be found despite the existence of several dozen boxes of documents. These were extracted from safe storage and a small team of us shifted though them to find documents that supported BG's expenditure on the project. These were needed to underpin BG's position on the value it was asking for in the sale negotiation. The Pexco team would need to visit BG's head office in Reading to review the documents. BG also stipulated that the Pexco team could not take any of the documents or copies with them. So, over two wintry days in late 2011, a Pexco delegation visited BG's head office to comb through the documents. They found this insistence on a physical visit and the restrictions, not only odd but difficult and frustrating. They wondered why BG was acting in such a paranoid manner. Their frustration grew as they reviewed the documents. Some documents were missing or incomplete and, in some cases, it was hard to understand how some of the amendments to the licence had come about. To the Pexco team, it was not clear what they were actually buying with Gaza Marine. What rights would they acquire? The licence was flawed. The Pexco team speculated that BG's paranoia was driven by a fear that Krishnan would go behind its back and ask the PNA directly for the licence and force out BG. There was some basis to this speculation. My colleagues and I did see a risk that the PNA would take away the Gaza Marine licence and re-award it to Krishnan. There was sufficient ambiguity about whether BG had fulfilled its obligations and doubts about BG's commitment to give the PNA a pretext for withdrawing the licence.

As well as placing restrictions on Pexco's access to documents, BG also insisted on complete confidentiality during the negotiation phase. My colleagues and I asked Pexco and its affiliates to avoid contacting the PNA and CCC. The Pexco team appeared put out by this demand. They wanted to build relations with PNA and create rapport as a prelude to the formal request for approval for the sale which would have to be made. We wanted to minimise the chances of a separate approach to the PNA but also prevent another risk. BG also judged that there was a high chance that if the PNA knew that we were trying to sell our interest, they would attempt to frustrate the deal before a sale agreement could be signed between BG and Pexco. As well as these risks specific to the Gaza Marine sale process, there was also a matter of long standing policy. The mergers and acquisition team within BG was managing the sale process and as matter of course they did not want news of any transaction to leak before BG were ready to announce the deal to the market.

This policy was based on the need to conform with the laws and regulations governing listed companies. BG preferred to present the PNA with a sales agreement and then ask for their approval. Pexco acquiesced to BG's knowledge of how the PNA might react gained from the long relationship that BG had with the Palestinians. After several months of discussions, Pexco put a serious and acceptable offer on the table in the spring of 2012, despite all the risks surrounding the project. Pexco offered $90 million for BG's 90% stake in the Gaza Marine licence. The offer was in the middle of the range that BG had set as a target. BG accepted the offer and a conditional sales and purchase agreement was signed. The agreement was conditional because at this point, BG was obliged to inform both its partner, CCC and the PNA. CCC possessed what is known as a pre-emption right i.e. it could acquire BG's stake on the same terms as the Malaysian buyer. Such pre-emption rights are typical in agreements governing such partnerships. CCC had one month in which to decide to exercise this right. Before CCC could make that decision, they needed to know the terms that BG had accepted. Also, both CCC and the PNA needed an opportunity to meet Pexco and assess its plans for Gaza Marine. Both CCC and PNA would have to work with Pexco if the sale went through. More immediately, BG and Pexco required PNA approval for the deal they were proposing. So, my colleagues and I at BG arranged for Pexco to meet CCC and the PNA. PIF executives would represent the PNA as they did at most meetings related to Gaza Marine.

This was a crucial meeting for both BG and Pexco. My colleagues and I knew that success of the deal depended on the meeting. In particular, it was important that Pexco came across as credible and a suitable replacement for BG as an equity owner in the Gaza Marine licence. We assessed that there was a high risk that the PNA and PIF would reject Pexco as the company did not have sufficient experiencing of developing an offshore gas field. We would have to put in a great deal of effort to improve the chance of success. Amongst ourselves at BG, we thought hard about the most difficult questions that PIF would ask, the weak points in our proposition and the strongest possible answers in response to PIF's concerns.

Before the meeting with CCC and PIF, we held a separate meeting with Pexco to agree the responses to PIF, rehearse the answers and coach the Pexco representatives on how to handle the meeting. Pexco was represented by its CEO, Sean Guest and its lawyer, Sheree Ford. At the meeting also, was the CFO for the company that owned the power station in Egypt and representatives from Bumi Armada, a well-known oilfield services company that Pexco were planning to use to undertake the engineering on the project. We saw the inclusion of Bumi Armada in the meeting as positive. This was a company that PIF and CCC would know and would add credibility to Pexco's case. The preparatory meeting went well. The Pexco team readily agreed to our responses and agreed with our advice on how to handle the meeting.

The preparatory meeting followed by the meeting with CCC and PIF took place at BG's central London office in the boardroom at Eagle House on Jermyn Street. The meeting was a disaster. The Pexco team did not stick to the script and seemed to ignore most of the advice we gave them. Instead, they gave vague answers to PIF's questions and did not put forward a convincing case to PIF. The BG representatives at the meeting were Sami Iskander, BG's chief operating officer, Paul Warburton, the project manager, Alejandro Figuero, from BG's legal department and me. At one point, Sami leaned over and wrote on Paul's notepad, "*Is this the best they can do?*" At the end of the meeting the BG team was deflated. We knew the Pexco team had blown the opportunity and would not get another one. Gaining PNA approval now seemed highly unlikely.

Before the PNA made its decision though, CCC had a decision to make: whether or not to exercise its pre-emption rights. CCC used the whole month to ponder its decision and informed BG just before the deadline was due to expire. In the end, CCC declined the chance to match Pexco's offer. Now, BG and Pexco could formally submit a request to the PNA for approval for the sale. On 23 December 2011, BG wrote to the PNA to request approval for transfer of its share of the Gaza Marine licence to Pexco's subsidiary Aquedo International. Under the terms of the licence agreement, PNA had an absolute right of refusal and did not have to explain its decision. This was not typical of such clauses. More typical is a format where the licensing authority cannot withhold approval without reasonable cause. The PNA was under no such restriction. It came as no surprise to BG when the PNA did not approve the sale. We had also feared that the PNA would be slow to make a decision or perhaps even refuse to give a definitive answer and keep us in limbo. However, the PNA came to its decision quickly and this helped sweeten the pill of rejection. On 7 February 2012, Dr Mohammad Mustafa in his capacity as economic advisor to President Abbas, wrote to BG informing the company of its decision not to grant approval in a brief three line letter. Although it did not have to reveal the basis for its decision, the PNA did so in a subsequent meeting with BG. In the PNA's opinion, Pexco did not have the same status and experience as BG. Pexco seemed surprised by the decision. The company's ultimate owner, Ananda Krishnan was reportedly very surprised and disappointed. He believed that his profile and connections would ensure PNA approval. However, as far as BG understood, he had not made full use of any existing relationship with the PNA to advocate for approval of the deal, even after BG lifted the bar on contact. Furthermore, BG was not aware that Krishnan or any of the Pexco management asked the Malaysian government to intervene on its behalf with the PNA. Such advocacy may have made a difference to the PNA. One of the items on the PNA's wish list from a foreign investor was a readiness to mobilise its home government in support. The PNA may have felt more confident about having a less experienced investor such as Pexco in place, if they knew that the Malaysian government was ready to intervene for the Gaza Marine project.

CHAPTER 10

ECONOMIC PEACE
(2011-2013)

The failure to complete the sales process with Pexco sparked a new phase of activity that would eventually lead to renewed efforts to find a market for the gas. CCC were keen to push ahead with efforts to develop the field. First, though the sales process highlighted some ambiguities in the status of the licence that needed resolving. Under the original agreement signed in 1999 and the outline development lease that the PNA granted in 2002, BG was obliged to relinquish areas of the licence not needed for the field's development. This requirement obliged BG (and CCC) to relinquish two tranches, each of 25% of the licence area. Such relinquishment obligations are a normal part of licence agreements. They allow the licensing authority to offer new licences for the acreage for further exploration. The PNA suspended this relinquishment obligation as part of its 2002 efforts to prevent BG declaring force majeure after the outbreak of the second Intifada. Removing the suspension was entirely at the PNA's discretion. As part of the relinquishment process, BG was also obliged to submit a report setting out the data available on the relinquished area. This would be provided to any future bidders for an exploration licence. Also, the 25 year clock of the development lease had now been ticking for 10 years. The 15 years remaining was insufficient to obtain approval for development, design, build and install all the facilities needed, produce the gas and then dismantle and remove all the facilities at the end of the field's life. So, an extension to the licence was needed.

On 24 April 2012, the PNA's Dr Mustafa wrote to BG's Sami Iskander notifying BG that it was lifting the suspension of the relinquishment obligation. The letter asked BG to prepare a report setting out the proposed areas for relinquishment (with maps) and the analysis of the remaining potential for exploration in the licence area. The PNA's letter provided BG with an opportunity to clarify some of the ambiguities related to the Gaza Marine licence and seek a licence extension. Sami and Paul wanted confirmation from the PNA that BG had fulfilled all of its commitments on the licence i.e. that BG was no longer under any obligation to conduct any further exploration work such as drill another well or acquire more data.

So, on 24 May 2012, Sami replied to Dr Mustafa to start the process of resolving these issues. Those of us working on Gaza Marine (Sami, Paul and I) agreed that it was worth spending some time and effort to resolve these issues and reach an agreement with the PNA. If another opportunity came along to sell BG's stake, then the licence would be in better shape and more attractive to a buyer. Our strategy was to agree a package deal with the PNA. We anticipated that in return for agreement on a licence extension, the PNA would revive their long standing demand for an increased share for PIF in the licence. There was a deal to be done. As for the relinquishment obligations, this was something BG was ready to agree to in return for clarity on the licence's status. First, it was a contractual obligation and second, it would create some goodwill ahead of what we expected to be tough negotiations on licence extension and increased PNA share.

Dr Mustafa replied to Sami's letter on 20 June 2012. The PNA did not seem ready to negotiate a deal. Their reply was terse and legalistic. The letter stated that the relinquishment obligation was driven by the end of each exploration phase and was not conditional on completion of the work programme. The PNA suspended the obligation in 2002 and was now exercising its right to lift that suspension and giving BG

14 days to comply. The letter also stated that no licence extension is required in order to carry out the relinquishment obligation. The letter also asked BG to prepare a report on the remaining exploration potential and provide all the relevant data. In the letter, Dr Mustafa stated that there was *"no link between the Developer's [BG] compliance with this obligation and the issues mentioned in the BG letter"*. The letter left BG with little choice to comply on the relinquishment obligation. BG had already set in motion the process of compiling the report. This report set out the proposed areas for relinquishment, BG's assessment of the potential for further discoveries and the relevant data. BG duly delivered the report to ensure that it met its contractual obligations. BG did not want to do anything that risked the PNA revoking the licence. While, Gaza Marine was no longer material to BG's business, the company did not want notion that it did not honour contracts.

The PNA had not linked relinquishment to other issues facing the Gaza Marine licence including BG's demand for a licence extension and the PNA's own demand for an increase in its eventual share of the project. In discussions with BG, the PNA continued to press for a greater equity share of the licence. Under arrangements reached in the early days of the licence, the PIF, on behalf of the PNA, would receive a 10% share in the licence after a final investment decision was made on developing the field. Since Salam Fayyad became Palestinian prime minister in 2007, the PNA sought a doubling of that share to 20%. The PNA wanted to demonstrate that it was standing up for Palestinian interests and maximising the economic return from Palestinian assets. A 20% stake would give a larger slice of the profits from the field once production started. The PNA would also be liable for 20% of the costs of developing and operating the field. The PNA was unlikely to have the funds to finance this level of costs. Once revenue started to flow from the field, the reality of the situation was likely to be that revenue due to the PNA would first be used to cover its liabilities. At this stage though, the PNA's ability to meet any Gaza Marine financial obligation was theoretical as there was no immediate prospect of the field being developed and no change in the licence ownership structure was agreed between the PNA, BG and CCC at this stage.

The demand for a doubling of the PNA's direct stake in the Gaza Marine licence reflected a view held by some within the PNA that they had not secured a good deal for the Palestinian economy. CCC's Yasser Burgan wrote to BG's Paul Warburton in late June 2012 asking for help to make the case to the PNA that the Gaza Marine terms compared favourably with terms in other countries. Burgan and his CCC colleagues were determined to correct this misperception. Burgan reported that, "*There are those within the PNA that make comments that (in comparison), Gaza Marine is not fair to the PNA and we want to stop this discussion before it starts.*" Burgan asked for BG's help "*on an urgent basis*" to provide a comparison with neighbouring countries, especially Egypt. Burgan wanted a comparison of the government's share of the value that the fiscal terms would produce. A BG economist produced a comparison of Gaza Marine with countries where there were similar fiscal terms. In replying to Burgan, Warburton made the point that Egypt was not a fair comparison as it used a different model and the government share was therefore calculated with a different method. Egypt used a production sharing contract system whereas the PNA used a tax and royalty regime similar to that used by the UK, the US and many other countries. BG's estimate was that under the existing terms i.e. with the PNA taking a 10% direct share, along with a 12.5% royalty and 25% tax rate, the PNA's effective share would be 45%. In BG's comparison chart, this share compared favourably with similar regimes. The chart had Ireland at one end with a share of 26% and the US at the other end with 56% and the UK on 50%. The PNA was comparable to New Zealand, also with a 45% share.

The aborted sale of BG's share to a Malaysian billionaire had prompted a surge in activity on the Gaza Marine project. It was not the only development that injected new energy into efforts to reach an agreement on Gaza Marine. Israeli Prime Minister Benjamin Netanyahu made a public commitment to renew discussions on Gaza Marine. He made this commitment in February 2011, but it took more than a year for those talks to become a reality. BG, CCC and the PNA were distracted by the sales process but there were other factors at play. As 2012 progressed, BG's Gaza Marine team conducted two parallel sets of discussions. The first with the PNA on a package of measures to agree an increase in the PNA share and a licence extension. The second with the Israeli government to gain approval for Gaza Marine's development.

Economic Peace

On 4 February 2011, Tony Blair and Israeli Prime Minister Benjamin Netanyahu held a joint press conference at which they announced a package of measures to help the Palestinian economy. Amongst the measures announced was a promise to restart negotiations on the development of Gaza Marine. These negotiations were to start *"immediately and conclude within three months (by 4 May 2011)"*.[44] The talks did not start immediately as neither the Israelis nor the Palestinians were prepared. First, both had to appoint negotiating teams. While Gaza Marine was the first project listed in the package of measures and improving the situation in Gaza was given priority in the package, there were more urgent measures to implement. Blair and his team's priority was to improve access for goods and people in and out of the Gaza Strip and relax restrictions on movement in the West Bank. The focus on movement was understandable as this was a more immediate need and would deliver benefits in the short term. Gaza Marine was a long term prospect. Even, in the unlikely event, the talks concluded within three months with agreement on the

---

44 Report for the Meeting of the Ad Hoc Liaison Committee On OQR Action in Support of Palestinian Authority State- Building, 13 April 2011, Brussels

field's development, that would be only the start of work that would continue for at least three years until the first molecule of natural gas flowed along a pipeline to a power station and the first revenue flowed to the PNA. Relaxation of movement restrictions would have a positive impact the very next day and would cost much less than developing Gaza Marine.

One other party was also not ready for negotiations to start immediately. To BG, this announcement came out of the blue. The company had not been consulted by Blair or his team. This put BG in an awkward position. BG's position on developing Gaza Marine had not changed. The company still had no appetite for pushing ahead with the project. At the same time, the BG Gaza Marine team realised that the company could not be seen as an obstacle and thereby block progress towards better Israeli-Palestinian relations or even an eventual peace deal. More positively, this initiative could provide an opportunity for BG, as it may attract a potential buyer for BG's share of the licence and allow BG to rid itself of an unwanted asset in its portfolio. At this stage, BG had not received the offer from Ananda Krishnan. So, BG expressed support for re-starting discussions on Gaza Marine. However, BG wanted to ensure that it did not waste time and resources on discussions that were not going to make progress. So, BG informed all the parties involved: Blair, the Israeli government, the PNA and CCC that it had one important condition for resuming discussions on Gaza Marine. BG demanded that the Israeli government appoint a negotiator who had the confidence of the Prime Minister and had sufficient seniority and a mandate to make decisions on Gaza Marine. This communication happened through the British government. There was no direct contact with Blair's team or the Israeli government at this stage. BG did not want to appear too keen to restart discussions. Israel also did not appear keen to discuss Gaza Marine. No name was forthcoming from the government. Meantime, Blair and his team were focussed on implementing other parts of the 4 February package.

In its September 2011 report to the Ad Hoc Liaison Committee (AHLC),[45] Blair's team noted that there had been *"no progress"* on the *"preliminary discussions . . . on the development of the "Gaza Marine" gas field"*. The report did, though, note that, *"The GoI [Government of Israel] has formally communicated to the PA that it is willing to commence talks and has identified a lead representative. The PA has also identified its team. The two teams have not yet met."*[46] The identity of Israel's lead representative had, though, not been communicated to BG and the company had not met either team. At the next AHLC meeting in March 2012, there was no mention of Gaza Marine in Blair's report to the committee. There was better news by the time of the next report to the AHLC in September 2012. This time, Blair's team were able to report, *"The OQR helped facilitate Israeli Government approval for the development of the Palestinian gas field, 'Gaza Marine'. This gas field, once developed, will support the energy requirements of the PNA and will generate significant fiscal revenues for the Palestinian Ministry of Finance. The private partners are now in high-level discussions with the PNA and the Government of Israel (GOI) about development options for the gas field."*[47] This report was a little optimistic. At this stage, the Israeli government had not yet, given *"approval for the development"* for Gaza Marine but the *"private partners"* i.e. BG, were in discussions with the Israeli government.

In late June, BG received notification of the Israeli official

---

45 The AHLC is a 15 member body established in 1993 to co-ordinate international policy and support to the PNA. Norway chairs the body and its other members are: the US, European Union, United Nations, IMF, World Bank, Russia, Japan, Saudi Arabia, Canada, Palestinian Authority, Israel, Jordan, Egypt, and Tunisia. It meets twice yearly, alternating between Brussels and New York.

46 Report for the Meeting of the Ad Hoc Liaison Committee on OQR Action in Support of Palestinian Authority State- Building, 18 September 2011, New York

47 Report for the Meeting of the Ad Hoc Liaison Committee, Reinvigorating Palestinian Economic Growth and Institution-Building, 23 September 2012, New York.

appointed to lead talks with the company. The news came via the British Ambassador to Israel, Matthew Gould. Israel had nominated Yitzhak Molcho to lead the discussions on the Israeli government's behalf. The BG Gaza Marine team assessed that Molcho was exactly the type of person that fulfilled the conditions that it had set. Molcho was a lawyer, a close aide to Benjamin Netanyahu and had good relations with the Palestinians. This seemed promising. So, in the summer of 2012, BG resumed discussions with Israel on Gaza Marine.

BG sent a team of three to hold an initial meeting with Molcho in August 2012. The team consisted of Sami, Paul and me. At that initial meeting, Molcho was accompanied by a representative with responsibility for energy on Israel's National Security Council and a government lawyer. The meeting was held at the Prime Minister's office in Jerusalem. My colleagues and I approached the meeting with a great deal of scepticism. There had been many false dawns on the Gaza Marine project, and this could be just another to add to the list. Obtaining Israeli agreement to go ahead with Gaza Marine had been impossible when the country needed the gas. Now that it had discovered enough resources to make it self-sufficient in gas and to consider exports, it had no need for Gaza Marine. Why would Israel change its position now and allow the project to go ahead? This was the question uppermost in our minds as we sat down with Molcho and his colleagues. Molcho was friendly and welcoming. He set out Israel's position and wanted to know what BG needed to make progress. Molcho explained that while Israel had been blessed with extensive gas resources, these were all in the hands of one consortium: Noble and Delek. As things stood, Israel would rely on one gas supplier for the foreseeable future and for the next few years would rely on one supplier from one field using one pipeline. This was not a comfortable position for Israel and its energy security.

Molcho wanted to know what BG needed to allow Gaza Marine

development to go ahead. Sami outlined the conditions that would need to be fulfilled: a creditworthy buyer who could commit to taking the bulk of the production, a sovereign guarantee from Israel and an umbrella agreement between the Israeli government and the PNA to set the regulatory framework to cover issues such as how the project would be taxed and how other "cross border" issues would be managed. Molcho considered the first two conditions were reasonable but he had reservations about the third. On the creditworthy buyer, he asked whether IEC would fit these criteria. Sami replied that it probably would. Molcho also undertook to set in motion the process for obtaining a sovereign guarantee. This would require liaison with the Ministry of Finance. On the third condition, he made the point that this should be a commercial arrangement and there was no need to make it political. This became his mantra in the series of meetings we held with him.

Molcho also set out Israel's red lines. He made it clear that Israel would only accept Gaza Marine gas landing in Israel. It did not matter whether the final market was Israel itself, Egypt or somewhere else such as Jordan. Gaza Marine gas would only reach that market via Israel. Israel would not agree to a pipeline direct from the Gaza Marine field to the Egyptian shore. Molcho also made demands on the revenue for the PNA. Israel wanted control here. It did not want revenue to flow direct to the PNA. Instead, Molcho proposed that the Israel would pay for the gas in kind through the provision of goods and services. BG was sceptical that the PNA would accept payment in kind.

The answer to our central question seemed to be that although Israel did not need the gas, it wanted to break the monopoly of the Noble and Delek partnership. This appeared to be a rational answer to the question, but scepticism remained. As well as emphasising the commercial nature of the relationship, Molcho also stressed the monopoly gas supply situation that Israel faced. To the Israeli government, this situation was uncomfortable and politically untenable. The government, he explained, was anxious to find a solution. He went on: allowing Gaza Marine gas into the Israeli market could form part of that solution. The monopoly on natural gas supply would become a hot political topic and come close to bringing down the Netanyahu government. The government's handling of the issue would lead to intensive political interference into the natural gas sector, severely tarnishing Israel's reputation as a stable destination for investment. That was all still to come.

Sami, Paul and I left the first meeting with Molcho pleased but not totally convinced. We had confirmed that we were talking to the appropriate representative of the Israeli government; he clearly had a mandate to negotiate and seemed willing to make things happen with the government system (for example the sovereign guarantee). He had also set out a good case for why Israel wanted Gaza Marine gas to enter the market. While, we thought it was a good case, we still did not consider it compelling. We needed to verify the extent of government concern over the monopoly situation and ensure that we were not just being sold a story to keep us talking and allow the government to demonstrate that it was living up to its commitment to Blair. We talked to a variety of other contacts to get to the bottom of the monopoly question. We talked to BG's Israeli legal advisors, the British Embassy, Israeli consultants and NGOs. We received a consistent message: the monopoly concern was genuine and of political significance. Molcho seemed to be negotiating in good faith. The new dawn for Gaza Marine was looking a little less false.

The resumption of discussions on Gaza Marine also meant renewed contact with the PNA. BG had maintained a line of communication with the PNA through its office in Ramallah. At no point during the hiatus had BG come under pressure from the PNA to resume talks. BG's interlocutor on the PNA side was Mohammad Mustafa. He was head of the Palestinian Investment Fund (PIF), which would own the PNA's share of project. He was also economic advisor to the PNA president Mahmoud Abbas. For a period, Mustafa would also serve as deputy prime minister in the PNA cabinet and later prime minister. There was a conflict of interest in Mustafa's dual role as head of PIF and presidential advisor. There was little BG could do about this as he was the PNA's point of contact. The only action BG could take was to ensure that we were open in our dealings with him.

As with Israel, BG had conditions for making progress on the discussions with the PNA. The most important of these conditions was an extension to the Gaza Marine licence. The licence extension was required as the clock on the licence had been ticking since 2002. Under the outline development plan agreed in 2002 to prevent a declaration of *force majeure* when the second Intifada started, BG and CCC had 25 years in which to develop the field, produce gas from the field and then decommission the field at the end of its life. The assumption on the part of BG, CCC and the PNA was there would be least 15 years of production. Development of the field would take at least three years (and possibly four) from the moment that the project was sanctioned. With almost ten years passed since 2002, there was now insufficient time left on the licence. BG also questioned whether PIF would be able to fund its share of the project and so a mechanism would have to be found to ensure payment. BG would also demand clarity on the precise corporate vehicle that the PIF would use to hold its project share.

The PNA's central demand remained that the PNA's share be increased from 10% to 20%. The PNA was under domestic political pressure to ensure the best possible deal. In particular, the PNA was under pressure from Hamas to demonstrate that it was acting within the interests of all Palestinians. A perception that the PNA was not getting maximum value for the Palestinian economy risked it losing even more support to Hamas. The PNA also had other demands. The PNA was also anxious that some of the gas be used to fuel the Gaza power station.

It was clear that there was a deal to be done: agreement on licence extension in exchange for an increased PNA share in the project. This would require an agreement between BG and CCC as the licence holders and PIF. First, BG and CCC would have to agree to cede a further 10% to the PNA. Assuming that the two companies did agree to do this, they would then have to decide how to allocate the PNA's additional share from their own equity stakes. There were many possible combinations. BG or CCC could give up 10% of their own holding. They could allocate the equity in proportion to their current shareholdings (90/10) or in what would have been their final shareholding (60/30) or even in some other proportions (e.g. 50/50). CCC's opening gambit was that it was not prepared to reduce its equity. It wanted to remain a 30% shareholder in the final project structure. In this case, the final shareholders would be BG (50%), CCC (30%) and PIF (20%). This was not acceptable to BG as it would dilute the value BG would receive and risked deadlock in decision-making. As operator, BG wanted to maintain a majority shareholding so that it could not be outvoted by the other partners on project decisions. This was a long-standing BG position related to all projects where it was the operator rather than specific to Gaza Marine.

BG's negotiations with Israel and the PNA were conducted on two separate tracks as both the Israelis and the Palestinians were reluctant to engage directly on the Gaza Marine project. The Israelis did not want to be in a situation where they may have to offer compromises. The Palestinians feared the political price they would be asked to pay in return for allowing the project to go ahead. It suited both sides to have BG in the middle. BG was able to arrange one joint meeting in a hotel in Tel Aviv. Present at the meeting were representatives of BG (including me), CCC representatives, Molcho and PIF representatives. The atmosphere was civil if slightly tense. Both the Israelis and the Palestinians were polite to each other, referring to "*my colleagues*" or "*our friends*". However, each seemed reluctant to refer to the other by their actual name. The Israelis did not want to seem to utter the word "*Palestinian*" and the Palestinians did not seem to want to say the words "*Israel*" or "*Israeli*". The one hour meeting had passed the halfway mark before one side cracked. Molcho could not find another circumlocution and said "*Palestinian*". The tension in the room eased several notches.

The two tracks of discussions, one with Israel and the other with the PNA, carried on for the rest of 2012 and into 2013. There was an early hitch on the Israeli track. Molcho's acceptance of the need for a sovereign guarantee had surprised BG. However, at a subsequent meeting, he made it clear that after consultations with government officials, he had over-promised. It was not Israeli government policy to offer sovereign guarantees for such projects. This had nothing to do with Palestinian involvement. It was a blanket policy. BG's consultations with others confirmed the Israeli policy. It also became clear that extensive discussions would be required with the Israeli energy regulator. These would cover the terms under which Gaza Marine gas would gain access to the Israeli gas transmission system.

During our discussions with Molcho and others, the BG team, got the sense that the Israeli government had another reason for wanting Gaza Marine to go ahead. Israel was keen to support the Palestinian prime minister Salam Fayyad. They wanted him to stay in office as he was someone they could do negotiate with. Molcho and others in the Israeli government had developed good personal relations with Fayyad. The Gaza Marine project offered the chance for Israel to give Fayyad a win and show that he could deliver for the Palestinian economy. Sami thought this desire to help Fayyad was a strong thread in Israel's approach to Gaza Marine. Molcho spoke approvingly of Fayyad and made clear that he was Netanyahu's liaison with Fayyad. He could pick up the phone to the Palestinian prime minister at any time. We also, though, got the sense that Molcho and the Israeli government would only secure a win for Fayyad on their terms. It was not at any price. Israel was not prepared to compromise on its total control over the project. Molcho also made it clear that Israel would only allow a development scheme that landed the gas on Israeli

221

territory (not the Gaza Strip or Egypt). This would give Israel ultimate control over the flow of gas. If necessary, they could intervene (with force if required) to shut off the gas. Molcho did not state this in such bold and dramatic terms but in his deliberate and assertive way, he made his meaning clear. Israel would also want control over the flow of revenues. During the various meetings, Sami, Paul and I held with Molcho and his colleagues, he floated various proposals for the payment mechanisms. These included an offshore escrow account and payment in kind for the gas. Payment-in-kind appeared to be Molcho's preferred option. This was not a new proposal and had been floated before. BG had not changed its view of this: it was a non-starter.

At the same time, dark clouds were gathering in the background. The ceasefire that ended the Gaza War (Operation Cast Lead) in January 2009 reduced the level of violence but had not stopped it. Hamas rocket attacks on southern Israel steadily increased and Israeli forces conducted raids on targets in the Gaza Strip. The Israeli Navy also tightened restrictions on Gaza's fishermen, severely limiting the waters in which they could operate. This had a devastating impact on their catch and ability to supply an important food source to Gaza's population. Hamas set a condition that the rocket attacks would cease in return for removal of restrictions on the fishermen. On 14 November 2012, Israel staged an air attack that targeted and killed Hamas military leader Ahmed Jabari. The air raid marked the start of an air assault that Israel termed Operation Pillar of Cloud (often translated in English as Pillar Defence).[48] Hamas named its response Operation Stone of Shales.[49] The military action lasted eight days with a ceasefire brokered by Egypt and the US coming into force on 21 November. Israel did not use ground troops this time around

---

48 The Israeli name was a reference to Exodus 13:21-22 which describes a cloud pillar that protected the Israelites on their journey to the Promised Land.

49 Quran 105:4

but undertook an intensive series of air raids intended to weaken Hamas' operational ability and especially its ability to stage rocket attacks. As in Operation Cast Lead, civilians comprised a significant proportion of the casualties. In one attack, ten members (including five children) of the same family were killed in their own home. While the air raids damaged Hamas' operational capability, it also damaged much civilian infrastructure in the Gaza Strip including private homes, schools, clinics and factories. The conflict did not provide a decisive victory to either side, brought no fundamental change to the situation either in Gaza or in Israel and highlighted the futility of military confrontation.

Following Barack Obama's re-election as US president in November 2012, there was an opportunity for a new initiative to bring a long term solution. Obama's new Secretary of State, John Kerry embarked on a bid to bring about a final settlement between Israel and the Palestinians. The Molcho-BG negotiations had started as part of an initiative by Tony Blair to push for improved economic relations between Israelis and Palestinians but became wrapped up in a new push for a comprehensive peace process. The Blair-Netanyahu proposals for an economic peace, launched in February 2011 now became a strand in the Kerry peace process. BG came under immense pressure from both the US and British governments to co-operate and revive the Gaza Marine project which would be the centrepiece of the economic track of the peace process. Blair and Kerry's team wanted periodic updates on progress and were keen to intervene to help. BG provided the updates but was also anxious to manage expectations. It did not want to create expectations that agreement would be reached because it did not believe it would. However, the prospect of an agreement was an advantage to BG. It made the asset more attractive for eventual sale. BG's strategy was to get as close as possible to a deal and then put Gaza Marine up for sale again.

To support the Kerry peace process, Blair and his team re-fashioned the economic peace plan into the *"Palestinian Economy Initiative"*.

This was launched in August 2013 and presented to both the PNA and the Israeli government for their approval. The plan was intended to drive Palestinian economic growth by *"catalyzing private sector-led growth in the West Bank and the Gaza Strip"*.[50] It set out a three year plan covering eight economic areas, including energy. The plan recognised the need to provide a reliable electricity supply to both the Gaza Strip and the West Bank and to ensure that future growth in energy demand could be met. The plan envisaged a crucial role for Gaza Marine in meeting growing Palestinian energy demand, *"These new sites will need to be fueled by natural gas, which requires finalizing long-term gas supply contracts with either Israeli or Palestinian gas companies. The development of the Palestinian Gaza Marine gas field will play an important part in this latter effort to expand the energy sector."*[51] Gaza Marine was also included in a list of infrastructure projects included in the plan. Implementation of the plan was dependent not only on the Kerry peace process but Israeli government approval and working with the PNA for technical inputs and to secure donor funding. A year later at the AHLC meeting in September 2014, Blair and his team were not able to report any substantial progress, mainly due to the military conflict that had just finished by the time of the meeting. Indeed, AHLC meetings were usually held every six months but the spring meeting had not taken place, and this was the first meeting since the plan's launch. By the next AHLC meeting in May 2015, there was no mention of the Palestinian Economic Initiative. Instead Blair's team called for urgent action to help Gaza and re-fashioned their priorities into five areas, one of which was *"Reliable Infrastructure"*. Under this heading, a new project was launched to bring a more reliable energy supply to Gaza. This was called *"Gas for Gaza"* and there was no longer any mention of Gaza

---

50 AHLC September 2013

51 Ibid.

Marine.[52] The implications of this new focus for the development of the Gaza Marine field are examined in the next chapter.

In the meantime, BG had come to a preliminary agreement with the PNA on a change in the equity position that would follow project sanction. To reach this agreement, BG had to circumvent Mustafa and reach an understanding with the Palestinian Prime Minister Rami Hamdallah, who had replaced Salam Fayyad in 2013. The agreement marked a compromise. The PNA's share would increase to 17.5% (rather than the 20% originally demanded). The additional 7.5% would be split between BG and CCC's share 5:2.5. So, BG's share would fall to 55% (as opposed to 60% as originally envisaged) and CCC's share would be 27.5% (rather than 30%). The understanding was sealed with handshake between BG's senior vice-president Mark Rollins and the Prime Minister in his office. I also attended that meeting. It was then set out in a follow up letter to put it on the record. We knew Mustafa would not be pleased but would have to defer to his political masters.

In the end, the Gaza Marine discussions fell victim to the collapse of the wider peace process. However, before the discussions ended, an elegant solution to Gaza Marine had emerged which was a win for all involved. Palestinian efforts to gain international recognition as a state including applying to the UN angered the Israelis and by mid 2014, Kerry's peace process had collapsed. Underlying the collapse was a lack of trust and political will on both sides. The solution for Gaza Marine that emerged in early 2014 revolved around Jordan.

---

52 AHLC May 2015.

CHAPTER 11

THE JORDAN OPTION
(2013-2020)

Jordan, while not a large economy, depends on imports for 97% of its energy needs. For much of the history of Gaza Marine, it was a theoretical market for the gas but one that presented significant commercial and practical difficulties. On the practical front, the gas would have to cross at least one country, either Israel or Egypt to reach the Kingdom. As long as either of these countries could use the gas, they had no incentive to allow this to happen. Also, the extra distance that the gas would have to travel, and the resulting transit fees would make Jordan a less commercially attractive market. Nevertheless, Jordan has significant demand for gas as most of its electricity generation is gas-fired. In 2013-14, its gas needs were around 500 million cubic feet per day, around three times the volume that Gaza Marine could produce in a day. The Kingdom faced a serious threat to its energy security and increases in the cost of importing gas. It had imported gas from Egypt via the Arab Gas pipeline since 2004. This gas had fuelled around 80% of the Kingdom's electricity generation. The pipeline runs across the Sinai Peninsula and under the Red Sea to the Jordanian port of Aqaba.

In the aftermath of Egypt's 2011 revolution, the pipeline suffered a series of attacks which severely disrupted supply. At the same time, Egypt was struggling to meet its export commitments due to increased domestic demand for gas. In 2012, supply through the pipeline stopped altogether but resumed at a much reduced level in 2013. In August 2014, the Egyptian state-owned gas company EGAS announced the permanent suspension of gas supplies. The Kingdom faced limited options to replace the lost Egyptian gas supply and all of them more expensive. The government invested in a floating LNG import terminal at Aqaba and sourced LNG on the world market. While this is an expensive option to receive gas, it has the advantage that Jordan was not reliant on any one country for its gas supply. This was not intended to be a long term solution but to provide a temporary answer. The other option was to switch to liquid fuel, such as diesel, to generate electricity. This is also an expensive option and has a greater environmental impact. There was a third option for Jordan: source gas from its other neighbours. The Kingdom has almost no oil and gas resources of its own but sits in an energy rich region. Its neighbours Iraq, Israel, the Palestinian territories and Syria all possess gas resources. There are plans for the construction of a pipeline from southern Iraq to supply oil and gas to Jordan as well as provide another export route for Iraqi hydrocarbons.

For Israel, there were strong political drivers for securing Jordan as a customer for some of its abundant gas discoveries made in 2009 and 2010. The Israeli government has been quick to recognise the foreign policy opportunities afforded by its newfound resources. Gas exports to its immediate neighbours can provide Israel with leverage over those countries and tie them closer to Israel's interests. The Israeli government has divided future use of its gas resources into three: first domestic use, second over the horizon exports and thirdly exports to immediate neighbours as part of an energy diplomacy strategy. In the case of Jordan, Israel sees the Kingdom's stability, including its economic stability and prosperity, as making a crucial contribution to its own security. Israel and Jordan signed a peace agreement in 1994. Relations between the two have never been warm but there was close co-operation between the security forces. There is though still a great deal of popular antagonism towards Israel in Jordanian society. So, while Israel can offer Jordan gas at a competitive price (especially in relation to imported LNG), the Jordanian government is likely to pay a high political price.

On 26 September 2016, the Jordanian state-owned power generator NEPCO signed an agreement with the Noble-Delek consortium for the supply of gas from the Leviathan field. The agreement was for an initial supply of 45 billion cubic metres of gas over a 15 year period in a deal reportedly worth $10 billion with the gas supply scheduled to start in 2019 and the agreement has options to increase the amount of gas supplied. News of the agreement provoked a peaceful demonstration by around 2000 people in central Amman. However, the Jordanian government appears to have timed the announcement to minimise the political fallout. The deal was announced the week after parliamentary elections had taken place and before the newly elected parliament had convened. In this way, the government avoided the deal becoming an election issue and subject of parliamentary debate.

While the deal to buy Israeli gas from Noble and Delek was announced in September 2016, this agreement had been under discussion for several years. The Jordanian government had long been concerned about its energy security even before the disruptions to Egyptian gas imports had started. The Jordanians had long been concerned that reliance on one source of gas supply was not a sustainable position. As well as talking to the Israelis about gas supply, the government had also looked to its other neighbours including the Palestinians. Buying Palestinian gas was much more politically acceptable to most Jordanians, many of whom have Palestinian origins. Tens of thousands of Palestinian refugees fled to Jordan in the aftermath of the 1948 and 1967 wars. Jordan, unlike many other Arab, countries integrated these refugees into society, giving them citizenship in many cases. Until the early 1970s, Arafat's PLO, was based in Jordan and launched raids against Israeli forces from Jordanian territory. King Hussein expelled the PLO after it threatened the Kingdom's stability. Arafat and the PLO decamped to Beirut and then later to Tunis from where Arafat made a triumphal return to Gaza following the Oslo Accords.

The import of Gaza Marine gas provides one possible strategy for the Jordanian government to gain political cover for the import of Israeli gas and to bolster its energy security. For Palestinian gas to reach Jordan, it could cross Israeli territory and use the same pipelines installed to transport Israeli gas. As the deal with Noble and Delek would be insufficient to meet all of Jordan's gas demand, there appeared to be scope for the Palestinians to supply Jordan from Gaza Marine. BG's discussions with Molcho revealed that Israel was enthusiastic about this scheme. Israel was committed to helping the Jordanian economy as it saw this as clearly in its national interest.

For BG, the Jordan supply option was also attractive. Jordan presented a long term market that offered sufficient demand, a competitive gas price and the means to pay. If BG could reach an agreement in principle, then it would make Gaza Marine a more attractive asset and increase the chances of finding a credible buyer for BG's share. For CCC, it was also an attractive proposition. Not only did it seem to present an opportunity to develop Gaza Marine, but Jordan was a country where they had significant interests and this would reinforce their presence and relationships in the Kingdom. So, in April 2014, a joint BG-CCC delegation travelled to Amman to open discussions with Jordan. The BG members of the delegation were Mark Rollins, a senior vice-president who had been given responsibility for Gaza Marine, Victoria Farrelly, a commercial manager and the author. This would be my last involvement in the Gaza Marine project. I had elected to take voluntary redundancy and would be leaving BG in June 2014. CCC's representatives were Stephen Byers, the former British cabinet minister who CCC retained as an advisor and Yasser Burgan, one of their commercial managers who had long worked on Gaza Marine. CCC used their existing relationships in Jordan to arrange meetings with the government.

The delegation was welcomed with open arms and gained an audience with the Prime Minister and a senior advisor to the King at short notice. This was no doubt testament to both the strength of CCC's relationships and the Jordanian government's anxiety about improving its energy security. Palestinian gas to Jordan provides an elegant solution. It provides revenue to the PNA, contributes to Jordan's energy security and provides political cover for Israeli gas imports.

Although the Jordan option appears to satisfy everyone, it has yet to come to fruition. Once more, Gaza Marine fell victim to external events, both those connected with the Israeli-Palestinian peace process and developments elsewhere. By April 2014 when BG and CCC made that initial visit to Amman, the Kerry peace process was in trouble. Kerry had set the end of April as a deadline for a breakthrough in the negotiations. The deadline passed without a breakthrough and the Kerry process came to a halt. While BG continued discussions with Israel for a while, it was clear that there was no longer any enthusiasm to reach an agreement on Gaza Marine. Molcho stepped back from the talks and directed BG towards the regulator and IEC. Without the high level political influence that Molcho possessed, these talks were not going to make any progress. As well as having little enthusiasm to continue the talks, two of the key participants, BG and Israel were about to face distractions which would once more push Gaza Marine to the back burner.

The breakdown of the Kerry peace process did not lead to an immediate upsurge in violence. The period since the end of Operation Pillar of Defence in November 2012 was one of the quietest in terms of rocket attacks from Gaza since the Hamas takeover in 2007. The trigger for an escalation in violence occurred in the West Bank rather than in the Gaza Strip. On 12 June 2014, three Israeli teenagers were kidnapped in the West Bank. Netanyahu blamed Hamas but without providing any evidence and subsequently evidence emerged that Hamas had not ordered the kidnap. The IDF launched a campaign in the West Bank, Operation Brother's Keeper to find the teenagers, capture the kidnappers and damage Hamas' capability in the West Bank. In response, Hamas launched rocket attacks from Gaza. On 8 July, Israel launched air raids on the Gaza Strip, setting off the longest and bloodiest military campaign against Gaza at that time. Israel named the assault, Operation Protective Edge. It lasted for 51 days until 26 August and also involved incursions by ground troops. More than 2000 Gazan residents were killed and more than 10,000 injured with the UN estimating that 65% were civilians. Israeli casualties were 67 military personnel and five civilians (one was a child). As in previous Israeli military campaigns, considerable damage was done to the fabric of Gaza. The UN estimated that more the 7000 private homes were destroyed. Agricultural land and livestock also suffered considerable damage. The military confrontation heaped the pressure on Gaza's fragile infrastructure, especially basic services such as health, water and energy. Hamas again suffered damage to its operational capability but not fatal damage. Although Gaza's civilian population endured the worst effects of the confrontation, it did not undermine popular support for the organisation. Polling in the aftermath of the conflict showed strong levels of support for Hamas and support for their actions.

Despite the unpromising political environment, the team at BG were not going to give up easily. While they had no allocated budget for business development activities for Gaza Marine and no mandate from the Board or Executive to pursue any opportunities, the business development team at BG carried on discussions with the Jordanians and Palestinians. BG's chief operating officer, Sami Iskander was sympathetic to the project. He authorised business development costs for the Gaza Marine project. Sami had taken part in the first few rounds of talks with Molcho, was sympathetic to the Palestinians and knew the kudos that would come his way if a deal could be agreed. A deal, of sorts, did emerge. BG, the Jordanian government and the PNA agreed an outline deal in late 2014 and early 2015. In August

2014, BG and the Jordanian state-owned power generation company NEPCO reached preliminary agreement on supplying gas from the Gaza Marine field to Jordan. The agreement was to negotiate a letter of intent (LOI) for supply of 150-180 million cubic feet per day with supplies to start in 2017. The LOI would be a skeleton of a full agreement in which many of the final terms were not agreed in full but would form the basis for the next stage of negotiations. BG and the Jordanian state power generation company, NEPCO, signed the LOI for supply of gas in May 2015.

The LOI, as signed, called for the supply of between 100 and 140 million standard cubic feet of gas per day for at least 12 years. The next step was to turn this into a gas sales and purchase agreement (GSPA) that would contain the detailed terms and conditions for sale, including precise volumes, price and other key terms. The agreement represented the first significant commercial breakthrough for many years for Gaza Marine. It demonstrated that there was a commercially feasible market for this gas. Some of those involved in the project were anxious to maintain the momentum. Within twenty four hours of the agreement's signature, Yasser Burgan of CCC was firing e-mails at BG's Victoria Farrelly demanding to know when she would be sending out the draft GSPA. One of the BG team involved described how Mohammad Mustafa, chairman of PIF and economic advisor to President Abbas, was beside himself with joy. This seemed to be a breakthrough and the Palestinians would get their gas field after all. There was still a lot of work to do to turn the LOI into a watertight and legally binding contract. The proposed volumes of gas for sale to Jordan did not represent the full potential volumes from Gaza Marine. There was more gas available. The Palestinians wanted some of the gas for their own use. Also, supply of Gaza Marine gas to Jordan still faced the practical difficulties already noted. The gas supply would still have to cross another country. Israel was the only real option. Israel would not allow any other option.

So, Victoria Farrelly and the BG team had to negotiate two other agreements. The first was with the Palestinians for supply of gas. The second was for access to the Israeli natural gas transmission system to transport the gas to Jordan and the Palestinian territories. The Palestinians' demand for use of some of the gas had formed part of the Gaza Marine project from almost the start. The demand, had though, previously focussed on supplying the gas to the existing power station near Gaza City, which was owned by CCC. The Palestinians now had new plans. The PNA and CCC now wanted the gas supplied to the West Bank. In 2015, there were no power stations on the West Bank. The territory's electricity supply came from Israel (largely) with some from Jordan. CCC, through its Palestine Power Generation Company (PPGC) was developing plans to build a gas-fired power station at Jenin in the northern West Bank. On 15 June 2015, BG and CCC signed a LOI for the supply of gas to a future Jenin power station. The terms of this LOI were vaguer than the Jordan document. No volumes were stated despite CCC indicating that it sought around 64 million cubic feet of gas. Gaza Marine's expected production would be able to supply both Jordan and Jenin at the respective volumes, especially if there was some flexibility in the contracts. BG were taking a cautious approach to CCC's Jenin power station idea. It existed only in their minds and there were enormous hurdles to overcome before it became a reality. CCC had presented this idea to BG several years before and in the intervening time, had made almost no progress on the project. Amongst the many obstacles to surmount, was the need for Israeli approval and co-operation throughout the construction and operation of the power station. Israel had a number of reasons for withholding co-operation: security, its control of the Palestinian economy and the competition to its own commercial interests as the state-owned power company, IEC, was the largest electricity supplier to the West Bank. The Palestinians were valuable customers for Israeli electricity.

BG required Israeli co-operation to access Jordan and use Israeli infrastructure deliver the gas to the Kingdom. BG proposed to pipe the Gaza Marine gas to a newly built facility at Ashkelon on Israel's Mediterranean coast. The gas would then enter the Israeli transmission system and an equivalent volume of gas would be exported to Jordan through the pipeline that connects Israel to its neighbour. On one level, this was a straightforward commercial transaction. BG and Israel would need to agree a tariff for the use of the Israeli pipeline system. This was politically and legally complicated. Israel at the time had no developed system for what is known as "*third party access*" i.e. allowing others to use the pipelines. The Israeli pipeline network was a state-owned and operated system and previously had no need for third party access regulations. This is the case in many countries where the state owns and controls the infrastructure. It is only usually in liberalised markets such as the UK, where sophisticated third party access regulations exist. So, BG would have to obtain either a change in the Israeli regulations or at least the granting of an exemption. It would be asking for this on behalf of Palestinian gas which many in Israel see as a threat to Israel and providing funds for terrorists. So, on another level, this project also had a political filter over it.

While the signatures of the LOIs with Jordan and the Palestinians had followed in quick succession, there was no quick follow up with an outline agreement with Israel. The Israelis seemed to be dragging their feet and appeared reluctant to negotiate a deal. The day after signing the LOI with the Palestinians in mid-June, CCC were chasing BG for progress and blaming BG for any delay. Sami, on BG's behalf, made it clear that BG was not the cause of the delay and that both companies were now waiting for the Israelis. BG representatives were scheduled to meet the Israeli side at the end of July 2015. While in the region, the BG delegation was also planning to meet Dr Mustafa in Ramallah. At the same time, the BG Chief Executive Helge Lund was due to meet the Palestinian Prime Minister Rami Hamdallah who was scheduled to visit London. BG were treading carefully through the web of Palestinian politics in arranging meetings with both Hamdallah and Mustafa at the same time. BG learnt from CCC that Hamdallah was trying to restrict Mustafa's role in government and make him focus on his role at PIF. Mustafa was reportedly trying to get an invite to the London meeting by claiming that BG were demanding his presence. BG was making no such demand as they were quite happy to meet him in Ramallah while meeting the PM in London.

Sami, Victoria and the rest of the small team at BG working on the Gaza Marine project were also navigating internal BG politics. The BG executive, under Lund, were not filled with joy when the team reported on the agreements with the Jordanians and Palestinians. They were impressed that the team had been able to reach any sort of agreement that made economic sense. The BG executive was given a formal chance to consider the Gaza Marine project in September 2015. The team presented a paper to BG's Executive Committee requesting funds to pursue the negotiations and turn the LOIs into fully fleshed agreements. Victoria produced an accompanying presentation for Lund which, like the paper itself, set out the political, technical and economic background, described the commercial concept of the project and outlined the risks. The paper asked for a budget of $15 million and authority to sign LOIs. The BG executive did not though give the go ahead to pursue this opportunity and there was still no budget for this project. Instead, the team were told to drag their feet over any future negotiations. So, the BG team had to push back on the enthusiasm of the Palestinians, the Jordanians and CCC to turn the LOIs into a legally binding gas sales and purchase agreement. BG had a perfect excuse for the go slow and it had nothing to do with Israel. While the team had been negotiating with the Jordanians, elsewhere in BG, negotiations of a very different variety had come to fruition.

On 8 April 2015, the super major oil and gas company Royal Dutch Shell announced a takeover of BG Group. The takeover was completed in February 2016. During this period, BG was pre-occupied with the takeover process and then with the integration into Shell. With the takeover of BG Group, Shell was set to acquire the 90% stake in the Gaza Marine licence. As with all takeovers, Shell had to obtain approval from each of the jurisdictions in which BG or Shell had interests, that included the Palestinian territories. The PNA had no hesitation in giving this approval. They were exchanging one FTSE 100 oil and gas company for an even larger FTSE 100 oil and gas company and a much better known global brand name. As part of the takeover, Shell committed to making savings and "*synergies*" to use the corporate jargon. This included selling non-material assets. Gaza Marine was in this category. Shell had no interest in developing Gaza Marine and getting involved in Israel. Doing business with Israel even in support of a Palestinian project would threaten its much more material interests in the Gulf and its ambition to re-enter Iran one day.

Gas for Gaza

While Shell was absorbing BG, Blair's team as noted above were re-thinking how to bring a reliable gas supply to the Gaza Strip. The project was named Gas for Gaza (G4G) and was based on building a pipeline to supply Israeli natural gas to the Gaza power station. The project's first stage was a feasibility study on the technical aspects, including the route for the pipeline to bring gas from the Israeli gas grid. Support from the Dutch and Qatari governments would underpin the project. In August 2015, Blair's team established a task force in conjunction with the PNA and in September received approval in principle from the Israeli government. In its report to the April 2016 AHLC meeting, the Quartet team set out a timetable for the project which scheduled construction to start by Q1 2018 and gas to flow along the pipeline in 2020. This report was issued in the name of the Office of the Quartet and not in the name of Blair. There had been a significant change. Tony Blair resigned as Office of the Quartet Representative in May 2015.

The Quartet team made some progress in implementing its Gas for Gaza project. It undertook a series of studies on the legal and commercial aspects of the project. The team also saw a new opportunity to make progress on Gaza Marine as part of its plans. The Shell takeover of BG seemed to offer the chance of a breakthrough. In its report to the September 2016 AHLC meeting, the team stated,

"As a priority, energy security in the West Bank and Gaza can be significantly improved through development of indigenous resources. The Gaza Marine gas field is a national Palestinian resource that could meet Palestinian energy demand for a number of decades, reducing reliance upon energy imports and generating considerable revenues for the sector (saving some $100 million annually in diesel fuel costs). It is therefore imperative for investment to be made to develop the Gaza Marine gas field. There is now the opportunity to expedite the development of this field, following years of stalled progress. This opportunity has been triggered by the recent change in ownership of the field".[53]

This was a misreading of the situation in light of Shell's lack of interest in developing the Gaza Marine field.

In its May 2017 report, the Quartet team was able to report that the technical, commercial and legal feasibility studies were complete and the start of the next phase. This was the planning and permitting phase. This would first require mapping out the planning processes for the pipeline with both the Israel authorities and the PNA. The relevant Israeli regulatory authorities, the Israeli Natural Gas Authority and Israeli Natural Gas Lines, were members of the project task force. The project team estimated that this phase would take approximately two years to complete. At the same time, the team would work with the PNA to map out its planning process. In the meantime, the energy situation in the Gaza Strip deteriorated with the Gaza power station struggling to get access to diesel fuel, in

---

53 AHLC September 2016.

part due to a dispute between the PNA and the Hamas government in Gaza over the taxation of fuel. Also, the optimism over the breakthrough on Gaza Marine was misplaced. In its September 2017 report, the Quartet team stated, "*The development of Gaza Marine – an indigenous Palestinian gas field – is a long-term priority. To date, progress has been slow with the field's development, due to ongoing political and security challenges to date but prospects for development remain positive. Development of Gaza Marine would greatly enhance the Palestinian territory's energy independence and could generate revenues for the PA of USD 2.5 billion over its 25-year production lifetime.*"[54] The team's figures for revenue and the production came from a report from the Washington DC-based Brookings Institute.[55] These numbers appear to be based on a misreading of previous accounts of the Gaza Marine field. The revenue figure of $2.5 billion is given in previous reports as the low end of the range of total revenue.[56] The licence granted to BG in 2002 was 25-year development licence, this includes the period of developing the field and decommissioning at the end of the field's life. BG and it partners planned on a 15 year production lifetime.

By September 2018, the Quartet was able to report further progress on its Gas to Gaza project. The task force overseeing the project had agreed a draft commercial proposal. Also, the task force had a new member with the EU providing support. Two obstacles remained to making the pipeline a reality. The first was agreement on the details of the commercial arrangements for the pipeline, including which entity on the Palestinian side would be the gas buyer. The second was money. The Quartet needed to secure $80 million to finance the pipeline's construction. The lack of peace process, the threat of more conflict in Gaza and continued Palestinian internal political instability all acted as deterrents to further donor aid and finance

---

54 AHLC September 2017.

55 Boersma, Sachs (2015)

56 Henderson (2014)

from international banks. The timetable for the project was slipping. The Quartet had already pushed back the expected date for first gas deliveries to 2021. By the April 2019 AHLC meeting, the Quartet was giving a completion date of 2022-23. It reported progress on the pipeline's design and the economic, social and environmental impact assessment. All the work conducted so far could be done in an office. No on-the-ground physical work on the pipeline had yet taken place. The real test of whether the Gas for Gaza project could succeed would come when finance was secured and work could start on the ground to construct the pipeline. When this moment arrived, Israel's approval in principle would be tested. Will Israel allow work to go ahead? Also, will Hamas and the PNA allow work to go ahead?

Monopoly Controversy
With the breakdown in the Kerry peace process in April 2014, Israel lost any interest that it might have had in pursuing an agreement on Gaza Marine. Any deal with the Palestinians was going to be controversial and with almost no political value for the Netanyahu government. In any case, it was about to become embroiled in a separate controversy in the natural gas industry. The controversy, which would prove a distraction for Israel, surfaced towards the end of 2015 but had been bubbling away for some time. The issue of Noble and Delek's monopoly supply position came to a head in December 2015 and stirred up turmoil in the Israeli natural gas sector. To address the monopoly position, Noble and Delek had reached an agreement with the anti-trust regulator to sell some of their licences offshore Israel. In December 2015, the regulator reneged on the agreement and announced that he intended to re-negotiate. There was outrage from Noble and Delek as Netanyahu's government scrambled to find a solution. The government's proposed solution served only to stir up a political storm. Netanyahu proposed invoking never-before-used powers to override the regulator and take direct regulatory control of this matter. However, he could not get support from key ministers

in his government and parliament, the Knesset, demanded a vote on the issue. With a parliamentary majority of one, the maths would not add up for Netanyahu as three members of the government were forced to recuse themselves due to a potential conflict of interest. In a moment of high political drama, Netanyahu made clear that the vote would be one of confidence in his government. Given his slim majority, the emotions aroused by the issue and the implications of losing the vote, this was a high risk gamble. Losing the vote would trigger an election, which he risked losing. Netanyahu, who had a reputation for political adroitness, seems to have misjudged the situation and made the situation worse. In the end he blinked first. He postponed the vote and embarked on extensive negotiations to agree a new framework for the natural gas sector. The resulting agreement, finalised in mid-2017, imposed more stringent conditions on Noble and Delek but resolved the issue. However, the episode had caused immense damage to the sector. It caused an 18 month delay on the Leviathan project, leading to Noble and Delek freezing work, re-assigning people and in some cases losing skilled staff. Israel's reputation as a destination for hydrocarbon investment was tarnished, making it harder to attract new investors to counteract Noble and Delek's monopoly position.

New Kid on the Block
With the completion of its takeover of BG Group on 15 February 2016, Royal Dutch Shell set about finding a buyer for the 90% stake in Gaza Marine that it had inherited. As when BG had sought a buyer, it found the number of candidates very limited. There was though a new kid on the block and one who might be interested in taking on the Gaza Marine challenge. The company was Energean, a Greek-based oil and gas company. Energean had bought two licences offshore Israel from Noble and Delek as part of their sale of assets to meet the new anti-trust agreement. Shell and Energean were, though, unable to reach an agreement. Shell were driving a hard

bargain and demanding a price for Gaza Marine that Energean could not stomach. Also, the PNA were not enthusiastic about the deal. They did not want a company with strong Israeli ties also having a stake in its largest natural resource. More importantly politically, the deal would not go down well with Palestinian public opinion. First, it would highlight that Gaza Marine remained undeveloped and the PNA had failed to realise its potential. Second, large multinational companies doing a deal and making money out of a Palestinian asset while the economy got nothing was also politically unpalatable.

Instead, Shell agreed a deal with the existing partner in Gaza Marine, CCC, and with PIF. In effect, Shell handed back its 90% share to the PNA to be divided equally between CCC and PIF. The result was that, in theory, CCC now owned 55% of the Gaza Marine licence and PIF held 45%. However, CCC and PIF agreed that eventually this shareholding would change. Neither CCC, nor PIF, had the technical or financial expertise to develop an offshore gas field such as Gaza Marine. CCC and PIF had agreed to each take a stake of 27.5% in the Gaza Marine licence, giving them a total of 55% and find a new international partner for the remaining 45%. This division of the equity in the Gaza Marine licence was not accidental. It gave CCC and PIF combined a controlling stake in the licence. They could not be outvoted by any future partner. They had learnt one lesson from the BG days, who with their majority stake could outvote the other partners in the licence.

Shell did not simply hand back its share for free. Shell has not let go of the licence completely. As part of the deal to hand back its 90% share, it negotiated an overriding royalty interest. This means it still has a financial interest in the Gaza Marine licence. When the gas field is developed and gas (and crucially revenue) starts to flow, Shell will obtain a share of the revenue in payment for giving up its stake in the licence. This is an established mechanism in the oil and gas industry and allows a company to benefit in the future from a licence where it has invested but has yet to receive any return. However, Shell no longer has any direct influence over the gas field's development and will play no part in the decision-making process concerning Gaza Marine.

For the remaining Gaza Marine partners, while they both had an increased stake in the licence, they were now without a partner that had international prestige and more importantly, extensive experience in developing offshore gas fields and finding markets for that gas. CCC and PIF therefore started a search for a new international partner who could bring the technical expertise, gas marketing skills and international advocacy. Both the PNA (including PIF) and CCC viewed an international partner (first BG, then Shell) as playing an important role in reducing the political risks to the project. A company such as BG or Shell could mobilise its home government (i.e. the British government) and wider political support for the project. At the same time, involvement of an international partner reduced the risk of Israeli interference (in the view of CCC and PIF). For CCC as well, an international partner is needed to transact with the Israelis. While CCC can talk to the Israeli government, it would have found it difficult to enter into contractual arrangements with Israel. The CCC subsidiary that held the Gaza Marine licence is a Beirut-registered company and as Lebanon is still at war with Israel, cannot have commercial relations with Israel.

The prime candidate for international partner was Energean. Indeed, it may have been the only candidate. None of the major international oil and gas companies, such as BP, ExxonMobil or Total would be interested in taking on Gaza Marine. It is too small and too politically contentious. Despite the failure to reach an agreement with Shell, Energean still seemed keen to be involved in Gaza Marine. Its CEO, Mathios Rigas, told Reuters in July 2018 that Energean was ready to buy a 45% stake in Gaza Marine and act as operator. He did, though, add the caveat, "*if that is something the host governments approve*".[57] His reference to more than one host government suggests he sought approval not just from the PNA, as the host government for the Gaza Marine licence, but also from the Israeli government. The *"host governments"* did not give their approval. Energean's enthusiasm was not converted into any contractual role in the licence. The only companies with a formal stake in the licence remained CCC and PIF.

The need to have an international partner was, though, not urgent. There was no prospect of any progress on Gaza Marine's development. The political environment remained hostile to any improvement in relations between the Israelis and the Palestinians. There was no peace process and the Israeli government under Prime Minister Netanyahu was determined to isolate the Palestinians and Gaza in particular. Israel continued to impose a stranglehold on Gaza, with severe limitations on the ability of people and goods to leave or enter the territory. Gaza's residents were not passively accepting their situation. On 30 March 2018, around 30,000 Gazans gathered on the border to highlight their grievances and press their demands. The protest was named *"The Great March of Return"* by the activists who organised it. The purpose was to press their demand for the right of return of Palestinian refugees who had been forced to flee in 1948 and 1967. The protestors were also voicing their opposition to the restrictions placed on them and to US policy in the region. These protests were held every Friday for the next six weeks in the run up to 15 May. The day that marks both Israel's independence and the events that Palestinians call the *"Nakba"*, the catastrophe of their expulsion from their homes by Israeli forces in 1948. The protests in spring 2018 would culminate in mid-May as the Israeli-Palestinian conflict was once again pushed back to the top of the political agenda.

---

57 Reuters, 6 July 2018, https://www.reuters.com/article/ us-gaza-gas-energean-israel/energean-ready-to-take-gaza-marine-gas-field-stake-if-israel-palestinians-agree-idUSKBN1JW1D8

CHAPTER 12

"BETWEEN FANTASY AND REALITY"[58] (2020 - PRESENT)

Decisions made thousands of miles away in Washington DC would put the Israeli/Palestinian conflict back on the front pages and top of the news bulletins for the wrong reasons. The election of Donald Trump as US President in November 2016 and his subsequent approach to the Israeli/Palestinian conflict did not provide any hope of a breakthrough. Although he promised, *"the deal of the century"* to bring peace between Israel and the Palestinians, he did not deliver on that promise. He placed his son-in-law Jared Kushner in charge of delivering on this promise. Jared, who had no previous experience in international relations and diplomacy, soon found himself out of his depth and compromised by conflicts of interest with his business interests. Any hope that Kushner entertained of bringing peace was undermined by Trump's most significant and public intervention in the conflict. Trump recognised Jerusalem as Israel's capital and authorised the move of the US Embassy from Tel Aviv to Jerusalem. On 14 May 2018, the official opening ceremony for the new US Embassy in Jerusalem was held in the city. In Gaza on the same day, clashes between protestors and Israeli security forces resulted in 52

---

58 Maya Jacobs, CEO of Climate Net, quoted in the Jerusalem Post, 21 June 2023, see: https://www.jpost.com/business-and-innovation/energy-and-infra-structure/article-747139

Palestinians deaths, the highest single day death toll since 2014.[59] The footage of the protests with thousands of angry Palestinians and black clouds of smoke billowing from burning tyres overshadowed the formalities and backslapping of the ceremony in Jerusalem.

While the embassy move cemented the already rock solid relationship between Israel and the US, it punctured a hole in the already damaged relationship between the US and the PNA. The Palestinians already long suspicious of the close US-Israel relationship, were now in no doubt of the partisanship of the US. The credibility of the US and any *"deal of the century"* that it may concoct was in shreds. The US government was not finished with its interventions in the conflict. The US State department quietly downgraded the status of the Palestinian representation in Washington DC. More publicly, the US withdrew funding from UN agencies providing support to Palestinian refugees. In particular, the US stopped funding the UN Works and Relief Agency (UNWRA). This decision had a disproportionate impact on Gaza, where a significant percentage of the population rely on UNRWA for their livelihoods, health care or education and in some cases, basics such as food.

Meanwhile, there was no sign from the Trump administration of its much-hyped peace plan. Speculation filled the vacuum. The peace plan would favour Israel's interests. The *"deal of the century"* was a re-heated version of the 2002 Arab Peace Initiative. In comments in February 2019, Netanyahu suggested that the peace plan resembled the 2002 Arab peace plan. While the US had not yet published its *"deal of the century"*, it did seem to have worked behind the scenes to bring Israel and Arab states (but not the Palestinians) closer together. In 2017, there were a series of signs that Israel and key Arab states, especially Saudi Arabia, were inching closer together. Both sides made public statements that seemed to indicate growing ties. There

---

59 BBC News website, 14 May 2018, https://www.bbc.co.uk/news/world-middle-east-44104599

were setbacks. Most Arab states condemned the US Embassy move to Jerusalem and repeated their support for the international position on Jerusalem and the Palestinians' claim to East Jerusalem as the capital of a future state. The embassy move had been expected so only caused ripples in relations between Israel and the US on one side and the Arab states on the other. More serious was the Khashoggi incident in October 2018. The Saudi dissident journalist Jamal Khashoggi was murdered in the Saudi consulate in Istanbul apparently on the orders of the Saudi Crown Prince Muhammad bin Salman. The US had to distance itself from Saudi. However, the Arab-Israeli diplomatic warming resumed in November when Netanyahu visited Oman. The first visit by an Israeli prime minister to a Gulf state. The diplomatic offensive continued in February 2019 in Warsaw, when Israeli and Arab states (but again not the Palestinians) gathered round the same table to discuss efforts to resist Iran.

Following the Warsaw summit, Kushner headed back to the Middle East in his latest efforts to put together the so-called "*deal of the century*". This time his efforts would be focussed on an economic peace.[60] This focus on the economic aspects seemed to recall Blair's efforts at the start of the decade, where he (and Netanyahu) spoke about focussing on an economic peace. Blair put the Gaza Marine project at the centre of his economic peace plan in 2011. This idea was taken up by John Kerry in his peace efforts. Was history about to repeat itself? Had the State Department dusted off the Gaza Marine file? Was Kushner going to put the weight of the US government behind Gaza Marine? Was Gaza Marine going to experience another moment of hope or another false dawn? In any economic strand of a Palestinian-Israeli peace deal, the Gaza Marine project should feature. It is one of the Palestinians' largest natural resources and economic assets. It has the potential to make a significant contribution to

---

60   Al-Jazeera, 24 February 2019, https://www.aljazeera.com/news/2019/02/jared-kushner-heads-middle-east-promote-peace-plan-190224102141749.html

Palestinian economic development and to reshaping the relations between Israelis and Palestinians.

Kushner and the US government did indeed go down the cul-de-sac of *"economic peace"*. On 22 June 2019, the White House published its plan for economic peace, entitled *"Peace to Prosperity"*.[61] The plan claimed that more than $50 billion over 10 years could be attracted to the Palestinian territories and neighbouring Arab states (Egypt, Lebanon and Jordan) through a mixture of grants, loans and private sector investment. The plan was set out in two documents: a 40-page narrative document that was heavy on broad and visionary statements and a 96-page plan that contained more details on the projects envisioned including likely cost and timescale. Both documents mention Gaza Marine. In the 40-page narrative document, there is a brief mention of Gaza Marine on p17 in a five line paragraph on developing the Palestinian natural resources. In the 96-page document, a little more detail is given on Gaza Marine on p43, again in the natural resources section. The plan gives an estimated cost of $1 billion for the project, made up of $750 million of loans and $250 million from the private sector. The document also states that Gaza Marine is part of phase 2 of the economic peace plan and gives a timeframe of eight years.

The inclusion of Gaza Marine in the *"Peace to Prosperity"* documents provides tacit US government acknowledgement that the Gaza Marine gas resources are Palestinian property. As the documents were prepared by a US administration that has shown some of the strongest support of any US administration towards Israel, this makes it harder for any Israeli government, politician or activist to claim that the gas does not belong to the Palestinians. Indeed, the documents may well have been prepared in collaboration with the Israeli government or at least shown to Israel before publication. In that case, the *"Peace to Prosperity"* plan also provides tacit Israeli

---

61 https://www.whitehouse.gov/peacetoprosperity/

government acknowledgement that the Gaza Marine gas belongs to the Palestinians. This is a step on from the position articulated by the Israeli government in the 2001 court case, where they stated the gas was in "*no-man's waters*" and they did not know who it belonged to.

The "*Peace to Prosperity*" plan also lists several other energy related projects and indeed has a whole section dedicated to power generation. The plan recognises that the Palestinians and in particular Gaza's residents, face an energy crisis. The power-related projects include upgrading the Gaza power station and converting it to run on natural gas. The plan gives Gaza Marine as one of the potential sources of gas but also contains a project to construct a pipeline to connect the power station to the Israeli gas grid. Such a pipeline would not preclude Gaza Marine supplying gas to the Gaza power station. In the event that the Gaza Marine field is ever developed, the gas is likely to land first at Ashkelon in Israel. A pipeline connection to the Gaza power station would allow the gas to generate electricity for Gaza's residents. This was part of the development concept that BG envisaged for the field.

The listing of Gaza Marine and other energy plans in the "*Peace to Prosperity*" documents, even with an estimated cost and timeframe, did not bring them any closer to becoming a reality. The economic peace plan did not go into any further detail. The plan did not assign responsibility for its implementation and it was unclear who or what agency will undertake the plan. It was also not clear who will provide the grants and loans to finance the plan. There were no further details on where the $750 million loan listed for Gaza Marine will come from. Banks, both private sector institutions and development banks, are reluctant to lend to upstream development projects such as Gaza Marine. This reluctance has historically been due to the level of risk involved but increasingly is also due to a reluctance to invest in fossil fuels. This policy is driven by their response to the climate crisis. Oil and gas companies have typically financed the development of resources from their own funds and not relied on project finance from banks. The plan was also not clear on the source of the $250 million of private sector funding. This could come from the existing private sector partner CCC or a new strategic investor or both. In any case, it represents a smaller share than any private sector partner is likely to have in the project. Gaza Marine's eventual development is likely to be funded almost entirely from the private sector. Such funding would provide a real boost to the Palestinian economy. It would not just be an injection of money but demonstrate that the project was robust and that the economy can attract hard-headed investors.

The White House published the *"Peace to Prosperity"* documents as a prelude to a summit intended to promote the plan and attract some of the finance required for implementation. The summit was held in the Gulf state of Bahrain on 25 and 26 June 2019. Like the documents, the summit was heavy on rhetoric and style and light on substance. Both the Israeli government and the PNA stayed away. Indeed, there were very few Palestinians who were willing to attend the event. Palestinians representing a wide range of views condemned the summit as one-sided, a talking shop, lacking in substance and a fig leaf for reinforcing Israel's occupation of the Palestinian territories. Both the economic peace plan and the summit lacked credibility in the eyes of many Palestinians and external observers and commentators. Some participants at the summit, disputed Kushner's proposition that economic peace would lead to full peace. Christine Lagarde, managing director of the IMF, in her remarks to the event noted that a *"satisfactory peace"* is imperative for prosperity. She went on, *"It's a matter of putting all the ingredients together"*.[62]

The Bahrain summit did not lead to any immediate breakthroughs, either economic or political. There were no immediate injections of cash into the Palestinian economy, no major investment deals

---

62 https://www.aljazeera.com/news/2019/06/led-bahrain-workshop-palestine-latest-updates-190624092422392.html

signed, or loans granted. On the political front, Kushner and the US government did not publish their plan for comprehensive peace deal between the Palestinians and the Israelis. This was not surprising as the political climate remained hostile to any peace initiatives. Israel was in the midst of its own political crisis with acting Prime Minister Netanyahu unable to form a government after the April 2019 general election and facing possible indictment in three corruption cases. The political deadlock continued after a second general election in September 2019 with Netanyahu's Likud party losing seats and again unable to form a government. Meanwhile, the Trump administration lurched from crisis to crisis as calls for President Trump's impeachment grew until September 2019 when the Democrat-led House of Representatives' committees opened impeachment hearings. In a possible sign that a Palestinian-Israeli peace plan was no longer a US government priority, one of the key figures behind the *"Peace to Prosperity"* plan, David Greenblatt announced his resignation in early September 2019. On the Palestinian side, the PNA had few options as it was politically untenable for them to support the US initiative and they had little leverage to push for a peace process acceptable to them. Furthermore, deep divisions remained in Palestinian politics between the West Bank ruled by the PNA and Gaza ruled by Hamas.

As President Trump became embroiled in impeachment hearings in January 2020, he launched his so-called *"deal of the century"* to bring peace between the Palestinians and Israelis. It was the *"deal of the century"* for Israel and especially for Prime Minister Netanyahu, who could hardly disguise his glee as he stood by Trump at the press conference to launch the peace place on 28 January. The plan gave Israel almost everything Netanyahu wanted. Sub-titled *"A Vision to Improve the Lives of the Palestinian and Israeli People"*, it envisioned a de-militarised Palestinian statelet with no access to the outside world and not in control of its own resources, including its gas reserves. The US *"vision"* for peace included ignoring Palestinians' claim to East Jerusalem and offered Israel sovereignty over all of the city. It also offered Israel sovereignty over most West Bank settlements and a strip of land down the Jordan River Valley to create a security buffer zone. Crucially for Gaza Marine, the plan also foresaw Israeli sovereignty over Gaza waters, which would hand control of the gas resources to Israel and grant it control over their development. Drafting of the peace plan, was reportedly, co-ordinated both with Netanyahu and the Israeli opposition leader Benny Gantz. Both enthusiastically backed the Trump plan.

This time it was the Palestinians and the wider Arab world that rejected a US peace plan from the start. PNA President Mahmoud Abbas reportedly refused to receive a copy of the peace plan, so that the US and Israel could not claim that he had been consulted. Indeed, no senior Palestinian appears to have been involved in putting together the plan. Although a few Arab states were represented at the 28 January press conference, most expressed scepticism about the plan or outright hostility. This included key states such as Saudi Arabia, which had appeared to be becoming more closely aligned with US and Israeli policy towards the peace process. In the wider world, many other US allies including some European states also expressed scepticism or at best gave it a lukewarm reception. The PNA refused to co-operate with US over the peace plan and went further by withdrawing security co-operation with both the US and Israel. In the face of this hostility and lack of co-operation, the next steps for implementing the 28 January peace plan seemed unclear.

In any case, Israel was absorbed by its own internal political difficulties. By the start of 2020, Israel had held two inconclusive elections within a space of less than nine months. It faced a third election in early March. Following both 2019 elections, neither Prime Minister Netanyahu nor leader of the opposition Blue and White party Gantz had been able to form a working coalition government. The elections had also seen a notable surge in support for Arab parties as Israeli Arabs became more engaged in the political process. Adding to the sense of political crisis was Netanyahu's indictment on corruption charges. Gantz refused to include Netanyahu's Likud party in a national unity government while Netanyahu remained as leader. Likud continued to back Netanyahu. An attempt to unseat him was soundly defeated. The March 2020 election proved equally inconclusive. Likud and its allies won the most seats but were still short of an overall majority. Support for the list of Arab parties remained strong and they increased the number of seats to 15. Netanyahu was unable to reach an agreement with potential coalition partners, which did not include the Arab list. Gantz was given the opportunity to form a new government. While the Arab parties were potential power brokers, they refused to join a formal coalition with either Gantz or Netanyahu. They had significant ideological and policy differences with both. Also, some of the potential coalition partners refused to sit in a government that included Arab parties, most notably the right wing Israel Our Home party led by Avigdor Lieberman.

On the Palestinian side, there were signs of tentative moves towards bridging the gap between the PNA in Ramallah and the Hamas administration in Gaza. The two sides were inching closer together, driven by a common opposition to Trump, his support for Israel and his *"deal of the century"*. The first concrete sign of improved relations occurred in October 2017 with the visit of the PNA Prime Minister Rami Hamdallah to Gaza, the first such visit since Hamas took control in June 2007. The PNA proposed an agreement with Hamas under which Hamas would give back control over some aspects of Gaza to the PNA including control of crossing points, tax collection, the judiciary and the land registry. The counter proposal from Hamas was implementation of an agreement dating from 2011 (but never implemented) under which the two sides would form an interim unity government that would hold elections in both the West Bank and the Gaza Strip. In early 2020, the PNA President Mahmud Abbas announced his intention to visit Gaza and meet with the Hamas leader Ismail Haniyeh. Such a meeting could break the deadlock. Before visiting Gaza, Abbas wanted guarantees from

Israel that he would be allowed to return to Ramallah at the end of the visit. He had realistic fears that the Israeli government would not permit him to return to Ramallah and would confine him to Gaza in retaliation for trying to secure an agreement with Hamas. As Abbas prepared to send two of his senior officials to the Gaza Strip to lay the groundwork for his visit, a new challenge emerged that put all politics and indeed much of life on hold, the coronavirus pandemic. President Abbas did not make his visit to the Gaza Strip in 2020. There was no need for guarantees from the Israeli government. Like many people, as the full force of the coronavirus pandemic became clear, Abbas had to stay at home.

Israeli Gas Exports

On 1 January 2020, Israel made the first exports of natural gas to Jordan under the deal signed in September 2016 between the Jordanian power company NEPCO and the Noble-Delek consortium.[63] News of the start of Israeli gas imports sparked protests in the Jordanian capital Amman on 10 January and again on 17 January. Thousands of people took to the street to express their anger at the deal. Some also called for the dismissal of the government. In both protests the security forces prevented the demonstrators reaching a central Amman square and potentially attracting even greater numbers. Later in the month there were also protests against President Trump's Middle East peace plan. These protests showed the strength of feeling against relations with Israel. However, the Jordanian. Government remained firmly in control and the gas kept flowing. The government also successfully prevented parliament from intervening in the gas deal. The Jordanian parliament attempted to pass measures to block the deal and demanded that the deal was not valid until it received parliamentary ratification. The constitutional court ruled these measures unconstitutional as the deal was between private parties

---

63 https://www.reuters.com/article/idUSL8N2960Q9/

rather than between states and therefore did not require parliament's ratification.

A few days later, Israeli gas also started to flow along the East Med pipeline to Egypt. This was a result of a deal signed in February 2018 between the Noble-Delek consortium and an Egyptian company Dolphinus Holdings.[64] The original deal was for 64 billion cubic metres of gas over ten years, worth an estimated $15 billion. This was later extended to 85 billion cubic metres over 15 years. When the deal was first announced, it caused surprise in Egypt. This was a country with some of the largest gas reserves in the eastern Mediterranean and which exported gas. Why was it now importing gas, Israeli gas at that and what was this company Dolphinus? Very few people had heard of it. I had heard of it but that did not mean I had any particular insight into the company. In 2016, Dolphinus hired me on a short-term consultancy contract to represent them at an energy conference in Tel Aviv. It was difficult for any of the company's Egyptian principals to travel to Israel and their presence may have attracted criticism back home and put their friends in government in a difficult situation. At the time Dolphinus were attempting to show that there was a market for Israeli gas in Egypt and answer the question about why Egypt needed to import gas, especially as it had recently discovered the giant Zohr field. The short answer was that demand was outstripping supply and Egypt needed more gas, even with Zohr. I attended the conference, sat on a panel and networked. I wrote a briefing note for the company and a few weeks later travelled to Cairo to brief the principals in person.

So what is Dolphinus and who are its principals? Dolphinus Holdings is a company registered in the British Virgin Islands and seems to be only a vehicle for importing gas from Israel. It does not appear to have any other business. Who is driving this vehicle? The founders listed on its (out of date) website are Dr Alaa Arafa,

---

64 https://www.reuters.com/article/idUSKCN1G31BK/

Khaled Abu Bakr and Mohamed Khalifa. During my association with Dolphinus, I met all three. They are all Egyptian entrepreneurs. Arafa qualified as a medical doctor but then joined his father's textile business, Arafa Holdings of which he is now the Chairman and Chief Executive. His father was a close associate of former Egyptian president Hosni Mubarak. Arafa has good relations with the government and also with Israel. He was a member of the Egyptian team which negotiated with Israel to set up the Qualified Industrial Zones (QIZ). These were established in the aftermath of the 1979 Camp David peace agreement between Egypt and Israel to promote economic relations between the two countries. Businesses (mainly textile) operating in them enjoy tax holidays and preferential access to both markets and to the US market. Abu Bakr is a stalwart of the Egyptian gas sector. I had met him previously when I worked for BG Egypt. He brings the natural gas knowledge to Dolphinus. The third entrepreneur, Khalifa, sits on the boards of at least two European fashion companies and has a background in finance and investment.

When the deal between Dolphinus and Noble-Delek was announced in February 2018, there was some outrage but no street protests as seen in Amman. The Egyptian government would not tolerate such dissent. Relations with Israel and especially business deals were still controversial in Egypt. Opponents of the deal demanded that the government block it. The Ministry of Petroleum put out a bland statement that it was an agreement between two private parties, and they had no power to intervene. While Noble-Delek was a private company, there were suspicions that Dolphinus was not and was closely tied to the Egyptian state, if not owned by the state. Arafa, Abu Bakr and Khalifa appeared to be acting as a front for government agencies, possibly the Egyptian intelligence service.[65]

---

65 For a more detailed analysis of Dolphinus and other companies involved in importing Israeli gas, see: https://www.madamasr.com/en/2018/10/23/feature/politics/whos-buying-israeli-gas-a-company-owned-by-the-general-intelligence-service/

The gas that was flowing to Jordan and Egypt was coming from the offshore Israeli field, Leviathan. The field started production in the dying days of 2019 to meet the target set by its operator Noble. Israel was now a significant player in the eastern Mediterranean gas sector with the potential to emerge as a major supplier to world markets. The gas supply to Jordan and Egypt created mutually beneficial relations. Israel gained a new important source of revenue and a demonstration that there was a market for any future gas discoveries. For Jordan, the gas made a vital contribution to its energy supply and provided a more affordable source of energy than imports from the Gulf or further afield. For Egypt, the gas supplemented its own production and reduced the risk of shortages at times of peak demand, especially in the summer months. The contract between Dolphinus and Noble-Delek was for an "interruptible" supply. The gas did not have to flow constantly. Egypt could choose when to take the gas. Even with access to Israeli gas, Egypt would still face shortages and just as events had disrupted the gas flow in the other direction in 2011-12, events later in the decade would also cause disruption.

For Gaza Marine, the start of Israeli gas exports was, in theory, good news. It strengthened the argument that the Israeli government could no longer stand in the way of Gaza Marine's development, gas production and the PNA's choice of market for the gas. The argument went: Israel was now to all intents and purposes self-sufficient in gas, and it had secured export markets for that gas. Therefore, what right did the Israeli government have to stand in the way of the Palestinians developing their own gas resources and earning their own revenue. The counter argument revolved around the long-standing concern that the revenue could be used to fund terrorism against Israel. While a real concern and threat, the use of a mechanism such as an escrow account with independent oversight could deal with this argument.

Gas for Gaza
In June 2020, I was invited to work again on Gazan gas, albeit

remotely due to the restrictions imposed as a result of the Covid-19 pandemic. This time I would be working on the Gas for Gaza project rather than Gaza Marine. The invite came from an environmental consultancy who were bidding to act as a consultant to prepare the environmental and social impact assessment (ESIA) for the Gas for Gaza project. This was a stage that Gaza Marine has yet to reach: the preparation of a full ESIA.

The UN were administering the tender process for the ESIA on behalf of the Office of the Quartet, which headed the taskforce implementing Gas for Gaza. The Dutch government were providing the funding. The UN had issued a request for proposals which set out the context in Gaza, the scope of the Gas for Gaza project and the requirements of the ESIA project. The project would be in two parts. The first was an environmental and social scoping study, expected to take six months to complete and then the full ESIA which would take a further nine and a half months.

The proposal document stated that, "*The Gaza Strip has gone from a situation of full electricity access, with all associated benefits, to one of severe deprivation.*" It also stated that, "*The Palestinian territory faces significant energy security challenges, which are especially severe in the Gaza Strip. The Gaza Strip is suffering a humanitarian crisis, which is characterized by a severe shortage of both energy and water.*" Electricity demand had risen since 2010 to 500MW but supply was only 210MW at peak and rarely above 200MW. The solution proposed was, "*An increased and reliable power supply is urgently needed to address the energy crisis. The supply of natural gas to the Gaza Strip is the central component of the solution to develop the Gaza's Strip energy sector.*"

The gas supply would initially come from Israel, but the proposal document recognised that, "*In the long term there is the possibility for the Gaza Strip to be supplied by the Gaza Marine gas field*". The context section of the proposal concluded, "*The eventual development of the 1.2 TCF Palestinian gas field, could allow for the substitution of Israeli gas with Palestinian gas, improving the Gaza's Strip overall energy security and self-sufficiency. Developing the Gaza Marine gas field is of great importance for Palestine's energy independence and economy. The G4G pipeline project will enable Gaza Marine reserves (directly or via swaps) to be used by Palestinian power plants, heavy industry and transportation consumers. This will reduce Palestinian dependence on IEC electricity in favor of lower cost Palestinian generated electricity."*

My invitation was to be part of the environmental consultancy's team as a sub-contractor. My role would be to produce analysis of the alternatives to Israeli gas supply, including a comparison of the benefits of each alternative and the risks facing each option. I would also provide some support on stakeholder engagement. In the meantime, I provided some input into the bid document. This was a competitive process, so there was no guarantee that I would end up working on Gazan gas issues again. The consultancy was very experienced in this sort of work, had put together a strong team of experts and proposed a compelling case. So, we were optimistic about our chances. The bid was submitted on 20 July 2020.

On 1 November, we got the good news that we had won the bid, after having been asked to reduce our proposed budget by 10%. We had submitted the strongest technical bid but also the most expensive. There would though be a slight delay before the project started as the OQ were waiting for the funding to come from the donor, the Dutch government. Work on the project did not really start in earnest until the new year. The slow start was a sign of things to come. The first phase of the project, the scoping study, took almost a whole year rather than the six months originally envisaged. The constraints imposed by the pandemic were partly to blame but so was slow decision-making by the OQ and the PNA. Both organisations had to approve all materials for the project, and this was time consuming. The second phase, the actual ESIA never happened. Like the Gaza Marine project, the G4G project never got beyond the theoretical stage.

The Egyptian Option 2.0

Since April 2018, when Shell handed back its interest in Gaza Marine to CCC and PIF, the two remaining partners had sought a new international partner. They needed an international partner to bring technical expertise in developing and operating an offshore gas field. Neither of the existing partners had such expertise. By February 2021, the search seemed to be over. They had secured a new international partner. It was a company that had considerable experience developing offshore gas fields, working with international partners and came from a country that had relations with both the Israelis and the Palestinians, including both the PNA and Hamas. It was the state-owned Egyptian Natural Gas Holding Company (EGAS). On 21 February 2021 during a visit to Israel and the West Bank, the Egyptian Minister of Petroleum Tarek El-Molla signed a memorandum of understanding with CCC and PIF to develop Gaza Marine.

The MoU between the Egyptian minister and the Gaza Marine partners was a statement of intent rather than a legally binding commitment. The agreement appeared to be a revival of the plan to export the Gaza Marine gas to Egypt's LNG facilities and onward to world markets. During the same visit, El-Molla agreed with his Israeli counterpart, the energy minister Yuval Steinitz to construct a pipeline connecting the Leviathan field with Egypt's LNG facilities. Both agreements were potentially win-win situations for all the parties involved. The Palestinians would secure expertise to develop Gaza Marine and a route to market; Israel would secure an export route for its largest gas field and Egypt would earn revenues from the use of its facilities and would take a giant leap towards realising its ambition to be a regional gas transit hub.

For CCC and the PIF, having the Egyptian state, in the form of EGAS, as a partner in Gaza Marine ticked many boxes. It gave them an ally with influence in both the Israeli and Palestinian governments who also had a direct commercial stake in the project's success and brought much needed technical expertise. For EGAS, it would mark the first step in realising an ambition to build a portfolio of overseas investments in the gas sector. In doing so, it was hoping to emulate some of its peer state gas companies in the region such as Qatar Petroleum and Abu Dhabi's ADNOC which have substantial international portfolios. EGAS was dipping its toes in waters it knew well as a start. The MoU with CCC and the PIF also represented a potential leap forward. While EGAS had acquired plenty of experience in developing offshore gas fields, this was entirely in its own backyard and where it was in partnership with experienced and well financed international players such as Shell and BP. It was these companies that brought the technical expertise and finance. In becoming a partner in Gaza Marine, EGAS was graduating from apprentice to being the operator. While EGAS probably possessed the relevant technical skills, it was not clear that it had the experience for this project and more crucially the finance.

EGAS would not have to call on its technical expertise and limited finances immediately. There was still a lot of talking and negotiating to do before the MoU signed in February 2021 could be turned into a substantive agreement that would trigger work on Gaza Marine and the spending of money. As well as the commercial terms on which EGAS would acquire a stake of up to 45% in the Gaza Marine project, there was also a need to neutralise any opposition to the deal, particularly from Hamas, who still controlled the Gaza Strip. Hamas denounced the MoU when it was first announced as they had not been a party to the deal. As in previous Gaza Marine deals, the MoU had been signed with the PNA in Ramallah, as the recognised Palestinian government. The Egyptian government also maintained contact with Hamas in Gaza in order to manage affairs on its north-east border and prevent any trouble in Gaza spilling across the border into the Sinai and mainland Egypt. Cairo did not want to become responsible for Gaza's problems.

The prospect of a deal on Gaza Marine, a deal that did not include

Hamas, triggered a reaction in Gaza. On 13 September 2022, Hamas staged a protest on the Gaza City waterfront, with the title, "Right to Natural Resources and Gas Fields". The protest was aimed not just at the PNA, Egypt and Israel but the international community. The protest included billboards, proclaiming, "*Our gas is our right*" in Arabic and English. There were also slogans in Hebrew alongside pictures of Hamas fighters. Armed drones flew over the protest and Hamas fired missiles into the sea in symbolic attack on offshore gas facilities and vessels. Hamas was making sure that its interests would not be ignored and showing that it had the capability, in theory, to disrupt Gaza Marine's development.

By October 2022, the negotiations over Gaza Marine had not reached a conclusion. The negotiations between Egypt, the PNA, Hamas and Israel were broader than just the gas project. They also included a reconciliation agreement (the latest of many with previous ones failing to have any impact) and talks over delineating the maritime border between Egypt and Gazan waters. On 14 October, one of these strands reached a conclusion with the PNA and Hamas signing a reconciliation agreement. This would have the same impact as previous similar agreements, none. On 26 October, El-Molla announced that a final agreement on Gaza Marine would be signed before the end of March 2023. About a month later, the Washington Post reported that there had been a breakthrough with Egypt, Israel and the PNA reaching a provisional agreement on developing Gaza Marine. While Hamas was not party to this agreement, it had been consulted and acquiesced. A final agreement was now expected before the end of February 2023.

The last day of February 2023 came and went, as did the 31 March, without any sign of the final agreement to develop the Gaza Marine field. It was mid-June before there was any substantial development and this time it came from the Israelis and specifically from the Office of the Prime Minister, Benjamin Netanyahu, which on 18 June issued a brief statement:

"In the framework of the existing efforts between the State of Israel, Egypt and the Palestinian Authority (PA), with emphasis on Palestinian economic development and maintaining security stability in the region, it has been decided to develop the Gaza Marine gas field off the coast of Gaza.

Implementing the project is subject to coordination between the security services and direct dialogue with Egypt, in coordination with the PA, and the completion of inter-ministerial staff work led by the National Security Council, in order to maintain the security and diplomatic interests of the State of Israel on the matter." [66]

The statement appeared to give Israeli approval for the development of Gaza Marine. This was not the final agreement promised earlier in the year. It did though seem to be a step in the right direction, despite being heavily caveated and announced without any fanfare such as a press conference or even quotes from the Prime Minister, or any of his ministers. This was a much more low-key announcement compared to the one back in February 2011 when Netanyahu and then Middle East envoy Tony Blair held a joint news conference to announce putting Gaza Marine development at the heart of an economic peace package for the Palestinians.

The statement did appear to be a step in a carefully choreographed plan. Two days later, an anonymous Hamas source stated that it *"in principle"* would allow the PNA to reach a final agreement to develop the Gaza Marine field. Hamas also made clear that it expected Gaza to directly receive a share of the revenues once production started and that it awaited the details of any final agreement. The PNA and Egypt did not make any official comment. Any deal to develop Gaza Marine was still very fragile. While there had been a notable lowering of the temperature in the region, with no significant escalations in violence, there was still a great deal of hostility towards Hamas from both the PNA and Israel. There had been a short flare up in violence

---

66 https://www.gov.il/en/departments/news/spoke-gas180623

in May and Hamas had captured two Israeli citizens who had strayed across the border and held the remains of two Israeli soldiers.

So why had Netanyahu and his government chosen this moment to offer an economic olive branch (albeit low profile) to the Palestinians, including Hamas? This was one of the most right-wing governments in Israel's history and committed to making no concessions to the Palestinians and especially Hamas. As well as fitting into the long-term pattern of Netanyahu preferring to offer economic measures, it also fitted into a more immediate pattern of events. In October 2022, Israel and Lebanon had reached a US-brokered deal to delineate their maritime border in order to facilitate gas exploration and development on both sides. This deal was not part of a wider peace agreement but a focussed measure that would benefit both sides economically. The offer to approve Gaza Marine's development shared some features with the Lebanon deal. As well as being brokered by a third party, it related to gas development and was not part of a final peace settlement.

Israel's provisional Gaza Marine approval may also have been sending a signal to all parties involved, including Egypt and the US that it was prepared to respond positively to the lower tensions that the region had experienced in late 2022 and the first half of 2023. Egypt, with the help from the US, was having separate discussions with both Israel and Hamas about a long-term ceasefire (*hudna* in Arabic). The US government had criticised recent announcements by the Israeli government over building illegal settlements in the West Bank. While no formal peace process was in place, nor was one even being discussed, there was a sense that the situation was calmer than for many months and perhaps this offered an opportunity to build trust and make some tentative moves towards maintaining lower tensions.

The calm persisted over the summer months. On 14 September, the head of the Palestinian Energy and Natural Resources Authority, Dhafer Melhem felt confident enough to announce that a final agreement would be announced within "five days" and that work would commence on Gaza Marine in October. Melhem's confidence was not entirely misplaced. Although no final agreement was reached, a preliminary agreement was reached by 18 September. The agreement covered issues such as the terms on which EGAS would acquire a stake in the project, the development phases and allocation of revenues. The agreement was not enough to allow work on the project to start the following month but did represent another step forward. However, there was no timetable for turning this preliminary agreement into a fully-fledged final agreement that could underpin Gaza Marine's development. The crucial agreement to turn the fantasy of Gaza and the Palestinian economy having access to its own energy resources and benefitting from the revenues remained elusive.

Shock and Awfulness
Reality intervened on 7 October, when Hamas launched a large-scale attack from Gaza. At dawn, Hamas fighters breached the security wall around Gaza in several places and hundreds of its fighters poured into southern Israel attacking towns, military facilities and a music festival. The attacks were savage and indiscriminate. Men, women and children were killed, hundreds of Israeli civilians (including women and children) and military personnel were captured and taken as hostages back to Gaza. Within a few hours, at least 1200 people, Israelis and foreign nationals were dead and more than 200 held hostage. It was the biggest and most brutal terrorist attack that Israel had ever suffered. The Israeli military and intelligence services had been taken by surprise. It was a massive intelligence and security failure on their part. For Hamas, it was a significant intelligence success. They had duped Israel and kept their plans secret despite extensive Israeli surveillance of Gaza.

Prime Minister Netanyahu vowed to defeat Hamas and to eliminate the organisation in Gaza. Israeli soldiers, tanks and other equipment gathered close to Gaza in the days that followed the 7 October attack and prepared to put Netanyahu's vow into effect. The Israeli response started on 10 October with air raids on Gaza. From 13 October, Israeli troops entered northern Gaza. Israeli warplanes, drones and naval ships bombarded the Gaza Strip. Israel ordered civilians to leave northern Gaza and head south. Water and electricity were cut. The Gaza Strip was sealed off. The fighting was fierce and brutal. Israeli troops worked their way through the densely built Gazan towns and villages. Tens of thousands of Palestinians (the majority civilians, including children) were killed, many more injured and hundreds of thousands of people were displaced. By early 2024, while aid convoys were getting into Gaza, food, water and medicine were in short supply and Gaza's people were facing famine. Most of Gaza's buildings and infrastructure was destroyed in the fighting.

Along with the conflict, casualties and chaos, also came the conspiracy theories focussing on Gaza Marine. The Gaza conflict was the latest attempt by Israel to seize control of Gaza Marine and access the gas for itself. "Blood Gas" was back. Self-proclaimed experts published articles and posted videos on social media with 'evidence' that the real purpose behind the war was Israel's desire to access the Gaza Marine gas reserves. These conspiracy theorists ignored several important aspects: the Prime Minister's Office had announced approval of Gaza Marine development on 18 June; Israel had not used previous conflicts to secure access to the gas reserves and Israel did not need to invade Gaza to secure the gas reserves. As noted in the "Blood Gas" chapter, if Israel really wanted to access the gas, it could station a platform above the field and extract the gas. It did not need to risk the lives of thousands of its soldiers and the hostages held by Hamas, undergo the expense of using millions of dollars-worth of equipment and attract stinging international criticism, even from strong allies such as the US and the United Kingdom.

The conflict did not stop efforts to develop the region's gas reserves. On 29 October, the Israeli energy minister announced the award of licences for gas exploration in Israeli waters. The winners included international major oil and gas companies including the British firm BP and the French company Total. This was the conclusion of a process that had started several months earlier, before the conflict. The announcement sparked protests against the companies concerned, who were accused of complicity in alleged human rights abuses committed by Israeli forces in Gaza.

Gaza Marine was not just the focus of conspiracy theories, there was also recognition that its development could and should play a role in Gaza's recovery, once the conflict is over. The revenues from the field's eventual development could make a significant contribution to the costs of rebuilding Gaza and its economy. In a late November 2023 visit to Israel, US President Biden's energy security advisor Amos Hochstein commented that Gaza Marine could go a long way to helping the Palestinian economy. He stated, *"it can absolutely be a revenue stream for a Palestinian government, and to ensure there is an independent energy system for Palestine."* In answer to a journalist's question about whether Israel would allow the Palestinians to exploit the Gaza Marine reserves, he acknowledged that the gas resources belonged to the Palestinians and not to Israel, *"I am very confident, there is no reason for them not to, it is not theirs [the Israelis], the gas belongs to the Palestinian people."* This was not the first time Hochstein had engaged on the Gaza Marine project. During the Kerry peace initiative, he had engaged with BG, CCC, the PNA and the Israelis on the project.

Gaza Marine has faced many obstacles since the field was first discovered in 2000: conflict, lack of Israeli approval, lack of interest from BG and at times from the PNA, opposition from Hamas and unclear routes to market. To make a contribution to the rebuilding of the Gazan economy, it may have to overcome its largest obstacle so far and the newest: climate change. Natural gas is a fossil fuel and a major contributor to climate change. As economies around the world transition to energy sources that do not use fossil fuels, the Gaza Marine partners may find it increasingly difficult to attract the finance required (more than $1billion) to fund its development. Many in governments and civil society who argue the Palestinians cause and support the rebuilding of the Gazan economy will find it hard to argue for this based on the use of a fossil fuel. There will be a tension between the need to rebuild Gaza in an environmentally friendly and sustainable manner and the exploitation of natural gas to fund, in part, that rebuilding. It will make some Palestinians, their supporters and advocates uncomfortable that the future may be gas-fuelled. One of the many challenges facing a post war Gaza Strip will be the reconciliation of the need to transition away from fossil fuels and the imperative to allow the Palestinians the freedom to use their own resources to power their future.

CONCLUSION

The Palestinians possess a valuable resource in the Gaza Marine gas field. It is a resource that can be used to finance the rebuilding of Gaza and provide a reliable energy supply in the future. It is a resource that belongs to all of the Palestinian people. It belongs to the Palestinian people because it is located in their territory. Gaza Marine was not a gift from Israel or any other country. Accepted international principles hold that the resources of a state belong to that state. The only actors to have disputed the Palestinians' right to Gaza Marine have done so either out of extremist nationalist views or due to commercial interest. Politicians on the Israeli far-right deny the Palestinians' rights and claim rights over a "*Greater Israel*" and its resources. The Yam Tethys consortium challenged the PNA's right to award the Gaza Marine licence in the Israeli courts. In an unsatisfactory judgement, the court did not rule on that specific question but did accept the Israel government's position that Israel had no sovereignty claim on Gaza's waters. That has remained the Israel's government's position. No Israeli government since has challenged that position and has acted in line with that position. In the numerous rounds of negotiations with BG, Israel recognised that the gas was a Palestinian possession. The various "*economic peace*" initiatives by Israel, the US or Tony Blair are also based on the premise that the gas belongs to the Palestinians. The US government has stated publicly that the gas belongs to the Palestinians. The PNA has gone beyond simply claiming ownership of the gas resources. It has acted to cement that claim. The act of awarding the Gaza Marine licence is part of staking its claim. The PNA has reinforced its claim through its engagement with BG, the Israeli government and other stakeholders in the efforts to develop the Gaza Marine field. Even if there was a counterclaim to possession of the gas field, the Palestinians have also asserted their rights under the principle of first capture.

More than 20 years have passed since the PNA attempted to assess and exploit its natural resources through awarding an exploration licence to BG and CCC. In that period, BG spent tens of millions of dollars studying the rocks below the seabed, drilling exploration wells, analysing data, surveying pipeline routes and commissioning engineering studies. In addition, representatives of BG, CCC, the PNA, the Israeli government, IEC, the OQR and the British government have spent the equivalent of hundreds of days talking about how to develop Gaza Marine to the mutual benefit of both the Palestinian and Israeli economies and societies. Despite all that activity, money, time spent, and brain power exerted, the Gaza Marine gas remains in its reservoir thousands of metres below the seabed. The only gas that has reached the surface is the small amount that was produced during the drilling of the two exploration wells in late 2000. No other drilling activity has taken place since then. There are no facilities, such as production wells and pipelines, in place to produce any gas. The lack of gas production means that the Gaza Marine field has not generated any revenue. It has not generated revenue for the PNA, for BG or CCC. Israel, Jordan nor any other customer has paid any money to receive gas. No gas production also means that the gas is still available for the Palestinians to exploit and use for the benefit of their economy and the rebuilding of Gaza. The gas is still available for use as fuel in the Gaza power station and to give Gaza's residents a reliable and long-term energy supply. The gas is also still available to export to Israel, Jordan or Egypt and earn revenue that can be invested to rebuild Gaza after the ravages of war.

The gas remains in place below the seabed because of a series of failures. Some of these failures were deliberate political decisions, such as Sharon's decision to prefer Egyptian over Palestinian gas. Some of these failures were failures in political systems such as the Israeli government's failure to take a strategic approach to energy policy and to co-ordinate across government departments. For example, in March 2007, when the Ministries of National Infrastructure and Finance recommended a deal on Gaza Marine to the cabinet but, failed to secure the support of the foreign and defence ministries. Israel's most significant failure with Gaza Marine was a failure to understand the contribution that developing the gas field could make to Israel's security, not just energy security but overall security. This failure stems from the unresolved contradiction at the heart of Israel's approach to the Palestinians: to secure the Israeli state through exerting near total over the Palestinians or to separate as completely as possible from the Palestinians. Sharon started down the path towards separation but his collapse into a coma halted the journey. In the years since, successive Israeli governments have tried to do both: separate from the Palestinians but continue to assert total control. Israel's policy towards Gaza exemplifies this approach. Israel separated itself from Gaza with the imposition of a blockade but continued to assert control over the population including its energy needs. This attempt to straddle two paths is not sustainable and does not enhance Israel's long-term security and denies the Palestinians fundamental human rights.

The failures that have led to the Gaza Marine gas remaining under the seabed are not all Israeli failures. The Palestinians have also failed to act in their own best interests. The PNA failed to ensure that the Gaza Marine licence award process was transparent and in the national interest. Having secured one of the world's leading gas companies and discovered a valuable natural resource, the PNA failed to press their case both with Israel and with the wider international community for their right to exploit that resource for the social and economic benefit of Palestinians. This failure to press its case included times when relations were better such as after the end of the second Intifada and when the Israeli government had real concerns about its long-term energy supply. The PNA's failure to wholeheartedly press its case was caused by its concern for the political price that Israel would demand in return and fear over the internal criticism it would face. The PNA feared that Israel may take measures such as imposing other restrictions on economic activity or confiscating more land for settlements in return for granting approval for Gaza Marine's development. The PNA also feared it would face criticism from Hamas and other groups for striking a deal over Gaza Marine that was not in the perceived best interests of the Palestinian economy. The lack of transparency around the deal and suspicions of corrupt behaviour made it difficult to sell the deal to the wider Palestinian public.

BG also failed to act in its commercial interests. In the late 1990s as it considered bidding for the Gaza Marine licence, it failed to undertake sufficient research and analysis of the political and business situation it was entering, including the ability of the PNA to actually implement decisions, the extent of Israeli control over Palestinian affairs and the scope for corrupt activity. BG also failed to understand the divisions in both the PNA and the Israeli government over policy towards the Gaza Marine project. BG also failed to provide sufficient senior executive support to the Gaza Marine project team. This reflected internal doubts in BG about the wisdom of developing Gaza Marine. There was not universal or widespread support for the project in the company. It became a marginal project. BG also failed to harness the willingness of the British government and other bodies such as the EU and Tony Blair as Quartet Representative. BG could have corralled a posse of international actors to put pressure on both the Israelis and Palestinians to reach a deal on Gaza Marine. Such pressure had no guarantee of success but could have made a difference at points when the prospects for a deal improved.

So, was there ever a point when the Gaza Marine project could have gone ahead, achieved project sanction and led to the production of gas from the field? To reach this point, many threads needed to be woven together. Israel would need to give unambiguous approval and actively co-operate in the project development (e.g. through granting permits and security clearance). The PNA would need to approve the field development plan and also grants permits and permissions. BG would need cast iron agreements with Israel, PNA and CCC. Its Board would need to be comfortable with the level of risk in the project and that it was not being negligent with its shareholders' money. CCC would also need to be comfortable with the level of risk and BG's conduct of project activities. After the start of the second Intifada in late September 2000, there was no moment when the political and commercial interests of all the component organisations with a stake in Gaza Marine aligned to produce a machine capable of delivering the project. The violence of the second Intifada hardened Israeli government attitudes towards Arafat and the PNA. The PNA's failures to build popular legitimacy undermined its foundations and it did not feel strong enough to take tough decisions in the Palestinian national interest. For BG, the risk/reward balance was not attractive. The risks it faced in the Gaza Marine project outweighed the rewards. This was a modest gas field with very little prospect for significant business growth. There was unlikely to be significant more gas to be found offshore the Gaza Strip and the Israeli gas market was proving too difficult to access. Also, BG had set its sight on larger projects in Brazil, Australia and the US, which appeared to present less political risks. At any given moment in the Gaza Marine project, at least one of the three key parties (the PNA, Israel and BG) was not ready to take the next step. There was no point when all the threads were close to coming together and weaving a viable project.

While there are many threads that need to be woven together for the Gaza Marine project to succeed, Israel provides some of the main threads that will form the web and weft. Its failures and actions have blocked the development of the Gaza Marine field. Sharon's decision to favour Egyptian over Palestinian gas, the later failure to reach agreement on a gas price and the failure to build on the opportunity created by the appointment of Salam Fayyad as Palestinian prime minister are some of the significant factors that have blocked Gaza Marine. There are many others. The result is that BG and CCC were prevented from developing Gaza Marine. The failure to develop the Gaza Marine gas field means that Palestinians have lost economic value. They have lost their ability to earn revenue that could be used to build the economy and build support for coming to an equitable peace agreement with Israel. The Palestinians have lost the ability to secure their own energy supply and create a more sustainable economy and society.

The Gaza Marine project and the ability of the Palestinians to exploit one of their most valuable natural resources is also victim of the violence inflicted by both Palestinian militants and the Israeli armed forces. The second Intifada obstructed efforts to reach a deal. Israeli military campaigns in both the West Bank and the Gaza Strip also made it much harder to reach an agreement. The violence destroyed trust on both sides. Without trust, any deal on Gaza Marine was impossible. At no time was Israel's military campaigns against the Palestinians and especially those targeting Gaza aimed at securing control over the gas field. The Israeli government was not that co-ordinated. It showed many times that those responsible for security were not aware of what those responsible for energy supply were planning. The security agenda, especially the need to combat Palestinian militant attacks, drove the military campaigns. Gaza Marine was incidental to this. Revenue from the gas was not funding any terrorism as there was no revenue. Despite several military campaigns, Israel did not secure access to Gaza's gas resources. The military campaigns only served to block progress. In any case, after 2009 and 2010, with major discoveries in its own waters Israel did not need access to the gas. If Israel wanted to access Gaza's gas resources, it could have done so without military action. It could have undertaken its own drilling and engineering activities and developed the field. Instead, Israeli representatives negotiated with BG to purchase gas from the Gaza field and appeared (at most times) to be conducting those negotiations in good faith.

The repeated willingness of Israeli government and IEC representatives to negotiate to buy Palestinian gas is consistent with the trend in Israeli policy to separate from the Palestinian territories. Israel took the first separation steps with the Oslo Accords. Barak's action as Prime Minister to give Arafat the green light to award the Gaza Marine licence and to grant security clearance for exploration to go ahead. These actions were consistent with the Oslo Accords and in line with separating from the Palestinians. Separation means allowing the Palestinians to take control of their own affairs. Full separation will mean full sovereignty for a Palestinian state with control over its land, population and resources. Separation also means negotiating with the Palestinians to reach agreements for mutual interest such as buying Palestinian gas or allowing the Palestinians to use Israeli infrastructure to export gas to other markets such as Jordan or Egypt. Sharon, as Prime Minister, took another step towards separation with unilateral withdrawal from the Gaza Strip and four small West Bank settlements. Sharon appears to have envisioned this withdrawal as a first step in a wider separation plan that included giving Palestinians greater control over their affairs but stopping short of full sovereignty. Since Sharon's January 2006 stroke, Israeli policy has been in a coma. It has imposed an almost total blockade on Gaza but not allowed it any more control over its affairs. Israel exercised almost total control over Palestinian affairs, both in Gaza and the West Bank. This situation is not sustainable and damages both Israeli and Palestinian interests. It makes Israel responsible for the humanitarian crisis in the Gaza Strip that the blockade and then war has created. It makes Israel responsible for human rights abuses. It imposes an economic cost on Israel in terms of maintaining the occupation and damaging Israel's ability to attract investment. For example, in the spring of 2019, several major international infrastructure companies withdrew from the tender process of the second phase of developing the Jerusalem light rail system due to concerns over being complicit in human rights abuses. For Palestinians, Israeli control inhibits almost all aspects of their social and economic development. In the case of Gaza, there is considerable evidence that its population has suffered de-development even before the current conflict.[67]

After the war in Gaza has ended, whether Israel succeeds or not in defeating Hamas and driving it out of the territory, Israel faces a choice: undertake a meaningful separation from the Palestinians and negotiate the creation of a sovereign Palestinian state or absorb the Palestinians into a bi-national state with full rights and responsibilities of citizenship. The situation that existed before 7 October 2023 or the proposed US solution set out in its "*Peace to Prosperity*" document in early 2020 are not viable choices. Neither will resolve the underlying conflict and will perpetuate the damage to Israel and the Palestinians. Also, neither will create the situation where the development of Gaza Marine can go ahead. A sovereign Palestinian state or the one-state solution would enable a political environment that would allow Gaza Marine development. It would remove the ambiguities about the rights of the Palestinian state to develop the field and should provide a clear legal framework for the field, including for the flow of revenues. There would still be many issues to resolve but many of these would be commercial and would depend on the agreements reached to produce and market the gas.

What would it take for Gaza Marine to be developed? The first steps to Gaza Marine's development are all political. A united Palestinian government encompassing both the West Bank and the Gaza Strip that is recognised by Israel, the US and other international

---

67 Roy (2016)

players such as the EU is a necessary condition. That government would then have to negotiate a comprehensive peace deal with Israel that finally resolves the conflict. Any interim agreements, including *"economic peace first"* plans are not going to be sufficient. While Gaza Marine could be included in any confidence building measures, there would have to be a path towards a final peace agreement. Investors are not going to take the initial steps towards developing Gaza Marine without some assurance that they will get a return on that investment. Without the prospect of a final agreement, the Palestinians are not going to be able to secure the capital to develop Gaza Marine. Investment of more than $1 billion is needed. Along with the finance, a company is needed that has the experience and capacity to develop, commission and operate an offshore gas field. This company does not need to be one of the super majors. There are plenty of medium sized oil and gas companies with the requisite experience or it could be a state-owned energy company either from the Middle East such as Qatar Petroleum or from further afield such as one of the Chinese firms.

The start of Israeli gas exports to Jordan and Egypt in January 2020 is also an important step towards Gaza Marine's development. Israel has secured its energy needs so the production of Gaza Marine gas and use either by the Palestinians or its export does not pose any threat to Israel's energy security. Moreover, the existence of these export channels, provides a means for Palestinian gas to reach international markets. The future start of large-scale, over-the-horizon Israeli gas exports to international markets would turn this step into a giant leap for Gaza Marine. Israel would no longer have reason to block Gaza Marine's development. In these circumstances, preventing the Palestinians developing Gaza Marine while exporting their own gas would expose Israel to accusations of hypocrisy, bad faith and denial of Palestinians' human rights.

Developing the Gaza Marine field would bring benefits beyond energy security for the Palestinians and a welcome source of revenue (significant benefits in their own right). A secure and reliable energy supply in Gaza would strengthen the economy in many ways. It would allow businesses to thrive and expand, new businesses to start and provide reliable energy for essential services such as hospitals, water treatment and education. Companies would be able to operate for longer each day and to plan for the future. The West Bank would enjoy the same benefits if power stations are also built there and supplied with Gaza Marine gas. This would make the Palestinian economy more self-reliant and robust. A successful Palestinian economy is also in Israel's interest in the same way that successful Jordanian and Egyptian economies are in Israel's interest. Growing economies mean less unemployment, poverty and despair: the breeding ground for radicalising militants. A successful Palestinian economy would make a peace deal more likely to persist and gain popular legitimacy. Palestinian economic growth is necessary to make any final peace deal permanent. The two need to go hand in hand. "*Economic peace*" first will not lead to peace or a thriving economy. A strong economy will give Palestinians the resources to build a state and build mutually beneficial economic, social and political relations with Israel, Jordan, Egypt as well as economies and markets globally.

The failure to develop the Gaza Marine gas field represents more than a lost economic opportunity, it is a missed opportunity to change relations between Israelis and Palestinians and is a violation of the Palestinians' human rights. Gaza Marine's development at any time since BG discovered the gas field in 2000 provided an opportunity to add a positive element to Israeli-Palestinian relations with the potential to alter the balance of those relations. The field's exploitation and the supply of gas to Israel under a commercial agreement would create a mutually-beneficial economic link. In this scenario, Israel would rely in part on the Palestinians for its energy needs and the Palestinians would receive revenue. Such a deal would demonstrate the ability for both sides to reach and implement an equitable agreement. This arrangement would build trust on the back of a mutual dependence. It would also demonstrate that the Palestinians could exercise their human rights to control and exploit their natural resources for their own social, economic and political growth. This right has been denied to them through a combination of Israeli obstructions, poor leadership from their own government, corporate mismanagement and lack of international political will. The results is that Palestinians, especially those in Gaza are caught between the control of Israeli political power and an energy source to fuel their own economic and political future.

APPENDIX I

ABBREVIATIONS AND ACRONYMS

AHLC   Ad Hoc Liaison Committee
AMI   Area of Mutual Interest
API   Arab Peace Initiative
bcf   billion cubic feet
bcm   billion cubic metres
BG   BG Group plc (British Gas)
BPBC   British Palestine Business Council
CCC   Consolidated Contractors Company Ltd
CEO   Chief Executive Officer
CFO   Chief Financial Officer
CNG   Compressed natural gas
CRG   Control Risks Group
DFLP   Democratic Front for the Liberation of Palestine
EAPC   Eilat-Ashkelon Pipeline Company
EEZ   Exclusive Economic Zone
EGPC   Egyptian General Petroleum Council
EIB   European Investment Bank
ELNG   Egyptian Liquefied Natural Gas company
EMG   East Mediterranean Gas
EU   European Union
FCO   Foreign and Commonwealth Office
FCPA   Foreign Corrupt Practices Act

FEED	Front-end Engineering and Design
GSPA	Gas sale and purchase agreement
ICL	Israeli Chemicals Limited
IEC	Israeli Electric Corporation
IFC	International Finance Corporation
IPP	Independent power producer
LNG	Liquefied natural gas
LOI	Letter of intent
MBC	Middle East Broadcasting Centre
mBtu	million British thermal units
MNI	Ministry of National Infrastructure
MoU	Memorandum of understanding
MP	Member of Parliament
NGO	Non-governmental organisation
OPT	Occupied Palestinian territories
OQR	Office of the Quartet Representative
PBBC	Palestinian-British Business Council
PCSC	Palestinian Commercial Services Corporation
PIF	Palestinian Investment Fund
PLO	Palestine Liberation Organisation
PM	Prime Minister
PNA	Palestinian National Authority
tcf	trillion cubic feet
UK	United Kingdom
UN	United Nations
UNWRA	UN Works and Relief Agency
US	United States of America
V&E	Vinson and Elkins

APPENDIX II

TIMELINE

Date	Event
13 Sep 1993	Declaration of Principles signed in Washington DC
25 Feb 1994	Far right Kach member Baruch Goldstein killed 29 people at the Ibrahimi Mosque in Hebron
29 Apr 1994	Paris Protocol signed
4 May 1994	Agreement on The Gaza Strip and Jericho signed in Cairo
26 Oct 1994	Jordan and Israel signed peace treaty
27 Aug 1995	Protocol on Further Transfer of Powers & Responsibilities signed in Cairo
28 Sep 1995	Oslo 2 agreement signed in Washington
4 Nov 1995	Yitzhak Rabin assassinated in Tel Aviv. Shimon Peres succeeded as Prime Minister
20 Jan 1996	First elections held for PNA president and legislative council
18 Jun 1996	Benjamin Netanyahu became prime minister following victory in general election
April 1999	BG approached PNA with proposal to explore for gas in Gaza waters
6 Jul 1999	Ehud Barak became prime minister following victory in general election
10 Nov 1999	BG Group, CCC, PNA signed Gaza Marine licence agreement

The Gaza Marine Story

Jan-Apr 2000	BG conducted 3D seismic survey in GM licence are covering 1000km2, costing $3.5m
June 2000	Yam Tethys Group voiced opposition to BG drilling GM
25 Jul 2000	Camp David negotiations broke down
21 Aug 2000	Yam Tethys Group served injunction on BG to prevent drilling.
25-26 Aug 2000	Atwood Southern Cross rig moved to GM drill location
29 Aug 2000	GM-1 well spudded in approx 600m of water, 36km from coast
27 Sep 2000	BG announced discovery of Gaza Marine gas field
28 Sep 2000	Ariel Sharon visited the Temple Mount, sparking the second Intifada
16 Nov 2000	Drilling started on GM-2 well
22 Nov 2000	Hearing in Israeli court on Yam Tethys injunction found in favour of BG
12 Dec 2000	GM-2 well drilling completed
7 Mar 2001	Ariel Sharon became prime minister
27 Mar 2002	Suicide bomb in Netanya killed 30
28 Mar 2002	Arab Peace Initiative published during Arab League summit in Beirut
29 Mar 2002	Israeli forces launched Operation Defensive Shield, besieging Arafat in Ramallah
15 Nov 2002	BG announced second Gaza Marine seismic survey
17 Aug 2003	Sharon reportedly vetoed deal for Israel to buy GM gas
11 Nov 2004	Yasser Arafat died
9 Jan 2005	Mahmoud Abbas elected as PNA president
8 Feb 2005	Sharon and Abbas signed agreement marking end of the second Intifada
16 Aug 2005	Unilateral Israeli withdrawal from Gaza started
11 Sep 2005	Israel completed Gaza withdrawal
15 Dec 2005	Fourth (of planned five) round of Palestinian local

elections held. Hamas performed well

4 Jan 2006	Ehud Olmert took over as acting prime minister after Sharon suffered stroke and lapsed into coma. Olmert confirmed as prime minister in May.
25 Jan 2006	Second PNA legislative council elections held. Hamas won 74 of 132 seats
19 Feb 2006	Haaretz newspaper reported Olmert-Brown exchange of letters on GM
18 Apr 2006	Gaza Marine reserves certified as 1.04 tcf by DeGolyer & MacNaughton
May 2007	World Bank published report on Palestinian energy sector
14 Jun 2007	Hamas seized power in Gaza Strip
15 Jun 2007	Salam Fayyad appointed prime minister of PNA
27 Jun 2007	Tony Blair appointed Special Envoy of the Quartet after resignation as British PM
27 Dec 2008	Operation Cast Lead launched
18 Jan 2009	Operation Cast Lead ended with ceasefire
21 Oct 2009	BG held meeting with CCC and PIF
4 Feb 2011	Blair and PM Netanyahu announced start of discussions to develop Gaza Marine
23 Dec 2011	BG wrote to PNA to request consent for sale of GM share
7 Feb 2012	PNA wrote to BG to inform that no consent given for sale of GM share
20 Jun 2012	PNA wrote to BG removing relinquishment extension
21-22 Aug 2012	BG held first meeting with Molcho
14 Nov 2012	Israel launched Operation Pillar of Defence in Gaza
21 Nov 2012	Operation Pillar of Defence ended
6 Jun 2013	Rami Hamdallah replaced Fayyad as PNA prime minister
Jul 2013	BG closed Gaza City office
Dec 2013	BG, CCC and PNA signed MoU to amend Upstream

	agreement, extending licence to 2042 and changing equity split
8 Jul 2014	Israel launched Operation Protective Edge in Gaza
26 Aug 2014	Operation Protective Edge ended with ceasefire
8 Apr 2015	Royal Dutch Shell announced bid for BG Group
May 2015	BG signed letter of intent with Jordan for supply of gas
27 May 2015	Tony Blair resigned as OQR
15 Jun 2015	BG signed letter of intent with CCC for supply of gas to future Jenin power station
15 Feb 2016	Shell completed takeover of BG Group
30 Mar 2018	Gaza residents staged protest, "*Great March of Return*"
14 May 2018	US held ceremony to mark re-location of Embassy to Jerusalem
14 Apr 2019	Mohammed Shtayyeh replaced Rami Hamdallah as PNA Prime Minister
22 Jun 2019	White House published "*Peace to Prosperity*" economic peace plan for Palestinians
25-26 Jun 2019	Economic peace workshop in Bahrain
28 Jan 2020	President Trump published Middle East Peace Plan
21 Feb 2021	PNA and Egypt signed agreement to develop Gaza Marine field
15 Jun 2022	Israel, Egypt and the EU signed deal to boost gas exports to Europe
13 Sep 2022	Hamas stage protest in Gaza for "Right to Natural Resources and Gas Fields"
18 Jun 2023	Israeli PM's office issued statement directing development of Gaza Marine field
7 Oct 2023	Hamas launched surprise attack on Israel, killing over 1200 people and taking around 200 hostages

ACKNOWLEDGEMENTS

Many people agreed to be interviewed for this book and also shared documents and other relevant material. Some spoke on the record, while others preferred to remain anonymous. Some people, both ex-BG colleagues and those from other organisations declined to co-operate. I am grateful to all those who gave me their time, insights and memories of the Gaza Marine gas project. They include Julian Bessa, Charles Bland, Peter Crumpler, Ariel Ezrahi, Stuart Fysh, Steve Larcombe, Mike Lockhart, Nicole McMahon, Walid Najjab, Joseph Paritzky, Nigel Shaw, Alan Stott, Paul Warburton, Dov Weissglas, Matt Wilks.

I would also like to thank Max Scott of Nomad Publishing for agreeing to publish this book and guiding me through the publication process.

Finally, I would like to thank my wife Julie, my children Will and Francesca for all their love and support over many years and tolerating my absences for travel related to Gaza Marine, which sometimes meant I missed family events.

BIBLIOGRAPHY

Books

Barak, Ehud. (2018). *My Country, My Life Fighting for Israel, Searching for Peace*, London: Macmillan

Barr, James. (2012). *A Line in the Sand*, London: Simon & Schuster

Bergman, Ronen. (2018). *Rise and Kill First The Secret History of Israel's Targeted Assassinations,* London: John Murray

Black, Ian. (2017). *Enemies and Neighbours*, London: Allen Lane

Blumenthal, Max. (2015). *The 51 Day War Ruin and Resistance in Gaza*, London: Verso

Chomsky, Noam; Pappe, Ilan. (2011). *Gaza in Crisis*, London: Penguin

Filiu, Jean-Pierre. (2015). *Gaza a History*, London: Hurst & Co

Finkelstein, Norman. (2014). *Method and Madness The Hidden Story of Israel's Assaults on Gaza*, New York: OR Books

Khan, Mushtaq Husain; with Giacaman, George & Amundsen, Inge (2004). *State Formation in Palestine Viability and governance during a social transformation,* London: Routledge Curzon

Kimmerling, Baruch. (2006). *Politicide The Real Legacy of Ariel Sharon*, London: Verso

Landau, David. (2014). *Arik The Life of Ariel Sharon*, New York: Vintage

Lebor, Adam. (2007). *City of Oranges An intimate History of Arabs and Jews in Jaffa*, London: W. W. Norton & Co

Levy, Gideon. (2010) *The Punishment of Gaza*, London: Verso

MacIntyre, Donald. (2017). *Gaza Preparing for Dawn*, London: Oneworld

Murphy, Dervla. (2013). *A Month by the Sea*, London: Eland

Murphy, Dervla. (2015). *Between River and Sea*, London: Eland

Ross, Andrew. (2019) *Stone Men The Palestinians Who Built Israel*, London: Verso

Roy, Sara. (2016). *The Gaza Strip The Political Economy of De-development*, Washington DC: Institute for Palestine Studies

Shehadeh, Raja. (2017). *Where the Line is Drawn*, London: Profile

Watson, Geoffrey. (2000). *The Oslo Accords International Law and the Israeli-Palestinian Peace Agreements*, Oxford: Oxford University Press

Briefing Papers and Reports

Antreasyan, Anais. (2012). *Gas Finds in the Eastern Mediterranean: Gaza, Israel, and Other Conflicts*, Washington DC: Institute for Palestine Studies, vol 42, no 3, http://www.palestine-studies.org/jps/fulltext/162608

Arafeh, Nur. (2018). *Long Overdue: Alternatives to the Paris Protocol*, Al-Shabaka policy brief

Arnon, Arie; Bamya, Saeb (ed). (2016). *Economic Dimensions of an*

Bibliography

Agreement between Israel and Palestine: Summaries of Recent Studies and Lessons Learnt, The Aix Group, http://aix-group.org/index.php/2017/01/20/economic-dimensions-of-an-agreement-between-israel-and-palestine-summaries-of-recent-studies-and-lessons-learnt/

Baconi, Tareq. (2017). *How Israel Uses Gas to Enforce Palestinian Dependency and Promote Normalization*, Al-Shabaka, policy brief, https://al-shabaka.org/briefs/israel-uses-gas-enforce-palestinian-dependency-promote-normalization/

Balls, Ed; Cunliffe, Jon. (2007). *Economic aspects of peace in the Middle East*, London: HM Government, https://www.procon.org/sourcefiles/FCO.gov.uk.pdf

Bennett, A; Nashashibi, K; Beidas, S; Reichold, S; Toujas-Bernate, J. (2003). *West Bank and Gaza Economic Performance and Reform under Conflict Conditions*, Washington DC: IMF

Boersma, Tim; Sachs, Natan. (2015). *Gaza Marine: Natural gas extraction in tumultuous times?* Brookings Institute, policy paper number 36, https://www.brookings.edu/wp-content/uploads/2016/06/Gaza-Marine-web.pdf

Darbouche, Hakim; El-Katiri, Laura; Fattouh, Bassam. (2012). *East Mediterranean Gas: What kind of a game-changer?* Oxford: Oxford Institute of Energy Studies

De Boncourt, Maite. (2013). *Offshore gas in East Mediterranean: From Myth to Reality*, Paris: Institut Francais des Relations Internationales

de Leeuw, Lydia. (2017). *Beneath troubled waters: Noble Energy's exploitation of natural gas in the Eastern Mediterranean Sea*, Amsterdam: The Centre for Research on Multinational Corporations (SOMO),   https://www.somo.nl/wp-content/uploads/2017/05/Beneath-troubled-waters.pdf

de Soto, Alvaro. (2007). *End of mission report*,http://image.guardian.co.uk/sys-files/Guardian/documents/2007/06/12/DeSotoReport.pdf

Fidler, David. (1999). *Foreign Private Investment in Palestine Revisited: An Analysis of the Revised Palestinian Investment Law*, Case Western Reserve Journal of International Law, vol 31, issue 2, https://www.repository.law.indiana.edu/cgi/viewcontent.cgi?article=1654&context=facpub

Giannakopoulos, Angelos (ed). (2016). *Energy Cooperation and Security in the Eastern Mediterranean: A Seismic Shift towards Peace or Conflict?* Tel Aviv: The S. Daniel Abraham Center for International and Regional Studies, Tel Aviv University, https://dacenter.tau.ac.il/sites/abraham.tau.ac.il/files/Energy%20Cooperation%20and%20Security%20in%20the%20Eastern%20Mediterranean.pdf

Henderson, Simon. (2014). *Natural Gas in the Palestinian Authority: The Potential of the Gaza Marine Offshore Field*, Washington DC: The German Marshall Fund of the United States, http://www.washingtoninstitute.org/uploads/Documents/opeds/Henderson20140301-GermanMarshallFund.pdf

Kattan, Victor. (2012, August). *Oil. Religion. Occupation . . . A combustible mix*, Al-Shabaka, policy brief, https://al-shabaka.org/briefs/oil-religion-occupation-combustible-mix/

Kattan, Victor. (2012, April). *The Gas Fields off Gaza: A Gift or a Curse?* Al-Shabaka, policy brief, https://al-shabaka.org/briefs/gas-fields-gaza-gift-or-curse/

Mekelberg, Yossi; Shapland, Greg. (2018). *Israeli-Palestinian Peacemaking What can we learn from previous efforts?* London: Chatham House, https://www.chathamhouse.org/publication/israeli-palestinian-peacemaking-what-can-we-learn-previous-efforts

Mustafa, Mohammad. (2016). *Palestine's Oil and Gas Resources: Prospects and Challenges*, Ramallah: Palestine Investment Fund, http://www.pif.ps/en/article/36/Palestine's-Oil-and-Gas-Resources-Prospects-and-Challenges-

Parker, Eric et al. (2008). *Geohazard Assessment and Avoidance on the Gaza Marine Subsea Development*, Houston: Offshore Technology

Conference

Popper, Steven; Berrebi, Claude; Griffin, James; Light, Thomas; Min, Endy; Crane, Keith. (2009). *The Supply of Natural Gas and Other Options for Generating Electricity*, Rand Corporation

Power, Susan. (2014). *Preventing the development of Palestinian natural gas resources in the Mediterranean Sea Implications for multinational corporations operating in Israel's gas industry*, Ramallah: Al-Haq, http://www.alhaq.org/publications/Gas-report-web.pdf

Power, Susan. (2015). *Annexing Energy Exploiting and Preventing the Development of Oil and Gas in the Occupied Palestinian Territory*, Ramallah: Al-Haq, http://www.alhaq.org/publications/Annexing. Energy.pdf

Shapland, Greg. (2018). *Better Israeli-Palestinian Relations Are Possible*, London: Chatham House

Srouji, Fathi et al. (2008). *Investment Guide to Palestine*, Ramallah: The Palestine Economic Policy Research Institute, http://www.palst-jp.com/eg/pdf/inv/03/INVESTMENT_GUIDE.pdf

Stocker, James (2012). *No EEZ Solution: The Politics of Oil and Gas in the Eastern Mediterranean*, Washington DC: The Middle East Journal, vol 6, no 4, pp579-597

Tagliapietra, Simone. (2013). *Towards a new eastern Mediterranean energy corridor? Natural gas developments between market opportunities and geopolitical risks*, Fondazione Eni Enrico Mattei, https://www.econstor.eu/bitstream/10419/72977/1/73639771X.pdf

Tagliapietra, Simone. (2017). *Energy: a shaping factor for regional stability in the Eastern Mediterranean?* Brussels: European Parliament, http://www.europarl.europa.eu/RegData/etudes/STUD/2017/578044/EXPO_STU(2017)578044_EN.pdf

The Palestine Economic Policy Research Institute. (2010). *Palestine Investment Guide*, Ramallah: Palestine Investment Promotion Agency, http://www.pipa.ps/files/file/publication/Palestine%20 Investment%20Guide_EN.pdf

UNCTAD (2019). *The Economic Costs of the Israeli Occupation for the Palestinian People: The Unrealized Oil and Natural Gas Potential,* Geneva: UNCTAD, https://unctad.org/en/pages/PublicationWebflyer.aspx?publicationid=2505

UNCTAD, (2019, July). *Report on UNCTAD assistance to the Palestinian people: Developments in the economy of the Occupied Palestinian Territory,* Washington DC: UNCTAD

US Energy Information Agency. (2014). *Palestinian Territories Key Energy Statistics,* Washington DC: US Government

World Bank. (2007). *West Bank and Gaza Energy Sector Review,* Washington DC: World Bank, http://documents.worldbank.org/curated/en/731521468137110533/West-Bank-and-Gaza-Energy-sector-review

World Bank. (1993). *Developing the Occupied Territories: An Investment in Peace,* Washington DC: World Bank

World Bank. (2018). *Economic Monitoring Report to the Ad Hoc Liaison Committee,* Washington DC: World Bank

Wurmser, David. (2013). *The Geopolitics of Israel's Offshore Gas Reserves,* Washington DC: Delphi Global Analysis Group, http://jcpa.org/article/the-geopolitics-of-israels-offshore-gas-reserves/

Yaalon, Moshe. (2007). *Does the Prospective Purchase of British Gas from Gaza Threaten Israel's National Security?* Jerusalem: Jerusalem Center for Public Affairs, vol 7, no 17, http://jcpa.org/article/does-the-prospective-purchase-of-british-gas-from-gaza-threaten-israel's-national-security/

UN Country Team in the oPt. (2012). *Gaza in 2020: A liveable place?* Jerusalem: Office of the United Nations Special coordinator for the middle East Peace Process (UNScO)

.